T0330393

The Islamic Debt Market for *Sukuk* Securities

FOUNDATIONS OF ISLAMIC FINANCE

Series Editor: Mohamed Ariff, *Professor of Finance, Bond University, Australia and Maybank Chair Professor, University Putra Malaysia*

Islamic finance, designed to be compliant with Islamic legal principles and common law, continues to rapidly expand as a multifaceted niche market in 76 countries. Written by leading industry experts and scholars, the works in this series will prove an essential guide to the complexities of Islamic finance and its underpinning foundations as well as fundamental principles. Key concepts, practices and issues emerging from this relatively new sphere of *ethics-based financial practice* will be explored in-depth, encompassing themes such as Islamic banking, insurance, and investment funds.

The series will provide a comprehensive and authoritative reference tool for regulators, practitioners and scholars in the fields of accounting, economics, finance, money and banking, who wish to grasp a deeper understanding of the origins, current modes and functions of Islamic finance.

The Islamic Debt Market for *Sukuk* Securities

The Theory and Practice of Profit Sharing Investment

Edited by

Mohamed Ariff

Professor of Finance, Bond University, Australia and Maybank Chair Professor, University Putra Malaysia

Munawar Iqbal

Professor, King Abdul Aziz University and formerly Chief of Research, IRTI, Islamic Development Bank, Saudi Arabia

Shamsher Mohamad

Professor, INCEIF University, Malaysia

FOUNDATIONS OF ISLAMIC FINANCE

Edward Elgar
Cheltenham, UK • Northampton, MA, USA

Published by
Edward Elgar Publishing Limited
The Lypiatts
15 Lansdown Road
Cheltenham
Glos GL50 2JA
UK

Edward Elgar Publishing, Inc.
William Pratt House
9 Dewey Court
Northampton
Massachusetts 01060
USA

A catalogue record for this book
is available from the British Library

Library of Congress Control Number: 2012930590

ISBN 978 0 85793 620 2 (cased)

Typeset by Servis Filmsetting Ltd, Stockport, Cheshire
Printed and bound by MPG Books Group, UK

Contents

PART III   *SUKUK* MARKETS AND INDUSTRY PRACTICES

Figures

Tables

Contributors

Mohamed Ariff, a Professor of Finance at Bond University, held the finance chair for more than 10 years at Monash University, where he was for eight years head of finance and also held a post equivalent to associate professor at the University of Singapore. Ariff received his post-graduate degrees in finance at the universities of Wisconsin-Madison and Queensland after earning an upper II honours from University of Singapore. He is co-author of a leading McGraw-Hill textbook, *Investments*, by Bodie, Ariff, DaSilva, Kane and Marcus, and his research articles and books published internationally are well cited in literature. He has worked in the universities of Boston, Harvard, Melbourne, Tokyo, Evansville, and UCD of Ireland. He was elected president of the 23-year-old Asian Finance Association in 2004–07. He is a recipient of a large Australian Research Council Linkage grant (with two others) on Islamic banking research. He is a joint chair of the *sukuk* symposium that resulted in this book.

Meor Amri Ayob has progressively developed the Bond Pricing Agency over the last three years to be Malaysia's core business in market informa-tion disclosures to investors, making the agency the principal source of valuation and data reference for *sukuk* including the global *sukuk* industry as well as the conventional bond markets. Ayob has an MBA with a major in finance from the International Islamic University and a BSc in actuarial science from the University of Kent. Prior to taking his current position, he worked in the rating industry from 1994 with the Rating Agency of Malaysia.

Peter Casey is Director of Policy in the Dubai Financial Services Authority, having previously been responsible for the supervision of banking and insurance firms. Before joining DFSA, he was head of the non-life insurance department of the UK Financial Services Authority. Casey held senior regulatory posts in the Treasury, the Department of Trade and Industry and the Office of Fair Trading. He has wide experience of UK government, having also served in the Cabinet Office and Science Research Council and having worked in areas ranging from export pro-motion to the creation of computer misuse legislation. Casey was educated at Cambridge University.

Murat Çizakça is a leading world scholar in comparative economics and Islamic civilization. He is currently Visiting Professor at INCEIF, a global university for Islamic banking and finance. He obtained his higher degrees from Leicester University and the University of Pennsylvania. He has taught at the Bogazici University, in Turkey. He has been visiting professor at several universities, including the Australian National University, University of Western Australia and LMU in Berlin, Germany. His published work and his continuing teaching and writing on Islamic economics and finance are original contributions to the literature. His chapter on *sukuk* public finance and *gharar* is an excellent work on the idea of risk, and how this concept spread to the West and later emerged as the concept of risk.

Shamsun Anwar Hussein has a BSc in business from Boston University. He has 20 years of banking experience in the US, Malaysia and in off-shore banking. His specialist knowledge is in Islamic finance, gained over 15 years. He successfully structured and closed the first *Sukuk Al Ijara* in the international fixed income market as a global Islamic security, in addition to various Islamic financing deals totalling about RM20 billion (US$6 billion). This includes the landmark RM4.4 billion serial *Bai Bithaman Ajil Islamic* debt securities (BaIDS) in 1996–97, a transaction that led to the exponential growth of the Malaysian Islamic capital market.

Munawar Iqbal is an eminent freelance researcher, speaker and trainer in Islamic banking and finance. He is a professor at the King Abdul Aziz University, Jeddah, Institute of Islamic Economics. His career, spanning over 30 years, saw him in top management positions while teaching, researching and engaging in training activities. He was the foundation professor and foundation dean at International Islamic University Islamabad in 1984. As the chief of research at the IRTI of Islamic Development Bank Group, he saw its growth over several years before retiring. He has published 15 books and 30 papers on Islamic finance. He was the founding editor of *Review of Islamic Economics* and *Islamic Economic Studies*, a leading journal at the IDB. He has delivered lectures and conducted training sessions in Islamic finance throughout the world.

Salman Syed Ali Khan is a senior member of staff at the Islamic Development Bank and is a researcher-trainer at IDB's IRTI, a training and research institute.

Shamsher Mohamad is a professor of finance at INCEIF University. Prior to his current appointment he had been working at the University Putra

Malaysia for 28 years, and he was a professor of finance and held the position of Dean of the Faculty of Economics and Management. Much of the work on this book was completed while he was at UPM. He is a well-published Asian scholar with specialization on emerging capital market behaviour, especially of Malaysia. As a co-editor of the book, he also contributed and co-authored chapters in the book.

Sat Paul Parashar is the head of Center for Banking and Research at the Bahrain Institute of Banking and Finance. He has an M.Com from the Delhi School of Economics and earned a PhD from the University of Delhi. His teaching, training, research and consultancy experience spans more than 38 years. His professional areas of interests are banking, corporate finance, risk management, management control systems and corporate governance. He has published 50 papers and two books. His current areas of research interest are Basel II; integrated risk management in banking and financial services; Basel-II for Islamic banks; and implementation of good corporate banking. He is a member of the editorial boards of a number of international journals in the field of finance, business growth and competition.

Abdullah Saeed, at the University of Melbourne, is Sultan of Oman Professor of Arab and Islamic Studies and Director of the National Centre of Excellence for Islamic Studies. His teaching and research interests are: Islamic thought, Qur'anic hermeneutics, Islam in the West, and Islam and human rights. He has professional and research relationships around the world: he is on the editorial board of international refereed journals, a member of the UNESCO Commission of Australia, and a board member of Australia–Thailand Institute of Australia's Ministry of Foreign Affairs. His publications include: *The Qur'an: An Introduction* (2008), *Interpreting the Qur'an: Towards a Contemporary Approach* (2006), *Islamic Thought* (2006), *Freedom of Religion, Apostasy and Islam* (2004), *Islam in Australia* (2003), and *Islamic Banking and Interest* (1996).

Meysam Safari is a doctoral student at the Graduate School of Management at University Putra Malaysia. His current area of research interest is on the valuation of special debt securities with special attention on how contract specifications that changes the cash flows of a debt security should lead to different mathematical solutions to the valuation issue.

Nasser H. Saidi is the Chief Economist of the Dubai International Financial Centre Authority, and is the executive director of the Hawkamah Institute for corporate governance, Dubai. He is a member of the

IMF Regional Advisory Group for MENA and co-chair of the OECD Corporate Governance Working Group. Saidi established the Lebanon Corporate Governance Task Force. He was Lebanon's Minister of Economy and Trade and Minister of Industry between 1998 and 2000. He was a Member of the UN Committee for Development Policy for two mandates over 2000–2006. He is the author of *Corporate Governance in the MENA countries: Improving Transparency and Disclosure*. Nasser has a PhD and a MA in Economics from the University of Rochester; an MSc from University College, London University and a BA from the American University of Beirut.

Omar Salah is a PhD candidate at the TISCO Research Institute, Tilburg Law School, Netherlands. He is a lecturer on corporate finance, Islamic finance, and Dutch property law and has affiliation with the De Brauw Blackstone Westbroek law firm, and two universities, Leiden and Maastricht, where he is involved in Islamic law work. His research is on Islamic finance and more in particular on *sukuk* structure. His interest is whether it is possible to create a transnational legal framework for *sukuk* structures. Among his publications are: *Islamic Finance: Structuring Sukuk in the Netherlands* (2010).

Michael T. Skully came to Monash University in 1992 from the University of New South Wales where he was an associate professor in its School of Banking and Finance. Prior to this he worked for a US investment bank. His research and teaching is mainly in the area of financial institutions in Australia and the Asia Pacific region as well as in corporate finance. Skully has published widely in academic and professional journals. His books include *Merchant Banking in Australia*, *ASEAN Financial Cooperation*, *Financial Institutions and Markets in the South Pacific*, *Merchant Banking in ASEAN*, and *Merchant Banking in the Far East*. As a joint winner of an Australian Research Council award for research in Islamic Banking, he has found a new research interest in Islamic finance.

Foreword

The University Putra Malaysia (UPM) is known as a multi-faculty international research university of excellence in several academic disciplines. The literature the UPM scientists have produced in such diverse fields as tropical agriculture, meat science, tropical biology and marine biology is well recognized as authentic studies in respective fields of inquiry. UPM is also home to the Graduate School of Management (GSM) which is increasingly an international player in business training and research. Its thesis-based research activities and course work masters in business are greatly in demand.

In line with its reputation as a research university, the GSM's researchers have pioneered an effort to add authentic literature to the newly emerging sub-discipline, Islamic finance. As the academic head of the UPM, I have encouraged the entry of the GSM into research on business-related fields to enrich its literature. A commitment has been made by the university to encourage research over the next 10 years, and possibly beyond, to create literature that is produced as joint efforts of eminent scholars and experienced industry professionals. This must result in producing sound literature for the continued progress of Islamic finance. Islamic finance has established itself as a viable niche industry with banking, insurance, investment and debt instruments (*sukuk*) as well as Islamic capital markets that are designed to avoid interest-based transactions, as mandated by Islam. Islamic financial products are priced through (a) profit-sharing, (b) risk-sharing and (c) asset-backing principles, all of which are decidedly risk-reducing principles that make financial transactions of ordinary citizens safer for both demanders and issuers of financial securities.

This book on *sukuk* securities lays the essential principles of how these rediscovered debt-like instruments are designed on sound ethical principles of avoiding interest rate-based transactions in favour of risk-sharing, profit-sharing and asset-backing. The chapters of the book are written by eminent scholars and experienced industry professionals as commissioned papers, which were edited to shape as an authoritative book for the fast-developing Islamic debt instrument markets in about 12 locations around the world: Kuala Lumpur alone has 65 per cent of the market share. The only aim of this effort is to provide a well-researched book to serve the readers, be they in the universities or in the industry, as a guide for future reference.

I commend this effort, hopeful that this endeavour will lead in the longer run to a collection of authentic volumes of studies in the best tradition of modern scholarship and professionalism of serious researchers.

Prof. Tan Sri Datuk Dr. Nik Mustapha Raja Abdullah
Vice Chancellor, University Putra Malaysia

Preface

'Why this book?' is perhaps the main question to address in this preface. Islamic finance emerged some 50 years ago as a return to ethics-and-doctrine-based practices in financial transactions in the context of modern finance. Financial transactions in Muslim-majority societies in historical times were based squarely on a set of Islamic-ethics-consistent financial practices for *payment*, *financing* and *investment* activities. This rediscovered modern attempt starting some 50 years ago to reshape financial transaction contracts in Islamic countries, in line with ethics and doctrines consistent with Islamic principles of fairness, equity and full disclosures, led to the creation of a body of Islamic finance literature. That literature today is *mostly* description of what this new niche finance is all about with no or little attempt to provide a systematic introduction to its fundamentals to link those descriptions and principles to modern financial practices, in short to financial economics. After the entry of large modern banks into Islamic finance, following the Bank of England's landmark approval in 2002 to permit Islamic banks as new niche financial businesses, the Islamic financial product markets have grown rapidly in this niche business selling *new financial products* known to the world as Islamic finance, although it should be described more appropriately by such terms as 'ethics-based financial transactions' or 'profit-shared finance' to emphasize the central difference in the pricing mechanism away from interest rates.

It has also become evident that there is an urgency to create authentic literature – in the classic tradition of objective inquiry using standards of modern research in financial economics – to systematically attempt to lay the *foundation* of this new niche finance. This will help us to (i) understand this new little-researched field of inquiry; (ii) provide peer-reviewed authentic literature for research and teaching of this subject in so many tertiary institutions; and (iii) aid in the training of professionals being certified to practise this new profession.

Hence this is a book with a very different objective from the several titles around. Call this a start in a series to lay the foundation of Islamic finance. This book is the second in this series by the same publisher, who has encouraged, as they do in other new emerging fields of inquiry, publications relating to Islamic banking and finance. This book is on Islamic debt market instruments, the *sukuk* instruments, which are now issued and traded in some 12 financial markets with a market value in excess of US$1200 billion.

This book is among the foundation books that are planned to be published using the classic modern method of public discussion of ideas, peer-review process and authentic literature creation. Thus, the answer to the question 'Why this book?' is that this new discipline, born some 50 years ago, given its academic recognition in the last ten years has come of age for mainstream regulators, practising professionals and learned academics to collaborate in an attempt to speed the creation of knowledge relevant to this field. Collaborators include some prominent industry players funding the event to conduct open public discussion of ideas that will be harvested as books and journal articles. To that end, it is noteworthy that the collaborators in this effort are very senior professionals and regulators as well as eminent scholars in the field, all committed to a long-term project to have one volume on each significant topic on Islamic finance. This book is on the hot topic of Islamic *sukuk* or *shari'ah* (Islamic jurisprudence) compliant debt instruments, in instrument markets.

At a fundamental level, we can address this question from a historical perspective from an inquiry of human ethics: what is the historically evolved status of human ethics that govern human financial transactions? An answer to this requires a discussion of the evolution of financial ethics – call it 'foundation' – as embodied in financial transaction practices that guided the everyday contracting relationship necessary for payment, financing and investment activities of Muslim residents in societies under Islamic law and rules, which evolved incrementally in Muslim-majority societies, over 14 centuries. This was in addition to the largely Greco-Roman influences that Islam borrowed from in its early centuries, and built on those financial transactions modes already in vogue, except those that Islam prohibited outright, as consonant with Islamic religious doctrines. Hence both human ethics and Islamic doctrines influenced this subject.

Since the Renaissance, some eight centuries ago, as Europe emerged from the Middle Ages, Europe re-inherited and reshaped the Greco-Roman concepts of law and rules, while also preserving some ethical foundations that are shared via the Old Testament, the Gospel and the Qur'an. During the last three centuries, the laws and rules of conduct in Muslim societies have been slowly and surely replaced by modern concepts of financial laws and rules emanating from the latter day *secular* European societies. For example, usury laws in Europe were dropped, on the urgings of Bentham in England, and in other nations on the urgings of economists under the influence of a powerful banking lobby. Islam still continues to

forbid usurious funding; it goes one more step to require returns to investors as permissible reward *only* if the risk is shared in profit-shared contracts, just as it also cuts off funding to unethical or anti-society economic
activities, such as prostitution, gambling, and alcohol consumption.

Pertinent to this book is the fact that financial ethics have undergone
subtle changes as a result of secularization and, more importantly, the
lobby of banking institutions such that several religion-derived ethical
foundations *long established in historical times* have been dismantled and
replaced with secular laws, to influence everyday financial transactions
by humans. This influence, after replacing such religion-based norms in
European societies, spread to Muslim societies as secular laws and rules
evolving from the advent of modern banking in the last 250 years.

Modern banking has changed the very fabric of the foundation that
guided financial transactions for payments, financing and investments.
Careful observation of the history of banking suggests how the banks
have come to dominate and even set the agenda for financial foundation.
This book lays the human ethical foundations relevant to the *sukuk* debt
securities (whereas in other books we cover banking and other topics).
Just take an example: the historical ethic that borrowing by entrepreneurs
should be based on *asset-backed* lending was widely practised until 1657
in Amsterdam, then the world's central market for money. Today there
is a debate, as in this book, on how asset-backed and asset-based *sukuk*
transactions make funding (financing) safer for demanders and suppliers
of funds. Of course the Dutch model gave way to fractional banking where
there is no full asset backing especially in today's banking operations.
This *sukuk* Islamic debt market started just 12 years ago in its present
form with strong asset-backed lending, and already there are twelve
markets, including one in Kuala Lumpur with a two-thirds market share.
Around the world, this form of debt contracting is providing money on an
asset-backed basis with other ethical provisions consistent with three key
principles: fairness, equity and full disclosures in contracts.

During the last 250 years such principles as the ones just enumerated
have been slowly eroded so that corporations (entrepreneurs) could
borrow with no evidence of assets to back a loan (take the spectacular case
of failures, and test this hypothesis: Enron; Pharmalat; HIH Insurance;
Maxwell Corporation; Infosystem). Borrowing using asset-backing makes
financial transactions safer for lenders and borrowers, especially when
turns in the business cycle may expose the assets of a firm to too much
danger of funding with no stable assets to back. Historically, asset-backed
borrowing is a principle all humans adhered to in practice *except* in the
cases of (a) sovereign borrowers, who had future tax revenue as *likely
assets* and (b) poor people borrowing for sustenance but having no assets.

In the latter case, the Roman Church used to lend money to poor people as far back as the twelfth century, with no expectation of repayments. Islamic finance requires a small portion of loans of financial institutions to be made to such people, with no expectation of returns. This form of lending is called *Qardul Hasana*, or benevolent loan, and the source of this loan is a small part of profits and also alms-payments for the poor channeled to the banks as contributions from the wealthy.

In this book, we trace the foundation principles of how *sukuk* securities are designed, rated and marketed, and now contracts are framed in accordance with the Islamic principles of fairness, equity and full disclosures in borrowing-contracts for different purposes of economic activities. In so doing, we have attempted to draw from years of research and practices of regulators, professionals and eminent scholars in this field so as to give authenticity to the findings. Statements based on their insights are presented to the readers in this book. We hope the effort in this book is a welcome addition to the literature on this new sub-discipline of finance.

A book of this nature at the early stage of development of a new area of research owes its origin to thoughts of many people across the world in industry and in academia, with whom we came in contact over many decades. In a sense, therefore, this book owes a good deal of gratitude to them for their willingness to share their ideas freely. We would therefore like to dedicate this book to these several students of this new area of study falling within the new discipline of Islamic finance.

It remains now to thank specific persons and institutions who made the publication of this book a reality. We acknowledge the following institutions for providing support for this project. University Putra Malaysia's Graduate School of Management, GSM, for the funding of the conference; the Dubai International Financial Centre for hosting the event in their excellent conference venue in Dubai in May, 2010, in particular Aderi Adnan (now Advisor to Labuan Offshore Financial Centre); the Australian Research Council for a grant to Mohamed Ariff, Constant Mews and Michael T. Skully to research Islamic banking during 2007–2011; the National Centre of Excellence for Islamic Studies, in particular Abdullah Saeed, its director. The funding for the symposium that preceded the book came mostly from the GSM, so their generous financing is deeply appreciated by us.

At different stages of this project, we received advice and encouragement from several people over several years: Murat Çizakça, Mervyn Lewis, Tan Sri Datuk Nik Mustepha Raja Abdullah, Rodney Wilson, Syed Othman Alhabshi and several others who are among those whose collaboration, support and encouragement should be recorded with sincere thanks from us. Creating authentic literature is a challenging task, and their simple acts of encouragement and their guidance in accomplishing this task is very much appreciated. All along the publishers, Edward Elgar, had encouraged the creation of this literature as has been the case in the publication of an earlier Foundation in Finance book *Islamic Financial Institutions: Theory, Practice and Education.* We would like to thank the wonderful cooperation we had from staff: Alex Pettifer, Jo Betteridge, Emily Neukomm, Liz Wager, Bob Pickens and Yvonne Smith. We record our gratitude for the excellent editorial help of these people in England for the careful review and editorial work on the book.

Mohamed Ariff, Gold Coast, Australia
Munawar Iqbal, Islamabad, Pakistan
Shamsher Mohamad, Kuala Lumpur, Malaysia
15 January 2012

1. Introduction to *sukuk* Islamic debt securities markets

Mohamed Ariff, Munawar Iqbal and Shamsher Mohamad

1.1 INTRODUCTION TO THE BOOK ON *SUKUK* SECURITIES

This book is the outcome of a joint effort of a number of senior practising professionals as well as leading research scholars and educators in Islamic finance. The result is a reliable book on the subject of *sukuk* securities. Though this type of security is new to modern Islamic finance, it has its historical roots some centuries earlier as a novel instrument developed in the Turkish Empire based on earlier practices of government treasuries to raise money. *Sukuk* securities were first offered just about 20 years ago as part of a slew of new Islamic financial products to fund activities mostly over a finite horizon, since these are financing contracts priced not by using interest rates but by using returns on profit sharing-based contracts and asset-backing for the finance provided.

This is noteworthy since Islamic banking, a financial intermediation paradigm designed to use profit sharing, has taken some 50 years to establish credibility as a new model that is not only viable, but that also has many additional benefits. Accordingly, it has spread across the world. One of the differences between Islamic and conventional finance is that the pricing of Islamic financial products is based on sharing a portion of profits/returns (or as a secured fee) only *after* profit is earned: the only exception is in a particular product where no reward is to be asked from the borrower, unless voluntarily given. Hence a fund provider actually participates in the risk of funding an economic activity before getting a reward for financing. Islamic finance treats reward and entrepreneurship as a *conjoint* matter so no reward can be had unless the contract specifies a profit (or secured fee) that could be earned by the borrower *ex post*.

This contrasts with conventional modern funding arrangements, where investors secure a return based on *pre*-agreed rewards based on interest rates (which are externally determined and not related to profits to the entrepreneur from the use of funds) with no provision to participate in the risk of the economic activity to which the fund is applied. This essential aspect is common in all Islamic funding arrangements. To that key difference, we can add several ethical no-go zones such as restricting funding to only socially-conducive economic activities (no funds for operating a casino, for example). Relevant for the *sukuk* securities is the requirement that fund seekers will not be able to obtain financing if they have no assets to back funds raised. These and other principles form the *foundations* of Islamic finance. These are explained in this book in some detail. The focus of the book is also on how the *sukuk* securities industry functions in terms of institutional organization, rules, and operations of the market players.

There exists today a voluminous body of literature on several aspects of Islamic finance on the interpretation and applications of the basic *shari'ah* principles (Islamic common law principles) relating to investment, financing economic production and the modes of financial transactions as well as contractual matters. It must be mentioned though that many of the available publications in that large body of literature already available are products of serious rigorous research. There are also publications that promote the agenda of the sponsors of a particular researcher with scant reference to modern finance in general or even how Islamic finance ought to be grounded in the same processes applied in the mother discipline of financial economics.

A more concerting issue in the literature is the current trend of criticizing Islamic finance and the widespread view among many that the success of Islamic finance depends on how well it can replicate conventional finance! Islamic finance can learn from conventional financial contracts, and vice versa, but there is absolutely no need for Islamic finance to mimic every conventional contract or its conditions. That is one of the contributions of Islamic finance. The consumer has a wider choice-set, since the two models have a different modus operandi. If one understands that the pricing of financial products in Islamic finance is based on different principles, namely profit-and-risk sharing or fee-based charges, then one's understanding of how these pricing mechanisms could lead to market clearing prices that are socially welfare-promoting is easy to understand. This book is not a panacea for all issues mentioned but it adopts the classic method of modern inquiry in economics, deliberates the research outputs with peers qualified to do so, and then produces an authentic literature on a current hot topic in finance, the so-called Islamic bonds – namely the markets for *sukuk* certificates.

Hence, this book should enable one to have a clear understanding of what *sukuk* securities (so-called Islamic bonds) are, how these are designed, traded, how the securities provide incomes via profit share (and mark-up fee) to investors and how these are redeemed at maturity. The one important thing, hitherto not widely addressed in *sukuk* literature, is the inclusion of several chapters meant to elucidate concept development, state theory-type discussions and attempt some valuation principles based on sound modern financial techniques common in financial economics. It may not be an overstatement to suggest here that there has been a rush to make viable markets for this new type security in about 12 international locations, of which Kuala Lumpur in Malaysia has become the leader, with Bahrain and UAE following closely.[1] The result is that little attention has been given to the concept development and elucidation needed to understand this security type as a different class of instruments. Another deficiency in the literature is that little attention has been given to developing basic valuation equations for *sukuk* securities.

This situation is very serious because market participants assume that the revelation of market price in the process of buying and selling a *sukuk* instrument is the true indication of the *theoretical* value of this new type of security in Islamic finance. Needless to say, this is not the case. Continued absence of sound valuation theories is likely to retard the growth of the industry since investors and analysts also need valid pricing models to establish *fair* prices, in addition to the ubiquitous *market price*. The intrinsic values of conventional securities have been established over several decades of concept development over time, resulting in basic valuation models to guide practices and education.

We believe that this modest effort of ours is welcomed by (i) the industry and (ii) scholars as likely to lead the inquiry in due time to valid conceptual and valuation models. In the case of some types of *sukuk* securities that could not be traded in public markets, there are no market prices for them. Notional values have to be calculated, and this also requires valuation models.

1.2 STRUCTURE OF THE BOOK

To provide a sound introduction to achieve both concept development and to describe practice issues, this book is divided into three parts. In Part I the reader will find concept development and valuation issues that lay what we believe are the foundation principles of *sukuk* securities. *Sukuk* markets that operate in more than a dozen different locations in South-East Asia and the Middle East (as well as other locations) are regulated by authorities with special laws and regulations geared to orderly market development and price discovery. Because of limitation of space, we only cover the regulatory framework in Bahrain, UAE and Malaysia as examples of the regimes in other locations. This aspect is covered in Part II under the heading of regulations and governance.

Part III is intended as an introduction to the practices of the market place. There is a vast body of literature on this aspect; in fact this has been the dominant theme of most of the books and articles that appear in the press and are held in the libraries as well as found as non-reviewed materials in Internet sources. We made a judicious choice of only selecting the common themes under this topic. We cover the widespread practice of marking-to-market as the traded fair value of *sukuk* securities to provide a guide to the investors. We have a chapter on origination of *sukuk* securities from the design to marketing and listing for trade. This part also includes a chapter that highlights a number of unresolved issues undergoing discussions with a view to removing obstacles to the orderly development of the market.

1.3 CONTRIBUTIONS OF THE BOOK

Concept development is attempted in a chapter by Mohamed Ariff, Meysam Safari and Shamsher Mohamed. The central theme covered is the description of the fundamentals of *sukuk* securities as Islamic financial instruments for funding economic activities (i) via profit-sharing after income is earned through (ii) risk-sharing with the entrepreneur who raises funds using *sukuk*. An attempt is made to provide a valid classification of the wide-ranging *sukuk* securities so writers may focus on the basic types and the basic types could lend themselves to ease of modelling and valuation. The cash flow patterns are established before the fundamental principles are laid that should guide the development of valuation models, in so doing, broadly following the rigour of modern finance. There is an attempt to establish some valuation models to be tested in the market in subsequent research. Thus, this contribution establishes the link between fundamentals and theoretical valuation modelling.

In the next chapter written by Abdullah Saeed and Omar Salah, the reader will find a judicious treatment of how avoidance of usury and the meaning of interest rate are two relevant fundamental principles in the design and trading of *sukuk* securities. The authors are careful to explain how the contemporary narrow interpretation of avoidance of interest is a development over just about 100 years, which has equated interest with usury as the widely accepted idea in Islamic finance today. Historical evidence suggests that this contemporary modern concept is a recent development as a consensus building exercise to face the reality of modern banking and financial practices. This is a theory-relevant chapter for the readers, and the writers ably discuss and clarify the jurisprudential issues relating to interest and usury.

Munawar Iqbal gives coherence to the fundamental principles that should guide the design of *sukuk* (indeed any other) financial products in line with a set of what he calls ten financial engineering principles. The debate here is to build a theory to represent the core requirements in Islamic finance to guide professionals to design *shari'ah*-consistent *sukuk* and other financial products. This chapter is a crucial framework for the design of products while it also serves as a theoretical summary of the principles guiding Islamic finance. This chapter is an essential read for all practitioners as it marks the perimeters within which securities ought to be designed to be in line with fundamental principles of Islamic economics and finance.

The last chapter in this part is a contribution by Murat Çizakça, an economic historian, who traces how the concept of *gharar* (uncertainty) was handled in public finance *sukuk* practices in the Turkish Empire. The topic of Islamic public finance is a larger area, which is not covered in this chapter, yet the author gives archive-based evidence to show how public finance techniques underwent a new interpretation and yet are consistent with *shari'ah* laws applied to changing circumstances. His archival-based research paper is a very welcome addition that pinpoints the origin of *sukuk* as being traced to an era when modern banking did not exist, and that funding arrangements akin to today's *sukuk* were in vogue in an earlier era. *Sukuk* provided the massive funding for infrastructure projects in that empire after the devastations from crusades over two centuries of warfare. His discussion also includes how the concept of risk as it was known then crept into the Western literature as a useful concept in economics at that time. The role of *sukuk* in public finance needs a separate research effort: this is particularly important since sovereign *sukuk* issues are about a third to half of the market issues.

Part II has three chapters on regulation and governance issues. All *sukuk* markets are carefully regulated by authorities responsible for deposit-taking firms and for securities trading. Hence, this aspect of regulations and the extent to which regulations arc complied with by industry players answers the governance issues in this field. The first chapter describes the regulatory framework in Dubai, contributed by the chief regulator there, Peter Casey. His attempt to treat *sukuk* instruments as debt instruments is a simple way to get at the heart of this market for regulatory purposes. He describes the framework of such regulations, which is somewhat common in Abu Dhabi and Sharjah in the United Arab Emirates.

Bahrain has a different approach to regulations and this is described by Sat Paul Parashar to highlight the important aspects that guide this second largest important market. Michael T. Skully examines the *sukuk* securitization process as a special case of securitization in general. His attempt is interesting in that the differences are highlighted just to reveal that the principles applied under a set of general principles are workable.

In Part III, the contributors are concerned about practices, a major issue addressed in this book. This is attempted very ably by Nassar H. Saidi, a practising economist, who lays out the fundamental facts about *sukuk* markets. His take in his chapter is to highlight where the market is around the world as at 2010, what impediments to growth are and what actions are needed to grow the *sukuk* markets around the world. His helicopter view provides a broad-based introduction to practices before he goes on to indicate the strategy needed to achieve this growth.

The growth of the *sukuk* market in Bahrain is described by Sat Paul Parashar. His extensive analysis with statistics provides a simplified description of the growing complexity of this very new market, which is the second largest among the twelve in Islamic finance. Two practitioners (Meor Amri Ayob and Shamsun Anwar Hussein) respectively provide descriptions on how *sukuk* securities are priced with reference to market prices and how *sukuk* are originated and sold.

It is evident that there are significant differences in the manner in which a *sukuk* is designed as a consequence of the fundamental principles of Islamic finance that must be adhered to. Beyond that, there are important issues regarding how a Special Purpose Company (SPC) takes over some income-producing assets of a borrower to enable *sukuk* holders to have *real claims* on assets removed from the control of the borrower. This is a fundamental difference in *sukuk* to (i) only provide funding if there are income-producing assets (or a known value of such future assets could exist in the case of working capital finance) that could be immediately owned by the financer and (ii) limit the appetite for unwarranted leverage. This fundamental provision in Islamic financial contracts – we call this the principle of 'no assets no funds' – limits the ability of governments, firms and individuals to raise too much funding, which cannot be serviced later (a major cause of recurrent financial crises and hence this automatic break is another major contribution as a society-wide benefit of Islamic finance). The aspect of heavy leveraging by economic agents has been hotly debated since the 2007–2008 Global Financial Crisis (GFC) exposed the weaknesses of firms and especially of governments with huge debt overhang. This bad universal practice is one that the world has to grapple with in the near term to prevent a recurrence of the credit-explosion-led crises during the last half of the twentieth century as well as the opening crisis of this century at the time of the GFC and after.

Salman Syed Ali Khan's chapter is aimed at how the Islamic Development Bank (IDB) is helping to develop this new niche finance across its constituent countries, some 56 nations, by practising finance consistent with Islamic financial principles. This is an important chapter, which suggests that international institutions with such august aims as eradicating poverty (World Bank) should perhaps turnover a new leaf in the light of how this is ably done by the IDB using contracts based on profit sharing or fee-based charges instead of interest rates. IDB's major contribution is in trade financing using Islamic principles: about two-thirds of its activities are in that area. The last chapter is about unresolved concerns that require the urgent attention of theoreticians, practitioners and regulators if the development of this new niche debt market is to be furthered. It is evident that this new financial market has features that appear to moderate the appetite for debt, actual returns being conditional on profit-making and of course risk being shared, among others.

1.4 COMMENT

We firmly believe that there are many aspects of *sukuk* markets that could be covered in more than one book such as this. We have indicated the need to examine public finance[2] and to that we can add more topics, including a topic on measuring the risk of *sukuk* from the angle of asset transfer to *sukuk* holders via the SPC or from the angle of earnings volatility. However, this book has aspects of coverage that we term theoretical and fundamental in nature, more so than is found in many books. This contribution, we hope, will be appreciated by regulators, educators and professionals as reference book to assist them in their job of running the markets and for the serious students of Islamic finance to help them in their understanding of this market. More technical aspects need further research.

NOTES

1. Hong Kong, in line with its reputation as an international financial market, has lined up its first *sukuk* issue for 2011 using Chinese Yuan, while Seoul in Korea, Egypt, and several other locations are making an effort to create *sukuk* markets.
2. The editors are grateful to the anonymous reviewer of the manuscript for this comment. We agree that the historical use of the *sukuk* instrument to finance public expenditure is a topic that needs to be carefully verified. In addition, this instrument provides an

automatic break for too much debt issue by an issuer, because unfettered issue of debt by sovereigns cannot be made because holders of this form of securities require assets of the government to be set aside in SPCs as required by the *shari'ah* principle. In a sense, a firm issuing too much debt would have very little of its assets since each time an issue is made, the assets under the control of the firm will shrink.

PART I

Fundamentals of *sukuk* securities

2. *Sukuk* securities, their definitions, classification and pricing issues

Mohamed Ariff, Meysam Safari and Shamsher Mohamad

2.1 INTRODUCTION

Islamic securities are specially tailored financial products that conform to a given set of legal-common-law-based (*shari'ah*) financial transaction principles, which are deemed strictly applied when designing financial contracting terms covering such products. These principles are quite different from those used in the design of conventional securities. The principles guiding the design of these securities evolved over some two and a half centuries *without reference* to such doctrine-based principles as are applied in designing Islamic financial products in historical times. From the time fractional reserve banking established a strong acceptance by regulators around AD 1800 some four decades after the Papal edict made interest rate-based lending permissible by the Roman Church, the lion's share of production lending that existed for millennia on profit-sharing slowly gave way to a one-way contract where the profits and risk of a production loan became divorced. The entrepreneurs had to take the full risk of a venture, not the lender. This is not the case for the production of Islamic financial securities. The products thus designed under the Islamic label are found in publicly-traded bills, shares, debt-like *sukuk* and derivative markets or as privately-traded in financial institutions.

Broadly defined, Islamic financial products could be classified into four types:

(i) *musharaka* securities with ownership-*and*-control in the entire firm's assets via share ownership, which makes this class very closely similar to common share securities with claims to profits only if profits are earned after sharing in the risk of the project being funded;
(ii) *sukuk* securities, which mostly finite-period debt or funding arrangement contracts mostly *without* managerial control of the

project funded but with unique fractional ownership of a set of income-producing assets of a borrower set aside by the borrower as asset-backed or asset-based in a Special Purpose Company (SPC) owned by fund providers, whose pay-off is based on profit sharing from the assets of the SPC;

(iii)   a *takaful* contract, which is a risk transfer arrangement, an insurance contract with provisions that such insurance premiums as are collected from the insured party are to be invested only in *approved* (permissible by *shari'ah*) securities passing Islamic finance regulations;

(iv)   Islamic mutual funds, which are investment funds managed by managers on behalf of clients for a fee *and* recovery of costs incurred in management of portfolios, with provisions for return of profits after management costs.

Among these four, *takaful* is an insurance transaction, but it uses mutual insurance principles, so excess profits are distributed at regular intervals to members based on a pre-agreed profit ratio.

This simple four-category division of Islamic financial products may resemble similar respective conventional security classes, namely shares, bonds, insurance and mutual funds. But there are significant differences in terms of structuring Islamic financial products, in the mode of pricing them, and in collateralization as well as what form of economic production activities may have access to funds under Islamic finance. For example, pricing of Islamic securities is done via *profit-sharing* contracting, whereas conventional securities are priced by *interest*-based payments, usually pre-agreed, to investors or as dividend-based payments to shareholders. Some may have even special features, say, a strange form of diminishing principal-cum-profit payments called the 'diminishing musharaka'. These and other characteristics make Islamic financial instruments very different from conventional instruments, and the *appearance* of similarity is somewhat exaggerated by critics not knowing the important structural differences meant to safeguard both borrowers and the lenders and to ensure ethics-and-doctrine-based funding arrangements.

Since Islamic securities, once issued as public-traded instruments, are also traded in financial markets, we have to also include (v) Islamic capital markets as an area of research in Islamic finance. To this, one may add (vi) private equity or private *sukuk* or private *takaful* or mutual funds as a separate group of securities if such securities are not traded in public markets, so we may call them non-traded private Islamic securities. Thus, this is a simple and broad-brush six-category division of Islamic financial transaction modes which precedes our discussion in this chapter on only one of them, the *sukuk*. We proceed with this main task of this chapter by examining the *sukuk* securities as a class by itself.

The rest of the chapter is organized as follows. Section 2.2 provides a simple introduction to the fundamental principles, in some detail, that are applied to *sukuk* securities to conform to doctrinally-required *shari'ah* provisions. The different definitions of this security will also be highlighted in that section. The origin of and contemporary design of the instrument is next described in section 2.3. Due to space constraints, we cover only six basic issued types out of the 14 potential *sukuk* securities reported as feasible in the literature. The cash flow patterns and a classification of *sukuk* securities are presented in section 2.4. Issues relating to valuation of *sukuk* are attempted in section 2.5 with a view to providing a good starting point on this important issue of valuation models for all *sukuk* securities. In sections 2.6 and 2.7, we provide a description of the worldwide *sukuk* issues across several markets, all adding up to about US$1200 billion in assets. The chapter concludes in section 2.8.

2.2 DEFINITION AND FOUNDATION PRINCIPLES

The foundation principles for *sukuk* (we will refer to *sukuk* to mean *sukuk* securities in the rest of the chapter) have developed in conformity with Islamic legal principles based on Qur'anic commandments as elaborated in *shari'ah* (Islamic common law) provisions over centuries of development as handed down since the Islamic scripture, the Qur'an, was revealed during AD 610–32. The word '*sukuk*' is not found in the Qur'an, and it emerged as a development of the application of Qur'anic principles to the act of debt funding. Scholars applied the commandments therein to refine financial transactions over some 1300 years by the time of the late nineteenth century, when the use of *sukuk* appears to have slowly waned, being replaced with modern banking practices from successful colonization and introduction of the old and the new world.

It appears that the foundation principles are quite comprehensive to guide parties to a contract to apply the overall aim of broad Islamic principles such as fairness, equity and full information provision (no asymmetric information, so both parties have the same information) for executing a financial contract: such contracts are provided in a written form so they can be formally witnessed. In this section, we do not intend to describe these overarching legal principles – fairness, equity, justice, and full disclosure – therefore restricting our description to the foundation principles to cover *sukuk* securities.

To start with, the word '*sukuk*' is plural for a certificate (*sakk*) of ownership of a given class of assets of the borrowers given to the providers of funds as proof of ownership. Therefore *sukuk* security is an instrument that requires, first, the creation of assets in a separate entity, these assets being owned by the lenders, the fund providers, in proportion to the amount of funds provided. This is a fundamental principle of *sukuk* contracting. In a sense, it suggests that without the lender being able to create an arm's-length asset-backing to a funding arrangement to which the borrower has transferred income-producing assets, there cannot be any lending contracts in an *ethical* financial transaction. This suggests that all *sukuk* securities have to have this safety so that, from the start of the contract, the lenders have asset-backing for their funding. This makes *sukuk* security safer than the conventional bonds because the lender in a conventional debt contract would need the permission of the court of law to obtain right of ownership, and even that permission is only given if it is contested at the time of actual default of promised pay-off.

A *sukuk*[1] contract may thus be defined simply as a funding (debt) arrangement agreed to between a party providing the funds (investor) and the counterparty (a government or a firm or an individual) borrowing the funds for the purposes of using the funds to engage only in permissible economic production/services. Because some of these funding arrangements range from ownership-*and*-control based share-type securities to pure borrowing-type securities to leasing-type securities as described in the previous section, it is inaccurate to describe *sukuk* as an Islamic *debt* instrument, as is the widespread practice popularized by popular finance media.

Unlike in *sukuk*, in share-type *musharaka sukuk* securities issued to investors with right of control of the firm, the fund providers only get back agreed rewards in the form of a portion of profits based on a pre-agreed profit ratio. Also, if the ownership is assigned to all the assets of the borrower, whether the ownership entails control or absence of control of the enterprise, then this is called *musharaka sukuk*, meaning a share-like funding arrangement for a finite period of time. This type does not exist at present and may be thought of as a common share in a specific project with a finite period of life to produce an item and the fund to be paid back with profits. In conventional share funding, if another restriction is imposed to limit the use of such funds to produce permitted products/services, the result would be a common share, *musharaka* contract. If such issues are also issued for a finite period, this would be a new type of share, which is not found in conventional finance. All contracts with an *infinite* period and share-ownership-*and*-control of assets of the total enterprise are pure *musharaka* contracts.

Next, more commonly in practice, a borrower sets aside a portion of income-producing assets in a Special Purpose Company (SPC) and immediately makes those assets available as owned by the investors in proportion to the funding ratio; this would be a basic asset-backed *sukuk* contract. A simple *sukuk* security would be a funding arrangement for a finite period with the provision of ownership of a part of the borrower's assets set aside as owned by an SPC, which entity would service the investors over the contract period using incomes produced by the SPC.

Hence, one should consider finite period funding (debt) arrangement as a characteristic of *sukuk* funding while the second characteristic is the removal of part of the borrower's assets into a SPC to be owned by the fund providers from contract start time: current practice somewhat alters the asset-backing to asset-based contracting as a newer form. This is not the case with conventional bond-type lending since the lender has to contest, in a court of law, only if non-payment of pre-agreed interest payments occurs for the court to permit ownership of assets of the *total* firm. Not so in *sukuk* contracts. This makes Islamic funding arrangements a lot safer, and restricts borrowers from borrowing without assets to back the funding.

Asset-backing can be considered as a fundamental principle: *if there are no assets to back a loan, there is no funding*. This places quantity limits on excessive borrowing. Heavy reliance on borrowed funds has been associated with financial fragility in economic policy literature as the root cause of so many bankruptcies over centuries during crisis periods and also during business downturns across the world. A recent example of financial fragility is that of the Global Financial Crisis, which came from the non-recourse to fund providers of real assets of major banks and financial firms. Had there been this ownership factor, there would not have been the credit bulge over 1994–2006, which has been blamed for the start of the global crisis.

A third characteristic is the use of *profit ratio* in the contract to determine the rewards to investors. Since profit or loss is only known *after* a span of time that the borrowed fund has been applied to an economic activity, this introduces the very significant characteristic of Islamic fund providers sharing in the risk of a project before a reward is mandated and decided. One can see this quite clearly when a firm decides to pay dividends in the case of common shares at the half-yearly or annual profit reporting times *after* earning profits. If there is no profit in a period (if there has been a fire that reduced the value of real assets of an SPC) then there is no reward or part reward for that period.

In conventional funding arrangements, a bond holder is entitled to a reward *irrespective* of a profit or loss: not so in *sukuk* contracts. To the extent that the payment of reward is conditional on profits occurring, the nature of the payment is not fixed. Thus, to treat the rewards promised as fixed and applying a fixed-coupon-paying bond valuation model to value a *sukuk* security is not justifiable unless it is meant as a rough, not a precise, indicator of theoretical value.

However, there are two specific *sukuk* contracts requiring the amount of pay-off to be fixed to be paid periodically or permitting the pay-off to grow at a constant growth rate: the part that is paid is fixed, but the incomes of the SPC may be higher or lower. These two *sukuk* contracts are exceptions to the general rule of pay-offs being not fixed. These special arrangements are: *ijara* (lease-type) *sukuk* funding with pay-offs of a fixed rental-type arrangement; and *bai bithaman ajjal sukuk* (constant-growth profit-share starting with a fixed ratio) or BBA, which provides for pay-off to increase by a constant factor in each subsequent periodic payment. The latter may be an arrangement where the rental of the assets held by the SPC increases by a constant factor after the first annuity due payment is made. There are four other types of *sukuk* securities that do not share this fixed or constant-rate-growth characteristic, as will be described in a later section.

Another characteristic of *sukuk* funding is that, where there is only an initial funding, and there are no periodic rewards paid over the entire period of contract with the intention of repayment at the terminal period, such contracts have different modes of design. Some are designed with a pre-determined end-period payment formula whereas some are based on end-period value based on the market value of the SPC assets at the terminal period (for example, a debtor's buyback arrangement at a price, to reduce the risk of the market price being volatile). Hence, the reader may note that the conventional bond design does not permit this level of sophistication because the lender is treated as an outsider to the firm with no ownership of any part of the borrower's assets. To the extent there is ownership, though only to that portion of income-producing assets in the removed SPC, it is possible that there will be a market value (less or more, depending on the depreciation and replacement value of assets in the SPC). The important point is that the value of pay-offs could be in *excess* of the original funding to provide a return that is unspecified. Thus the pay-off is stochastic depending on the to-be-revealed market value of assets in the SPC, unless a buyback arrangement limits this. That is, for valuation purpose, the final repayment is indeterminate and not fixed (except in buyback contracting) and this introduces a new element in the valuation of such assets.

Finally, as in all Islamic financing contracts, the projects to which funding is supplied must be projects that are engaged in *pro-society* (legally-permitted or *halal*) economic production/services. This means

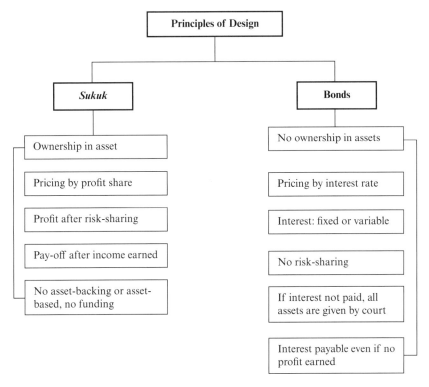

Figure 2.1   *Fundamental principles of* sukuk *security compared to conventional debt security*

that there are doctrinal restrictions to funding firms engaging in gambling, production of intoxicants for human consumption, offering prostitution, or producing pork for human consumption. Hence, *sukuk* financing will not be extended to those economic activities that are pre-determined to be not pro-society: this is an ethical principle very dear to a moral society. There are few other restrictions, one of which is that funding is made unavailable to firms engaging in usurious interest-rate-based activities. We are not going to delve into other characteristics since we discuss this in another section. Figure 2.1 provides a comparison of the fundamental principles underlying the contract specifications of *sukuk* funding against conventional debt funding contracts.

As a summary of the discussion in this section, the reader can identify six main differences in Islamic *sukuk* funding arrangements compared to the conventional bond-based or bank-lending arrangements. First, the pricing of the bond is based on how much of the *profit share* the borrower is willing to give, which of course depends on the riskiness of the project to which the fund is applied. A letter of credit to import a million dollars' worth of wood product may be less risky than to fund a project to build a toll road. Hence the profit ratio would be lower in the former case and higher in the latter case. In a conventional lending contract, be it a pre-agreed fixed or variable pay-off (or fee-based) loan, the pay-off is lower in the former case and higher in the latter case. There is a subtle difference. The fund provider in *sukuk* agrees to take no rewards if in a particular year there is no profit, unless the borrower is proven to have behaved fraudulently. That means that there is participation in the risk of the project. Even worse, the project may fail out of wilful neglect of the entrepreneur.

These two favourable aspects, namely profit-sharing and risk-sharing, may make *sukuk* securities have a higher risk than is the case of pre-fixing a pay-off in interest rate-based securities where there is no ownership of any assets until the project fails.

Hence the second and third characteristics are: *reward is given only if profits are earned*, and, if the project fails with no proof of wilful negligence, the *principal is lost to the extent of the market value* of the assets in the SPC, which is owned by the fund providers. Having access to ownership of income-producing assets from day one of the contract limits the loss of the entire principal fund. In conventional bond-type lending, haircuts are applied to the entire firm's assets and not just the assets transferred to the SPC.

Hence, during crises, *sukuk* contracts tend to take away or waste fewer assets than would be the case in conventional funding. The fourth characteristic is that, for a *sukuk* funder, only the assets in the SPC are accessible for sale, not the entire firm's assets. In a sense this provides a half-way house before bankruptcy, whereas under conventional funding, bankruptcy is the only course under civil laws in most countries. Even in the case of Chapter 11 protection (when a firm can apply to continue to operate while all assets are being taken away by lenders) under bankruptcy laws the unavailability of this limited-damage recourse to settle dispute saves assets not transferred to the *sukuk* holders via the SPC. Hence, at the aggregate level of the economy, there is no need to throw away large amounts of assets each time a crisis or recession occurs, because under *sukuk* contracting part of the loss is borne by *sukuk* funders and most assets are under the control of the owner of the firm. The haircut (the extent to which debt settlement is reduced) is limited to some part of the head, not the entire head!

The fifth characteristic is that *sukuk* provides special structures to match the special needs of the project cash flows. For example, in a working capital *sukuk* (*istisna*) the customer wanting to produce an item over a period may provide funds for that finite period for production of an item even before it is produced: This encourages entrepreneurship. But the contract must specify the exact nature of the product, so that the future existence of that product could serve as the value for the purpose of working capital funding. There are other more exotic designs such that the original sum funding a project will be repaid both as profit-share as well as part principal repayment in what is called diminishing *musharaka sukuk* contracts. Complexity of product design is a desirable characteristic in finance.

Finally the doctrinal restrictions on the application of the funds to pro-society activities constitute the sixth distinguishing feature of Islamic finance in general. Religious doctrine dictates that gambling, prostitution, consumption of intoxicants and production of pork meat for human consumption are not permitted (that is, these are prohibited or *haram*) activities. So, no *sukuk* funding will be made available if the intended use of the fund is to produce those items: this aspect introduces a high moral purpose to debt-contracting. This aspect is meant to starve the growth of such not-pro-society activities through denying investments in prohibited economic activities. If one uses one's own funds to carry out these activities, then it is a different matter of taking personal responsibility regarding breaking the doctrine relating to not-permitted activities. This is not an area for compromise under Islamic doctrine-based fundamental principle.

Hence, a brief examination suggests that *sukuk* are not bond-like funding contracts or bank-lending based on: (i) pre-fixed or variable interest rate, (ii) or merely profit share, (iii) non-risk-sharing contracting; (iv) principal guaranteed to be returned at the terminal period. (v) Basic conventional funding is not easy to structure in complex ways, at least as practised because of lack of an SPC, and (vi) there are no provisions for restricting only pro-society economic activities.

2.2.1   Definitions and Regulations

The regulatory authorities in each regime in which *sukuk* are issued have clearly defined the *sukuk* security and anyone may find these definitions on each regulator's website. However, in this chapter, we use international standard-setting bodies' definitions to define *sukuk*. International Islamic Financial Market (IIFM) defines *sukuk* as a 'commercial paper that provides an investor with ownership in an underlying asset'. Here the definition for paper can be extended to any finite period *sukuk*. The Islamic Financial Services Board (IFSB) defines *sukuk* thus: 'certificates with each *sak* representing a proportional undivided ownership right in tangible assets, or a pool of predominantly tangible assets, or a business venture (such as a Mudarabah). These assets may in specific project or investment activity be in accordance with Shari'ah rules and principles.' This definition is highly applicable to financial institutions, and it emphasizes the asset transfer and ownership, while ignoring the trading aspects.

A third definition is from the accounting standards setting body, AAOIFI (Accounting & Auditing Organisation for Islamic Financial Institutions) 'Certificate of equal value representing, after closing subscription, receipt of the value of the certificates and putting it to use as planned, common title to shares and rights in tangible assets, usufructs and services, or equity of a given project or equity of a special investment activity.'

These definitions identify a common theme: existence of SPC; asset ownership; real assets as well as usufructs. There is a plethora of definitions, but we prefer to quote only these three.

2.3   ORIGIN OF AND STRUCTURING OF *SUKUK* IN HISTORICAL TIME

Documented historical records allude to the creation of *sukuk* as a borrowing instrument that the Islamic legal scholars in the Turkish Empire helped to design when the emperor needed to borrow large amounts of money to reconstruct an empire after the devastation of crusades that ended in AD 1285. The innovation of fund-raising consistent with Islamic ethics of borrowing differed considerably from that of the practices at that time which were based on Babylonian and Greco-Roman laws. Under Islamic principles of borrowing/funding, a financial contract must have the following characteristics. Ownership-*and*-control-based contracts must be based on profit-shares via participating in the risk of the project so that the profit accrues to lenders after the fund is used: the profit earned is shared in proportion to an agreed share of profits. The important thing is that it is a share-like arrangement although the *sukuk* instrument is a borrowing instrument for a limited period of funding, where the rewards for funding depend on the outcome of the funds being applied with a mutuality of interest of both parties to secure good outcomes of the enterprise activity.

Where no ownership-*and*-control is involved on *all* the assets of an enterprise, a *sukuk* instrument is agreed upon with (i) the fund provider (lender) having a share of that part of the borrower's assets transferred to an SPC to be owned by the lenders and (ii) the borrower sells the set-aside assets to repay the borrowed money at the end of the contract period while (iii) the earnings of the SPC assets provide incomes to be paid as rewards at periodic times, if provided for such pay-offs regularly. In a sense, to borrow, a producer firm must have assets removed from its control so that the lender has incomes coming from those set-aside assets to pay the rewards to the fund provider.

Borrowing for any purpose other than economic usefulness to society is not encouraged, and the setting-aside of assets of a producer firm ensures an income as returns to the lender, which is meant to make the borrowing contract more secure than is the case in conventional bond markets. Borrowing in conventional bond markets is by and large based on the good name of the borrower; certainly assets are not owned from day one of the funding, nor is risk shared before pay-off occurs.

Such a *sukuk* contract, as described in contrast to a conventional bond, was agreed upon by the Turkish emperor to raise money by setting aside some of the Treasury assets to be owned by the lending public to rebuild the infrastructure of the empire.

Another characteristic in *sukuk* funding is that the rewards that a fund-provider gets from investment is from incomes that derive from the assets set aside by the borrower to both pay an agreed return (regular pay-offs) based on profit share and also to repay the borrowed funds at the end of the term of the loan contract. While *sukuk* funding is always as described above, the only borrowing that is considered exempted from such restriction is *individuals* borrowing for sustenance, in which case funds are lent without any promised pay-off over the funding period requiring only the repayment of the principal lent. This is called *ghard Hassan*, which is a form of bank lending with no interest and repayment of principals solely to fund household durable funding.[2] This is equivalent to the Roman Catholic Church's Papal lending that occurred in Italy during periods of famine and wars when the Church lent money without any interest and with no expectation of the principal being repaid. Lending for sustenance without expectation of rewards – even the forgoing of the principal amount – is clearly lauded in the Torah, the Bible and the Qur'an as desirable acts of the faithful.

2.3.1 Contemporary *Sukuk* Securities

The Islamic *sukuk* funding market was rediscovered about 22 years ago when in 1990 a private sector firm (Shell Malaysia Bhd) issued a *sukuk* borrowing instrument to raise RM125 million (US$40 million) through a private issue in Kuala Lumpur. Since then and especially from 2000, this market has grown, with private sector firms as well as government and government agencies raising money issuing *sukuk* securities not just in Kuala Lumpur, but in 11 other locations around the world. The Bank for International Settlements (BIS), which count both public traded and private issues, reports that the *sukuk* bond market around the world is worth about US$1200 billion (about 2 per cent of conventional issues). So, the private issues dominate this market because the government issues amount to less than US$100 billion in open markets in the same 12 locations. Of the twelve, the most active markets are found in just six: Bahrain, Dubai, Malaysia, Oman, Sharjah and Saudi Arabia. In 20 years to 2010, *sukuk* issues have grown to become about 2 per cent of conventional bond market value, and there is room for further growth of this market.

Scholars have different opinions on the character of the assets so transferred and jointly owned by the lenders. One school of thought is that as long as the assets transferred are not real assets, a *sukuk* contract is not likely to be secure. Chapra (1998)[3] provides this view that real assets must be backing funding contracts, although in practice usufructs and incomes of financial assets are used to secure income production. Over the last two decades, this provision is being watered down quite a bit such that some institutions get the nod from the *shari'ah* regulators to consider any assets as permissible so long as the assets or securities are income producing. One school of thought is that the assets must be owned, and the other school is that assets need not be owned, so that the contract provides for asset-*based* contracting. This issue is addressed separately in this book in another chapter.

The *sukuk* market has grown very fast only in six major locations that offer securities for investors to fund both private and public projects following the profit-share formula and SPCs having ownership of income-producing assets held by the lenders, at least at the start of the lending process. In the penultimate section of this chapter, we provide market statistics.

2.4   AN ATTEMPT AT CLASSIFICATION BASED ON PRACTICES

We mentioned that there is a tendency in the popular press to describe *sukuk* as Islamic bonds. The reader should be convinced by now that this is not an accurate description, especially because there is a profit-sharing formula for pricing risk, second, there is ownership of set-aside assets and third, the funds may lose all or part of the principal or profit share if the project fails due to no neglect of the entrepreneur or when profits did not accrue in a particular payment period. These essential fundamentals are lost if *sukuk* is described as a bond. So, *sukuk* cannot be classed as Islamic bonds.

The literature has provided references to 14 different *sukuk* instruments although only six are commonly used. These are classified in the literature in different ways, and our aim in this section is to discuss this issue and find a classification implicitly based on wider practice.

One popular classification is by reference to the issuer, as is also done in conventional bonds. So, we have (i) risk-free government issues as Treasury *sukuk* (there are a few different ones here). There are (ii) the agency *sukuk* issued by special-purpose institutions such as a government railway company. Then there are (iii) *sukuk* securities with risk higher than the last ones issued by private firms or institutions (say the Islamic Development Bank or World Bank). These private funding arrangements are rated by ratings agencies, of which the more common are Moody's, Standard & Poor's and RAM of Malaysia.

The agencies give ratings as excellent (AAA to AA), good (A to BBB), both of which are similar to conventional bonds, investment grades, and poor or not investment grade (BB to B). There is a fund of experience grafting the age-old common rating processes to the *sukuk* securities successfully learned over the last 15 years. The market accepts this rating process as reasonable to compute the similarities and differences in the art of rating. That is great for now, and is widely accepted by regulators and the *shari'ah* supervisors. The criteria used to rate a *sukuk* security based on largely existing criteria applied to the bond market are questionable. As is commented upon by Michael Skully in a separate chapter, *sukuk* have unique features, which do not lend themselves to be amenable to bond-type rating. There is good reason to believe that this widespread practice in the rating industry, while largely accepted at this stage of market development, needs to be modified at least in those contracts that do not fit squarely with the pre-agreed interest-based no-risk-shared bond securities.

Another way the *sukuk* have been classified is by market type. Primary issues are initial offers before being listed and traded. These are issued in the primary markets by investment banks after approval by regulatory authorities before being sold to any investors wanting to invest in a *sukuk* issue. Investment banking laws and rules are complied with as considered safe for investors and the process of formal application may reveal the bona fides of the issuers. Once issued, *sukuk* are traded in secondary markets, which are traded if the primary holders sell their holding in the market, either in stock exchanges or the over-the-counter (OTC) markets. Most *sukuk* securities are traded, whereas there are a few that can not be traded, as for example in Bahrain. Classification by market type is not meaningful since it does not reveal anything more than the fact that the listing has occurred.

We propose, therefore, to depart from these two classification methods by describing a way of classifying using the intrinsic nature of the *sukuk*

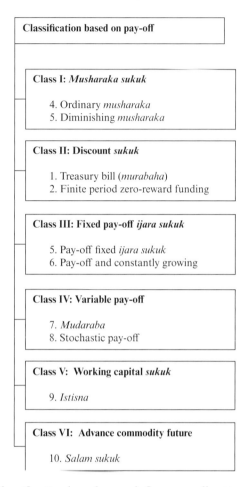

Figure 2.2   Classification based on cash flow pay-off patterns of sukuk
securities

terms as these are marketed in practice. This is summarized in Figure 2.2.
The classification is as follows:

- Class I: Share-like securities (*musharaka sukuk*) are with full control
  either over an infinite period, in which case it is the risk-shared profit-
  shared common share or simply *musharaka* contract. If the *musharaka*
  is over a finite period of time with some form of pay-off based on profit-
  share and risk-sharing, with the pay-off of rewards and principal being
  repaid at a diminishing rate, then this is a *diminishing musharaka sukuk*.

- Class II: Discount *sukuk* (no pay-off during intermediate periods) where the pay-off occurs at the end period, be it less than one year, in which case it is a *bill*, or more than one year, in which case it is a *loan arrangement*. There is no servicing of fund providers at regular periods in some of them. One thing that will be there for sure is the SPC responsible to provide a regular income that will ensure that the end value is higher than the received fund (the principal). Obviously, the sum paid is *indeterminate* until the end period is reached until a price is discovered in the market for the SPC.

- Class III: Fixed pay-off *sukuk* (*ijara* or lease) and constant growth pay-off (*bai bithamin ajjal sukuk*). Under this arrangement, the pay-off coming from the SPC is agreed as growing each period, after the first payment, at a constant growth rate. If the profit share is fixed at, say, US$100, the subsequent period's payment increases at the rate of, say, 5 per cent. In that case the second payment would be $100 $(1.05)^1 = \$105$ and so on. The SPC may have incomes far exceeding this amount, but the pay-off is set as fixed at a constant growth rate.

- Class IV: Variable pay-off that is determined by incomes of the SPC (*mudaraba sukuk*). A *murabaha* contract provides for mark-up and *not* profit-share, and is appropriate if the bank buys an asset at a price, then sells the item to a borrower at a mark-up so that the funding is equal to the price plus mark-up recovered over a period of time. A mortgage-reducing type of pay-off is worked out. In a case of variable payoff, the regular payments are variable but is determinable from the profit ratio at each period of payoff. A contract may have specified a profit-share but not the amount. Since the incomes of SPC's profits are variable, the actual pay-off at each pay-off period will be different, based on some benchmark (the London Inter-Bank Offer Rate, LIBOR, is used in 25 per cent of *sukuk* contracts). A *mudaraba sukuk* is an example of this type.

  It could be that there is no reward for funding (recall the sustenance loan) in which case the proceeds of sale of the SPC assets are used to pay the initial funded amount and the balance, if any is given back to the borrower. More commonly, a pay-off is given, in which case the fund provider gets a pay-off equal to the principal lent plus the profit share of the project as agreed.

- Class V: *Istisna sukuk* is a case of working capital funding where a fund provider provides capital to manufacture/produce an item. The full description of the item (say a toll road) is known and the payment is based on instalments of the pre-agreed amount. The final payment will be the extra payment to make up the market value of the item manufactured.

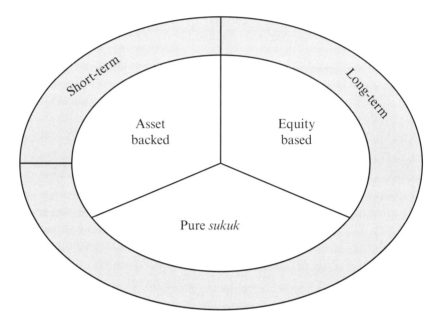

Figure 2.3   A simple classification of long-term and short-term sukuk
          securities

- Class VI: *Salam* contract is one where the item purchased will
  materialize in a forward period and a payment is made now to
  secure ownership of that item to be delivered at a future time. An
  ideal example is paying an agreed sum of money now on evidence
  of fruit on the trees to be delivered as a ripe commodity, say in 6
  months' time. It is widely used as forward contract in agriculture
  and extracting industries.

Short-term securities and long-term securities issued could be (a) equity-
based *musharaka* contracts as *musharaka sukuk*, which is a common-share
like issue over a finite period or (ii) asset-based *sukuk* as *ijara* to several
others or (iii) pure *sukuk*, in which case the pay-offs are fixed over the term
of the funding.

This simple three-way classification of the six classes discussed earlier
makes for easy understanding of the six different individual types: see
Figure 2.3. We are of the view that these last two classifications are based
on implicit provisions found in *sukuk* instruments as traded in several
markets. It is also fruitful to have a simple classification based on term of
the contracts using this three-way classification.

2.5   CASH FLOW PATTERNS, THE MARKET PRICE AND VALUATION MODELS

Valuation is a necessary process to discover the true worth of any security for investment purposes as well as in estimating performance. This is also true for conventional securities. By valuation is meant the process of reducing a financial contract to the cash flows, the pay-offs from an instrument, to understand the nature of the pay-offs as to whether the pay-off is fixed, variable, growing, or stochastic, and then applying an appropriate discount rate to find the present value of promised pay-offs. Thus, a pay-off (TREW = terminal reward) of $120 at the end of one year from now would be $110.09 if the discount rate for this pay-off is 9 per cent per annum (d = discount rate and N = number of periods).[4] Though very simple, there are a number of complex issues in arriving at a value, as may be guessed by the readers from comments made in earlier sections. Hence Equation 2.1 is:

$$V_0 = \frac{TREW_N}{(1 + d)^N} \tag{2.1}$$

Any security with fixed terminal payment of, say, principal plus profit share, TREW, at the end of next period and with no other payments in between can be valued simply as in Equation 2.1 above. A fixed cash flow of $500 000 received at the end of one year, $t = N$, with a current interest rate (or profit rate) of 0.05 per cent (d) will be equal to the present value of that sum discounted at the current interest rate: $476 190.48. This pattern of pay-off with no risk, such as a risk-free yield of an Islamic Treasury security, can be used to value the single discount problem as in Equation 2.1. This basic model is probably applicable to value pure *sukuk* with fixed pay-offs so long as the pay-off of the pure *sukuk* is *not* stochastic, and the end period payment is also pre-determined.

A slightly more complex *sukuk* could, instead of a one-year term, be a 10-year fixed *mudaraba sukuk* requiring fixed payments of US$REW over each of the next 10 years. This is Class II *sukuk*. The valuation will be a present value of $n = 10$ pay-offs, REW, discounted at the appropriate discount rate, d, and the present value of the terminal value of the SPC also discounted at the same rate, at the end period. The last value, M, must be pre-determined. The formula is as in Equation 2.2:

$$V_0 = \frac{REW_1}{(1 + d)^1} + \frac{REW_2}{(1 + d)^2} + \ldots + \frac{REW_N}{(1 + d)^N} + \frac{M_N}{(1 + d)^N} + \tag{2.2}$$

To keep our discussion brief and non-technical, we decided not to proceed to specify more complex *sukuk* security valuation models in this chapter. That task is left to be done as a separate scholarly pursuit to be attempted at a later date.

2.6   OVERVIEW OF GLOBAL *SUKUK* MARKETS

The revival of Islamic Financial Systems (IFS) since 1963 has led to an increasing demand for new securities in both Muslim and non-Muslim countries in organized Islamic Financial Markets (IFMs). The *sukuk* issues are the latest to come on the market rapidly in the last ten years. The trend has also opened up windows of opportunities for Muslim and non-Muslim investors around the world with high liquidity to invest in profitable ventures in Islamic finance instruments. The establishment of the Islamic Development Bank (IDB) in 1975 was followed in the 1990s by financial engineering for the Islamic capital market as a solution for liquidity and portfolio management for participants in the Islamic financial transactions.

The 2000s ushered in the introduction of asset-backed Islamic securities commonly known as *sukuk* (Baljeet, 2006) to solve the long-term invest-ment and financing needs of much-needed economic activities in Islamic majority countries. These are long-term *shari'ah* consistent instruments issued by both corporations and governments in global bond-like markets. For example, in the UK, *sukuk* have been recognized by the government as a good alternative to existing interest-based conventional bonds for raising funds. Most Muslim and non-Muslim investors invest in *sukuk* based on their yields *and* safety relative to conventional bonds with similar risk and not simply based on doctrinal compliance to a set of ethical dictates. Besides, current *sukuk* pricing results in higher yields for similar conventional bonds.

In general, *sukuk* is an Islamic funding arrangement and gets its name from the Arabic word *sakk* which means a certificate of entitlement (AAOIFI, 2002). Its issuance requires an SPC which helps in purchas-ing the productive assets so investors earn a share of the profits from the assets based on profit–loss sharing. Hence, earnings or pay-offs on s*ukuk* depend on the returns from the SPC and the maturity value of the s*ukuk* contracts depends on the term structure revealed in the market. This SPC-collateralization is another distinction of s*ukuk* compared with conven-tional bonds because all *sukuk* issuance requires collateralization, while not all conventional bonds are collateralized.

To gain a quick impression of *sukuk* instruments, it is useful to refer to

Six *sukuk* in practice:	Other possible *sukuk* structures:
1. Joint enterprise (*musharaka*)	1. Benevolence (*wakala*)
2. Partnership in profit (*mudaraba*)	2. Corporate farming financing (*muzaraah*)
3. Mark-up financing (*murabaha*)	3. Agricultural sector financing (*musaga*)
4. Project financing (*istisna*)	4. Advance payment for forward purchase of service (*milkiyat al khadamat*)
5. Lease (*ijara*)	5. Agricultural sector *sukuk* (*mugarasa*)
6. Advance payment for forward purchase of goods (*salam*)	6. Forward *ijara* (*ijara mowsufa bithimn*)
	7. Usufruct lease (*manfaah ijara*)
	8. Forward usufruct lease (*manfaah ijara mowsufa bithimn*)

Figure 2.4   Common sukuk *securities found in several markets*

a simple classification of the market types as below: see Figure 2.4 which lists all the *sukuk* securities. Overall, as in bond markets, *sukuk* markets can be designated as markets with short-term and long-term securities. But both have asset-backed or asset-based contracting arrangements as a minimum, so there cannot be a security market without this feature. Next, we can divide them, as has been discussed earlier in Figure 2.3, into equity-based *musharaka sukuk*; pure debt-like *sukuk*; and finally asset-backed *sukuk*. This simple three-way classification is a starting point for the reader to understand the more nuanced classification.

In this section, we attempt a brief introduction to public-traded *sukuk* issues. *Sukuk* certificates are issued by corporations, agencies of governments and by governments as public issues. Sovereign *sukuk* are similar to conventional fixed income bonds that are default-free, referred to as *sovereign sukuk*. These are debt instruments that represent cash flows (fixed or floating) which are guaranteed as payable during a specific time period. These provide capital market investors with short-, medium- and long-term investment opportunities for people with funds. With the development of this fixed-income bond-like market, asset-backed securities are also available usually carrying a fixed or floating rate.

For example, in September 2001 the first sovereign *sukuk* was issued by the Bahrain Monetary Authority for liquidity management purposes. This was closely followed by the first global *sukuk* issued by Malaysia in June 2002. Earlier in 1990 a private firm issued a *sukuk* in Kuala Lumpur. These default-free *sukuk* certificates carry a rate that is usually reset on a periodic basis based on the predetermined benchmark such as the 3-month EURIBOR (Europe Inter-Bank Offer Rate) or as the 6-month LIBOR (London Inter-Bank Offer Rate).

It should be noted that not all *sukuk* are asset-based nor are they indexed to these benchmarks. A classical assumption is that they are default-free and hence investors earn a default-free yield and a little liquidity premium.

The attractive return on *sukuk*-based funding has resulted in robust growth in demand and supply of different varieties of Islamic financial instruments in a number of capital markets though the total asset value of *sukuk* is a tiny fraction of the total international funding bond markets. According to the BIS, *sukuk* is worth $1.2 trillion during the first half of 2006: the world's international bond market alone is approximately $67 trillion (about 2 per cent) according to Merrill Lynch.[5] A total of 283 *sukuk* have been issued as at 2007: Bahrain Monetary Agency issued the first *ijara sukuk* in 2001; the Malaysia Total Mobile IMTN *ijara sukuk* 2007 followed later (Global Investment House, 2008). Issuance from Malaysia alone was 111; a figure that represents almost 40 per cent of the global issuance.[6]

A notable feature of Malaysian *sukuk* is that the issuances are mostly in Malaysian Ringgit (RM1.00 = US$0.32) in a market where both conventional and Islamic instruments are traded. *Shari'ah* scholars have yet to come up with an Islamic indicator of profitability since the profitability rate is indexed to the London Interbank Offer Rates (LIBOR) as is commonly practised. This practice has been seen as a distortion of the true market value of underlying assets, and hence their returns (as critiqued by Muhammad Al-Bashir, 2008). It is worth noting that out of the 111 sovereign issuances in Malaysia as at 2008, only 10 were indexed to LIBOR.

As at the end of 2007, Malaysia accounted for two-thirds of the world's outstanding *sukuk* estimated at $62 billion (RM213 billion). The establishment of the Malaysia International Islamic Financial Center in 2006 was aimed to facilitate more issuances of *sukuk* and to further position Malaysia as the global hub for the Islamic capital market.[7] As at June 2007, the Islamic Finance Information Service (IFIS) database showed that there was a growth of 71.4 per cent in the domestic *sukuk* market and 83.3 per cent in the international *sukuk* market over 2006. Sovereign *sukuk* grew by 521 per cent while Ringgit-denominated *sukuk* accounted for 70 per cent.[8] Moreover, the use of underlying assets and the application of a profit/loss sharing system embedded in the Islamic Financial System (IFS) based on *shari'ah* is probably an attraction. Conventional and Islamic markets are regulated by the Bank Negara *Malaysia* (BNM), but its interest rate policy may affect long-term bonds and their yield curves, including *sukuk* certificates, especially given the dual system in this market.

2.7 GLOBAL OVERVIEW ON SOVEREIGN AND CORPORATE *SUKUK*

Activities in the global *sukuk* market started in 2000 in Bahrain, later in Malaysia with Ringgit and US$ issues in 2002: soon after, Qatar, Pakistan, Dubai and Germany were launching their respective global *sukuk*. ABN Amro, Barclays, Société Générale, Deutsche Bank and UBS underwrote nearly 190 issues, accounting for funds of US$27 billion (Erik, 2007). Figure 2.5 shows the distribution of investors by continent. As at 2002, about 27 investors took part in the first global *sukuk* in Malaysia. Those deals were milestones, with 51 per cent of the funds coming from investors in the Middle East, followed by 30 per cent from Asia with half of this placed in the Labuan offshore market. About 15 per cent was taken by European investors and 4 per cent by US investors (Abdul Rais, 2003).[9] Some of the notable *sukuk* issues were:

- US$150 million world first global corporate *sukuk* of 2001 by Kumpulan Guthrie Berhad;
- US$600 million world first sovereign *sukuk* of 2002 by the Malaysian Government;
- RM500 million (US$132 million) first Ringgit *sukuk* of 2004 issued by supranational agency (International Finance Corporation, World Bank);
- RM2.05 billion (US$540 million) world's first Islamic residential mortgage-backed securities by Cagamas MBS Berhad;
- RM9.17 billion (US$2.86 billion) complex and innovative structuring which converts the issuer's (PLUS) debt into Islamic Financing, issued in 2006 by PLUS;

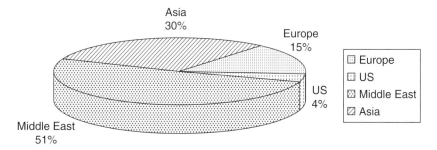

Source: Compiled from *Malaysian Sukuk Handbook* (2008).

Figure 2.5   Investors in Malaysian sukuk *by continent (2002)*

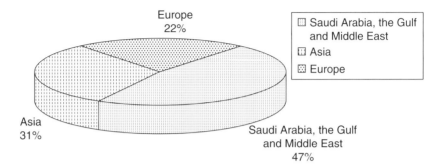

Figure 2.6 Investors in Pakistani sukuk *issues by continent (2005)*

- US$750 million world's first exchangeable *sukuk* issued by Khazanah Nasional (Rafflesia Capital) in 2006;
- RM8 billion (US$2.5 billion) first hybrid *sukuk* of 2007 issued by Nucleus Avenue;
- US$850 million largest equity-linked *sukuk* which recorded highest oversubscription issued by Khazanah Nasional (Cherating Capital) in 2007;
- US$300 million world's first international subordinated *sukuk* issued by Maybank Berhad in 2007;
- RM15.25 billion (US$4.8 billion) world's largest *sukuk* by Binariang GSM in 2007;
- RM1 billion *musharaka sukuk* by Toyota Capital Malaysia Sdn Bhd which is the largest Malaysian *sukuk* issued by Japanese-owned company.

The latest *sukuk* issues reported by the CEO briefing on Islamic Finance Industry discussion on 4 November in Kuala Lumpur are as follows: Bank Negara Malaysia RM3 billion *sukuk*; Celcom Axiata, US$1.3 billion *sukuk*; Cagamas, US$319 Tradable *sukuk* (Al Amanah Li Al Istithmar); Khazanah Nasional, SG$1.5 billion (largest and longest term *sukuk* issuance in Singapore); Malaysian Airport Holdings, US$318 million *sukuk*; and Islamic Development Bank, US$318 million *sukuk* (10-year *sukuk* on Bursa Malaysia).

Pakistan *sukuk* issued in 2005 were also widely accepted by investors. Investors from Saudi Arabia, the Gulf and the Middle East subscribed to 47 per cent in that issue. Information summarized in Figure 2.6 shows that Asia picked up 31 per cent, followed by Europe, at 22 per cent.

Government of Pakistan officials undertook pre-launch road shows in Saudi Arabia, Dubai, Bahrain, Kuwait, Switzerland, Singapore and

Hong Kong, offering the Islamic bonds.[10] The Pakistani Prime Minister said then that the 2005 *sukuk* issuance was a way of moving away from the International Monetary Fund's financing to the international bond and money market financing. The *sukuk* was priced at 220 basis points over the six-month LIBOR; the initial price guidance was 220–235 basis points above LIBOR. This *sukuk* issue was considered to be better than the costly Eurobond issued in 2004 that was marked by domestic criticism: see Figure 2.6.

Going by categorization of clients, 24.5 per cent were bought by state and government agencies, 23.45 per cent went to the asset managers, 20.3 per cent to Islamic banks, while other banks took 18.3 per cent, private banks 10.7 per cent, corporate organizations 2.0 per cent and insurance companies 0.8 per cent.[11]

Qatar issued its first *sukuk* to raise US$700 million in 2003 through an SPC using an *ijara* contract. The *sukuk* was rated A+ by Standard and Poor's (S&P) with a proposed application to list the *sukuk* on the Labuan International Financial Exchange (LIFE) as well as the Luxembourg Stock Exchange. The planned issue of $1 billion *sukuk* to finance investment in renewable energy in mid-2008 was postponed to 2009 due to the global credit crunch in 2008 and a lack of appetite by investors in dollar-based investments.[12]

As noted earlier, Bahrain was the first sovereign state to develop and issue *sukuk* despite a private issue in Malaysia in 1990 and in an earlier period in Pakistan and Saudi Arabia. The Central Bank of Bahrain has since 2001 issued 14 *sukuk ijara* worth US$2.05 billion, with US$1.27 billion outstanding as at the last count in 2008. An Islamic *sukuk* liquidity instrument has been developed by the central bank and the Bahrain Liquidity Management Centre to provide more liquidity to the *sukuk* market for both Islamic and conventional institutions[13] as a further market-deepening effort. It is also expected to promote an efficient pricing mechanism by providing fair prices to *sukuk* investors to enhance efficient primary and secondary trading on *sukuk* (Jamelah, 2008). Bahrain issued 24 *sukuk* in a year including the *sukuk ijara* and short-term *sukuk al-salam* (Ijlal, 2006). Lebanon is close to its first $200 million *sukuk*.

Emirates Islamic *sukuk* were issued in 2005: this was by an airline with a term of seven years and received subscriptions of US$824 million exceeding its initial target of US$550 million by nearly 50 per cent. This attracted wide investor participation from Europe as well as the Far East. The money raised was used to finance the new Emirates Engineering Centre in Dubai. The principal proceeds will be paid on maturity.[14] The world's largest *sukuk* bond was issued in November 2006 by the Nakheel

Table 2.1   Islamic sukuk *securities by country, 2006*

	Amount in US$ million	Percentage	Issues
Malaysia	9356	59.1	262
UAE	5205	32.9	6
Saudi Arabia	818	5.2	2
US	168	1.1	1
Pakistan	152	1.0	2
Kuwait	100	0.6	1
Indonesia	21	0.1	1
Total	15820	100.0	275

Group, a Dubai property developer, for US$3.52 billion. The Aldar Properties issued a US$2.5 billion issue on the London Stock Exchange. The Dubai Metals and Commodities Center issued a gold-linked *sukuk* (a commodity-linked *sukuk*, a special form of design) that allowed investors to receive payments in gold bullion or US dollars.[15]

Germany's first sovereign *sukuk* for 1 billion euros was issued by the state of Saxony-Anhalt in 2004, which also formed the first *sukuk* issued by a Western country. Citigroup and Kuwait Finance house jointly managed the deal. Investors from the GCC region took up 60 per cent of the deal while 40 per cent was taken by European investors. The *sukuk* was listed on the Luxembourg and Bahrain stock exchanges (Wilson, 2008). The first Islamic bond using hydrocarbon reserves as an asset class was issued by the US firm Gulf of Mexico, in collaboration with East Cameron Gas Company in July 2006. The *sukuk* of US$165.7 million was the first time the US entered the *sukuk* market (Abdel-Khaleq and Richardson, 2007).

The longest dated *sukuk* in history was issued by Saudi Basic Industries Corporation as Saudi Arabia's first with a maturity of 20 years.[16] Arabian petrochemical giant SABIC offered US$800 million *sukuk* in 2006 (Abdel-Khaleq and Richardson, 2007). The Islamic Finance Summit report 2006 shows that the global *sukuk* market was expected to be $24.251 billion at the end of 2006. Meanwhile, in recent data on *sukuk* from Dialogic Database adopted from *MIF Monthly*, the actual global *sukuk* at the end of 2006 totalled US$15.8 billion, and US$36.4 billion at the end of 2007 (see Tables 2.1 and 2.2). Malaysia was and is still the leading country in terms of number of issuances as well as in terms of amount in dollars. Although there was a reduction in the number of *sukuk* Malaysia issued in 2007 compared to 2006 figures, there was an increase in the value issued. The 2007 figures in Table 2.2 show the exigency for *sukuk*, almost all the

Table 2.2   Islamic sukuk *by country, 2007*

	Amount in US$ million	Percentage	Issues
Malaysia	17713	48.6	255
UAE	11018	30.2	15
Saudi Arabia	5716	15.7	5
Kuwait	775	2.1	3
Pakistan	635	1.7	16
Qatar	300	0.8	1
Bahrain	200	0.5	1
Total	36357	99.6	296

Table 2.3   Reporting of shari'ah *compliance assets*

US$ million	2007	2006	Per cent change
GCC region	178129	127826	39
Non-GCC MENA	176822	186158	30
MENA Total	354951	263984	34
Sub-Saharan Africa	4707	3039	55
Asia	119346	98705	21
Australia/Europe/US	21476	20300	6
Global Total	500452	386033	30

Source: Maris Strategies and *The Banker*, 2009.

countries increasing the amount issued in million dollars by 100 per cent compared with 2006.

Furthermore, there was an astonishing increase in the issuance from Saudi Arabia, Kuwait and Pakistan. Therefore, it may not be wrong to conclude that the *sukuk* in these countries is increasing rapidly compared to the rate in the Malaysian market.

There are about 524 Islamic financial institutions currently operating in about 75 countries worldwide, with more than 100 Islamic equity funds managing assets in excess of US$5 billion. The latest value of Islamic funds is said to be US$1.3 trillion while the Islamic financial market is estimated to be US$230 billion in size, with an annual growth rate of 12–15 per cent.[17] According to research conducted by *The Banker* in 2007 on the top 500 Islamic financial institutions, the geographical distributions of countries with Islamic financial institution that are reporting shari'ah compliant assets are as described in Table 2.3 and Figures 2.7, 2.8 and 2.9.

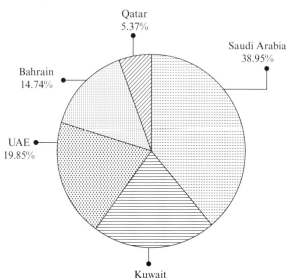

GCC reported total shari'ah assets in 2007: $178.13 billion

Qatar
5.37%

Saudi Arabia
38.95%

Bahrain
14.74%

UAE
19.85%

Kuwait
21.16%

Source: The Banker

Figure 2.7   Geographical distribution of reported shari'ah *assets in GCC,*
2007

2.8   CONCLUSION

The readers were introduced in this chapter to the Islamic bond markets
(more correctly Islamic *sukuk* debt markets): The Islamic bond market
is not an apt description for a very complex funding arrangement based
on doctrine-based fundamental principles guiding the design of *sukuk*
instruments. We noted that the market for this special funding instrument has started to grow very fast since 2000, when the traded markets
began to be established in Bahrain first and later in other legal jurisdictions with special laws and *shari'ah*-based supervision of product design
as well as trading. As at the end of 2010, this market has grown to a
size larger than US$1200 billion or 2 per cent of the international bond
market value as reported in 2007. The readers were also informed that
this form of funding was widely practised over fourteen centuries at
least and is found in the Ottoman archives as far back as the fourteenth
century.

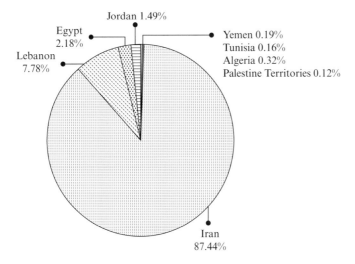

Source: The Banker

Figure 2.8   Geographical distribution in non-Middle East and North African countries

There are six general-type *sukuk* instruments that are actually offered and traded in different forms in the 12 market places where these have been issued. Another eight *sukuk* instruments do exist, but these are conceptual ones, not yet issued to date, at least as public issues, as reported in the literature. We noted six basic differences ranging from asset-backing to complexity that make these securities very unlike the bond securities in the conventional markets. Profit-sharing is used to price the security while pay-off or reward (return) range from fixed in two types to quite complex pay-offs that are not easy to track for valuation purposes. We also noted that there is no agreed theory about how to compute the discount rate. We suggested a six-category classification of the *sukuk* market securities as being consistent with the practices and descriptions found in the literature.

Also, we noted the important asset-backing principle that gave this market a distinct difference from other forms of debt. Valuation of cash flows (pay-offs or rewards as we termed them in this chapter) is very simple in two basic types (Class I) and in discount instruments (Class II). But the pay-offs that depend on the asset values and asset return of more complex

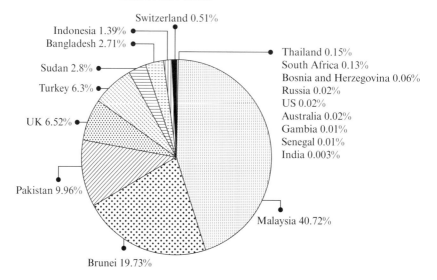

Geographical distribution of reported shari'ah assets,
Non-Middle East global, 2007
Total: $145.53 billion

Source: The Banker

*Figure 2.9   Geographical distribution in non-Gulf Cooperation Council
countries*

sukuk instruments do suggest that much more complex cash flow patterns
are at work, not easily fitting the existing bond valuation theories. That
means there is an important and urgent need to research the valuation
problem in order to resolve the pricing problem in this new debt market.

Overall, it is perhaps in order to suggest that this very young market
of only about a decade old, though growing at a fast pace, requires more
focused attention to create a reliable data base to track its growth than exists
in scant reports. Finally, there is an urgent need to pin down the nature of
the pay-offs so that appropriate mathematical routines can be identified to
price the theoretical value of some of the more complex *sukuk* securities.

NOTES

1.   Historical references suggest that the word '*sukuk*' was used as both singular and
     plural from the word '*sak*', meaning 'certificate'. So *sukuk* is the plural form of *sak*. A
     sak issued by a person is a certificate of ownership of assets so that the recipient of a

sak could make a claim on the assets. This mode of issuing certificates was practised a millennium ago in Damascus as a form of cheque-writing to pay for purchases. In this book, we use the term '*sukuk*' as both singular and plural as the context indicates.

2. For example, the National Australia Bank (the second largest Australian bank) has made available a large sum of money to a Muslim financial cooperative to lend to needy families to buy household durables without any interest payments. Traditionally, this form of lending was and is widely practised in communities whereby a society, bank or rich individual provide interest-free loans to needy families to obtain productive assets. Some reports indicate that banks do lend about one twenty-fifth of their funds for this purpose in Iran, for example.
3. Chapra, M.U. (1998), 'The major modes of Islamic finance', paper presented at the 6th Intensive Orientation Course on 'Islamic economics, banking and finance' in Kuala Lumpur. Archive on the INCEIF website.
4. The concept of discount rates is very complex in modern finance. There are some suggestions in Islamic finance literature to use such modern solutions, which we consider as inappropriate until a careful study is done to establish the correct discount rate given the more complex cash flow arrangements in *sukuk*.
5. PIMCO Bond Basics December 2007, available at: www.pimco.com, accessed 29 January 2009.
6. 'Sukuk: a new dawn of Islamic finance era', Global Investment House Research, January 2008.
7. http://www.imf.org/external/pubs/ft/survey/so/2007 accessed 8 May 2008.
8. 'Global *sukuk* market soars to \$24.5bn' *IFIS News*, August 2007, available at: www.ameinfo.com, accessed 8 August 2008.
9. Abdul Rais Abdul Majid is the CEO of IIFM.
10. 'Record "*Sukuk*"-Islamic Bond Offering – by Pakistan', Khaleej Times Online (2005).
11. Ibid.
12. *IIFF Newsletter*, June 2008.
13. Ibid.
14. 'Emirates Airline debut Islamic sukuk bond receive top honors at Airfinance Journal's 7th annual deal of the year award', *United Arab Emirates News online*, 5 April 2006.
15. www.bfinance.co.uk.
16. www.bfinance.co.uk.
17. Bursa Malaysia, 'The Islamic capital market', available at: icm@bursamalaysia.com, accessed 27 January 2008.

REFERENCES

Abdel-Khaleq, A. and C. Richardson (2007), 'New horizon for Islamic securities: emerging trend in sukuk offerings', *Chicago Journal of International Law*, **7**(2), winter, pp. 409–26.

Abdul Rais, A. (2003), 'Development of liquidity management instruments: challenges and opportunities', paper presented at the international conference on Islamic Banking: Risk Management, Regulation and Supervision, August, Kuala Lumpur, p. 15.

Accounting and Auditing Organization for Islamic Finance and Institutions (AAOIFI) (2002), exposure draft, '*Shari'ah* standard no. (18) on investment *sukuk*', November.

Amado, S. (2007), 'Malaysia: an Islamic capital market hub', 18 September, IMF Monetary and Capital Market Department, mimeo, accessed 30 April 2008 at www.imf.org/external/pubs/ft/survey/so/2007.

Amin, M. (2008), 'The new UK tax law on sukuk', 1 January, mimeo, accessed 26 February at www.newhorizon-islamicbanking.com/index.cfm.

AmIslamic Capital Market (2009), 'The bright side of downturn', *RAM Islamic Finance Bulletin*, 25, (July–September), pp. 1–33.

Anwar, M. (1992), 'Islamic banking in Iran and Pakistan: a comparative study', *The Pakistan Development Review*, **31**(4), Part 11, Winter, pp. 1089–97.

Ariff, M., F.F. Cheng and V.H. Neoh (2009), *Bond Markets in Malaysia and Singapore*, Malaysia: Penerbit University Putra Malaysia Press.

Baljeet, K.G. (2006), 'Raising capital through Labuan IOFC', presentation at Labuan Offshore Financial Services Authority promotional meeting, Labuan, Malaysia, 12 December.

Bank Negara Malaysia (2007), '*A Guide to Malaysian Government Securities*', 2nd edn, Monetary Policy Implementation Section, Investment Operations and Financial Market Department.

Bank Negara Malaysia (2008), *Malaysian Sukuk Market Handbook: Your Guide to the Malaysian Islamic capital Market*, Kuala Lumpur: RAM Rating Service Berhad.

The Banker Online (1998), accessed 5 April 2005.

Buhari vol. 3, Hadith 334.

Chapra, Umer M. (2008), *Muslim Civilization: the Causes of Decline and the Need for Reform*, Jeddah, Saudi Arabia: Islamic Foundation.

DiVanna, J. (2008), 'Will Islamic banking appeal to non-Muslims?', in 'Convergence: new directions in Islamic finance', *Arab Financial Forum*.

Erik, U. (2007), 'Islam is not the only driver for sukuk popularity', 30 April, *Financial Times* report accessed 26 February 2008 at www.ft.com.

Faisal, A. (2008), 'Overview of Malaysian sukuk market', *MIF Monthly*, February.

Fuad, A. and A. Mohammed (1996), *Islamic Banking: Theory, Practice and Challenges*, London: Zed Books, p. 99.

Global Investment House (2008), '*Sukuks*: a new dawn of Islamic finance era', *Global Investment House*, January 1–36.

Hassan, M.K. and M.K. Lewis (2007), *Handbook of Islamic Banking*, Cheltenham, UK and Northampton, MA, USA: Edward Elgar Publishing.

Hettish, K. (2007), 'Sukuk bond issue on the rise. . . .', *Daily Times*, May, accessed 17 March 2008 at www.bluechipmag.com/subarticledet.php?id.

Ijlal, A.A. (2006), ' "Sukuk" – Developing a secondary market', paper presented at the 5th Annual Islamic Finance Summit, organized by Euromoney Seminar, Dubai, UAE.

International Financial Service London (2009), 'Bond Markets 2009', *IFSL Research*, accessed 14 January 2010 at www.ifsl.org.uk.

Iqbal, Z. and H. Tsubota (2006), 'Emerging Islamic capital markets: a quickening pace and new products', in *The Euromoney: International Debt Capital Markets Handbook*, accessed 15 September 2008 at http://meeting.abanet.org/webupload/commupload/IC727000/.

Ishrat, H. (2006), 'The surge in Islamic financial services', Dawn Group Newspaper, Karachi, Pakistan, accessed 3 March 2008 at www.dawn.com/events/ifs/ifs.

Jamelah, J. (2008), 'Liquidity in the Malaysian sukuk market', *MIF Monthly*, June.

Jerry, U. (2002), 'Banking on Allah', *Fortune Magazine*, 10 June.

Jobst, A., P. Kunzel, P. Mills and A. Sy (2007), 'Islamic finance expanding rapidly', *IMF Monetary and Capital Market Department*, 9 September, accessed 30 April 2008 at http://www.imf.org/external/pubs/ft/survey/so/2007.

Khaleej Times Online (2005), 'Record *Sukuk*'-Islamic Bond Offering – by Pakistan', *Khaleej Times online*, 26 January, accessed 5 April 2008.

Mikharor, A. (2007), 'Islamic finance and globalization: a convergence', *Journal of Islamic Economics, Banking and Finance*, **2**(2).

Muhammad Al-Bashir, M. (2008), 'Sukuk market: innovations and challenges', *Islamic Economic Studies*, **15**(2), Islamic Development Bank, Jeddah.

Rating Agency Malaysia (2009), 'Market statistics', *Islamic Financial Bulletin*, 25, July–September.

Securities Commission Malaysia (2009), 'Malaysia Islamic capital market', *Quarterly Bulletin*, **4**(3), September.

Shamsher, M., H. Taufiq and Mohammad Ariff (2007), 'Research in an emerging Malaysian capital market: a guide to future direction', *International Journal of Economics and Management*, **1**(2), June, 173–202.

Shankar, S. (2007), 'Global capital flows', accessed 15 January 2008 at www.find articles.com/articles/mi_qa3715/is_2007.

Usmani, M.T. (2008), 'Sukuk and their contemporary applications', Accounting and Auditing Organization for Islamic Financial Institutions (AAOIFI) reference document, Bahrain.

Wilson, R. (2008), 'Islamic finance in Europe', *Journal of Islamic Economics, Banking and Finance*, **3**(2), July.

3. History of *sukuk*: pragmatic and idealist approaches to structuring *sukuk*

Abdullah Saeed and Omar Salah

3.1 INTRODUCTION

Sukuk are Islamic securities that are often translated as Islamic bonds. However, the term 'Islamic bond' does not entirely cover the substance of *sukuk*. A closer look at *sukuk* shows that *sukuk* have elements that might resemble both shares and bonds, depending on the applicable underlying Islamic financial contract terms and structures. In this chapter we will outline the backgrounds of *sukuk* providing a better understanding of *sukuk* as Islamic financial instruments.

This chapter is motivated to illustrate the discrepancy in the idealistic approach to *sukuk* structures. That is, how this financial product ideally should be structured from a *shari'ah* perspective, as compared with a pragmatic approach adopted at this early stage of the market development, in other words, how it is structured in practice.

In order to place *sukuk* in context, first some concepts associated with *shari'ah* that are relevant to any conceptualization of *sukuk* will be briefly mentioned in section 3.2. These include key sources of s*hari'ah* as well as concepts of *ijtihad*, *riba* and *gharar*. In the following historical overview of *sukuk* in section 3.3, we provide particular focus on the origins of the word '*sukuk*', its use in medieval times and the recent history of *sukuk*, known today as new financial instruments in financial and capital markets. Finally, the development of several forms of *sukuk* will be described, explaining a number of structures and mechanisms that have been developed in practice over the years, highlighting the tension between the idealist and pragmatic approaches towards *sukuk* structures today: this is found in section 3.4 before concluding this chapter.

3.2 *SHARI'AH*: BASIC FOUNDATIONS OF ISLAMIC FINANCE AND *SUKUK*

The *raison d'être* of *sukuk* lies in the *shari'ah*. *Shari'ah* literally means 'the way' and it is generally understood to be the body of Islamic religious law. Islamic law, in the context of Islamic finance, does not refer to the black-letter law of a particular jurisdiction. Instead, what is meant is a set of religious and moral principles, concepts and rules as developed throughout Islamic history based largely on the Qur'an and *Sunnah*. *Fiqh* (often translated as Islamic jurisprudence) is knowledge of the practical regulations and rules of the *shari'ah* acquired by reference to and in detailed study of the sources.[1] Banking and financial activities form part of the economic activities within one area of *fiqh* called *fiqh al-mu'amalat*.

3.2.1 Sources of *Shari'ah* (Body of Islamic laws)

In accordance with the classical theory of Islamic jurisprudence there are two primary sources and a range of secondary sources of Islamic law. The primary sources are the Holy Scripture of Islam, the Qur'an, which was revealed to the Prophet Muhammad. Some eighty verses of the Qur'an refer to strictly legal matters, although there are doubts as to whether the legal injunctions in these verses are obligatory or permissive.[2] After the Qur'an, the second most important source is the *Sunnah* (the normative behaviour of the Prophet) as documented in the *hadith*. The secondary sources include *ijma'* (the consensus of the scholars), and *qiyas* (reasoning by analogy).

Ijtihad is often referred to as a secondary source of Islamic jurisprudence. However, *ijtihad* is not strictly a source of law, but it is rather a method by which the *mujtahid* (the person) recognizes and makes known the legal meaning of the texts and rules of the Qur'an and *Sunnah*. While the *mujtahid* has the necessary freedom to propose interpretations of such texts and rules, it is only when the interpretations are supported by a subsequent *ijma'* (consensus) that they attain the necessary authority in Islamic law. *Sukuk*, for example, are not referred to in the Qur'an or in the *Sunnah*. The ideas that have been developed in relation to *sukuk*, how they are to be structured and their use are the result of *ijtihad*. Given the importance of *ijtihad* for any exploration of *sukuk*, a discussion of the concept of *ijtihad* is warranted.

3.2.2 Ijtihad (In-depth Discussion to come up with a Legal Opinion)

The classical view of ijtihad: *Ijtihad* is the process, as well as the mechanism, by which the law revealed in the Qur'an and *Sunnah* may be interpreted, developed and kept alive in line with the intellectual, political, economic, legal, technological and moral developments of society as it develops over time. Since the rules and instructions provided in the Qur'an and *Sunnah* are limited in number, and Muslims face new situations and problems at all times and in all places, the revealed law may not always be able to provide specific answers. This ultimately determines the necessity for *ijtihad* and makes it an essential instrument in the development of Islamic law. In relation to *sukuk* it is possible to argue that ideas about *sukuk* also developed today in such a context. The need for funding through the capital markets required an Islamic alternative to conventional bonds. Through the exercise of *ijtihad*, the contemporary scholars, together with bankers and lawyers, developed *sukuk* as a *shari'ah*-compliant – some would say still not consistent–alternative to conventional bonds.

Taken broadly, *ijtihad* began as an extremely flexible institution among the first two to three generations of Muslims. It then gradually became more rigid with the development and writing down of the *shari'ah* sciences like *hadith*, exegesis, law, theology, history and *usul al-fiqh* (principles of jurisprudence). In particular, Imam Shafi'i's success in formulating and propagating his *usul* and the further development of the *usul* by later scholars led to a gradual decline in the flexibility available to scholars of all persuasions.

The early lack of formalism in the first century of *hijra* (the century starting in AD 622) thus gave way to a more systematic, formal and rule-governed method. By the fourth century AH, *usul al-fiqh* methodology was well established in Islamic legal scholarship and, by the end of the sixth century, had reached its zenith in the works of eminent scholars such as al-Juwayni (d. 478 AH or AD 1200) and al-Ghazali (d. 505 AH or AD 1227). In the following centuries, serious attempts to question major aspects of *usul* were only made in rare cases.[3]

Ijtihad in the modern period: *Ijtihad* remained, from then on until the modern period, a formalistic, legalistic and literalistic practice. In the nineteenth and twentieth centuries AD, faced with Western concepts such as rationalism, historical criticism, development, nationalism and human rights, many Muslims, with varying degrees of skill in Islamic scholarship, began to question the suitability of the existing methods of *ijtihad* in Islamic scholarship. This new-found awareness and critical attitude is now widespread throughout the Islamic world. Considerable diversity exists and it would be foolish to claim that the concerns and perspectives of Muslim scholars throughout the world are one and the same. Local circumstances have a strong influence; internal and external threats, demographics, levels of development, contact with different cultures, educational opportunities, all vary. Scholars differ in their perceptions of the social, economic, political and legal problems facing their respective communities.

Today, three different forms of *ijtihad* can be identified. The first one is the text-based *ijtihad*. This is the method of *ijtihad* generally recognized in the classical period and still practised in traditional Islamic legal scholarship. It is based on the foundational texts as well as *ijma'* and *qiyas*, and relies on the rules and principles of *usul al-fiqh*. For the scholar, each new legal problem should be seen largely in isolation and does not have to be considered an element of a whole system. When a new problem emerges, the scholar identifies relevant texts of the *shari'ah* and attempts to apply the rules of *usul al-fiqh*. The new problem is then linked to an earlier ruling or a text and a decision is made as to its *shari'ah*-compliance or otherwise. The text could be a verse of the Qur'an, a *hadith* or a view of an imam. Literal reading of texts, strict application of the rules of *usul* and heavy emphasis on conformity and traditionalism are the hallmarks of this method.

Another form of *ijtihad* is referred to as eclectic *ijtihad*. In eclectic *ijtihad* the scholar faces a problem or issue and must decide whether or not it is acceptable from an Islamic perspective. Often, the scholar is convinced of the *shari'ah*-compliance of the issue and then attempts to justify his position by selecting texts such as verses, *hadith* or views of imams that support the scholar's preconceived position. Such a method is ad hoc, opportunistic and does not systematically follow principles or rules. No consideration is often given to *usul al-fiqh* methodology and the scholar often ignores possible textual or historical evidence to the contrary. As far as intellectual honesty is concerned, this is the most hazardous and problematic approach of all: hazardous because it has no clear boundaries, signposts or methods that can be conceptualized and followed. A number of examples of eclectic *ijtihad* are found in the emerging areas of Islamic economics, banking and finance as well.

The third form of *ijtihad* is the context-based *ijtihad*. Although it existed in an undeveloped form in early Islam, context-based *ijtihad* should be seen as a relatively new phenomenon. It is distinguished by the fact that it attempts to understand a problem in both its historical and modern contexts. If a problem emerges for which an Islamic view is needed, the scholar first looks carefully at the problem, identifying its features, purpose and function or role in today's society. If it is found that a related or similar problem existed in the time of the Prophet, the scholar will examine the historical problem (precedent) exactly as he would for the modern one.

In this the scholar is often guided by the concept of *maslaha* (generally translated as ('public interest' or 'common good'). The scholar is less concerned with the outward *form* of the problem, historical or modern. More emphasis is placed on the underlying objectives of the *shari'ah* in relation to the problem, such as fairness, justice and equity. A decision will then be made as to the attitude Muslims should adopt vis-à-vis the problem in today's environment. In context-based *ijtihad,* the scholar is not interested in specific *ijma'* formed in the classical period, or in certain *usul*-based tools like *qiyas*, but mainly conducts what we may refer to as a *context analysis* both for the modern situation and that of the classical period.

3.2.3   Islamic Financial Principles

Islamic law, in principle, recognizes contractual freedom, and all contracts and contractual provisions are allowed unless explicitly prohibited in the foundation texts. The obvious and crucial questions then are what these explicit prohibitions are and how they pertain to financial transactions. The foundation texts identify two explicit prohibitions: (1) the ban on receiving and paying *riba* (often translated as 'interest' in Islamic finance literature in contemporary period); and (2) the ban, to the extent possible, on *gharar* (uncertainty) in contracts.

3.2.3.1   *Riba* (usury)
Riba is often divided into three different forms: the *riba al-jahiliyya, riba al-fadl*, and *riba al-nasi'a*.[4] *Riba al-jahiliyya* has been prohibited directly in the Qur'an, while *riba al-fadl* and *riba al-nasi'a* have been prohibited in the *Sunnah* of the Prophet. *Riba al-jahiliyya* refers to the *riba* of the pre-Islamic period.[5] According to the practice in pre-Islamic Arabia, interest was charged at the maturity of debts from interest-free loans or credit sales, and compounded at later maturity dates.[6] This form of *riba* has been prohibited in the Qur'an.[7] In the Qur'an it is also mentioned that Muslims should abandon all remaining *riba*.[8] One of the most discussed verses on the prohibition of *riba* in the Qur'an is verse 2:275 according to which God has permitted trade, but prohibited *riba*:

> Those who devour [*riba*] will not stand except as stand one whom the Evil one by his touch Hath driven to madness. That is because they say: 'Trade is like [*riba*]', but Allah hath permitted trade and forbidden [*riba*]. Those who after receiving direction from their Lord, desist, shall be pardoned for the past; their case is for Allah (to judge); but those who repeat ([t]he offence) are companions of the Fire: They will abide therein (for ever).[9]

The prohibitions of *riba al-fadl* and *riba al-nasi'a* originate from the *Sunnah* of the Prophet Muhammad.[10] There are several *hadith* prohibiting both *riba al-fadl* and *riba al-nasi'a*. The most quoted *hadith* on the prohibition of *riba* is:

[Ubada b. al-Samit] ([may] Allah be pleased with him) reported Allah's Messenger (may peace be upon him) as saying:

Gold is to be paid for by gold, silver by silver, wheat by wheat, barley by barley, dates by dates, and salt by salt, like for like and equal for equal, payment being made hand to hand. If these classes differ, then sell as you wish if payment is made hand to hand.[11]

As appears from this *hadith* the essence of *riba* here does not concern interest over loans, but sales, that is delay or excess in exchange of certain types of property such as currency and foodstuffs. The phrase 'equal for equal' in this *hadith* establishes that certain goods of a single type can only be exchanged in equal amounts.[12] This is the so-called *riba al-fadl*. The phrase 'hand to hand' refers to the *riba al-nasi'a*; according to this form of *riba* the exchange of certain goods may only take place in the present and as instant barter.[13] Based on an explication of *riba al-jahiliyya*, *riba al-fadl* and *riba al-nasi'a*, many contemporary Muslim scholars have argued that all forms of interest are forbidden as *riba*.

Under the rules of s*hari'ah*, granting a loan is considered an act of charity, for example a personal loan.[14] If that is the case, it would be improper to make a profit on a loan by charging interest to the borrower. This does not mean that making a profit itself is forbidden within Islam. Quite the reverse – Islamic law encourages circulation of wealth, investment and profit.[15] But profit must be made through trade and other similar activities. A return on investment is only justified when the investor takes a commercial risk (shares in the risk of a venture before a return is sought). Lending money does not qualify as a commercial risk,[16] because the risk of non-repayment (poor debtor creditworthiness, for example) is deemed insufficient to warrant charging interest. Profitability requires taking a real commercial risk.

Given the *riba* ban, the concept of profit-and-loss-sharing is extremely important in Islamic finance.[17] Financiers generally do not receive interest on the funds they provide, but instead participate in the project to the extent that they share in any profits or losses made.[18] So unlike interest payments, charging for funding-based project participation can be justified, provided that the project yields a profit. (Hence Islamic debt instruments provide for profit-shared and risk-shared funding activities.)

But the *riba* ban reaches much further. *Shari'ah*-compliant transactions preclude making money with money. Money itself may not be a source of profit, because many scholars of Islamic economics argue that money has no intrinsic value within Islam.[19] The ultimate purpose of money, from their point of view, is to help fulfil basic needs, such as food, clothes and shelter. In this approach money must be seen (and used) as a means of exchange only, not as a basic need in itself.[20]

This position, for instance, is at the heart of the *bay' al-dayn* doctrine or trade in debt claims.[21] Most *shari'ah* scholars agree that the *riba* ban extends to this trade,[22] because trading in debt claims is similar to the forbidden use of money as a source of profit. In the case of *sukuk* therefore, they must be backed by tangible assets. Typically (and unlike in conventional forms of funding), *sukuk* certificate holders have (or should have) a claim to one or more tangible assets. These certificates can be traded on the international capital markets because their holders are entitled to the underlying tangible assets, and it is not only debt claims that are traded.

While the equation of *riba* with interest has become common-place among Muslims, there is still a significant number of scholars who do not believe that *riba* can simply be equated with interest. One such scholar, Mohammad Omar Farooq, notes that there are a number of problems with the 'orthodox' understanding of *riba* as interest. He emphasizes the following points: first, it is a misunderstanding that the prohibition on *riba* as interest is directly derived from the Qur'an.[23] There is no support from foundational texts (the Qur'an and *hadith*) that any conditions of an initial contract or agreement, including any stipulated excess over the principal, are covered by the Qur'anic prohibition of *riba*.[24]

Nor is there *ijma'* or consensus that *riba* equals interest, even though such a view is widely held.[25] The prohibition on *riba*, specifically pre-Islamic *riba* (*riba-al-jahaliya*) in the Qur'an (2:275) is primary referring to loans (presumably a particular type of loan that existed in pre-Islamic times).[26] Thus *hadith* concerning *riba* in the context of trade or credit sales cannot legitimately be used to broaden the scope of the prohibition on pre-Islamic *riba*.[27]

Moreover, the discussion on *riba* and loans in the Qur'an occurs in connection with transactions or contracts characterized by *zulm* (injustice and exploitation), with the broader context of the verse discussing spending and charity (sadaqa).[28] Thus, he argues, it is a certain type of *riba* – one that renders a debtor financially vulnerable to poverty or need – that is specifically prohibited.[29] Although this view has been supported by several scholars from a wide range of perspectives,[30] the view is not accepted in Islamic finance.

3.2.3.2 *Gharar* (uncertainty and asymmetric information)

The second ban in *shari'ah* in relation to Islamic finance is that of *gharar* or excessive uncertainty and risk. In contracts, *gharar* must be avoided as much as possible;[31] the *shari'ah* recognizes that ruling out uncertainty in financial transactions altogether is unrealistic.[32] For that reason, the *gharar* ban primarily concerns essential elements of contracts, such as price, deliverability, quality, quantity, and so on.[33] Therefore, the essentials of a contract may not remain unspecified.

The *gharar* prohibition is also somewhat related to the ban on *qimar*, which is strictly forbidden by the s*hari'ah*.[34] *Qimar* pertains to yields that depend solely on luck or chance, such as gambling.[35] Many Islamic economists would argue that excessive speculation and gambling are prohibited, because profits achieved through them cannot be justified.[36] Yet ordinary entrepreneurial risks are not included in this ban. Conventional derivatives contracts are considered in this context to contain elements that are akin to speculation.[37]

3.2.4 Approaches to Islamic Finance: Idealist, Liberal-pragmatic

When considering the principles of Islamic finance, it must be emphasized that the early idealistic vision of Islamic banking and finance, which existed in the literature in the decades prior to the 1970s, has changed significantly in practice. The idealism of the early period of Islamic banking during the 1950s and 1960s saw the development of models of Islamic banking and finance that adhered closely to ideas developed by the classical jurists. However, the reality of operating in contemporary financial markets, in a context very different from the classical period, has meant that modern scholars have been challenged to reconsider these conceptions. Although the ideal models still exist, other more pragmatic approaches have been developed.

Overall, three approaches to Islamic banking and finance have emerged that can be placed on a continuum: idealist to liberal-pragmatic. The idealist approach seeks to maintain the original vision of the Islamic banking literature of the 1950s and 1960s and to remain faithful to the instruments and contracts developed in *fiqh* as far as possible as was known to be in practice during the classical period. At the opposite end of the continuum are Muslim scholars who argue that interest is not inherently evil and *riba* does not include modern bank interest. This liberal approach even makes a case that there is no need for Islamic banks and financial products at all. Between these two extremes lies a more pragmatic approach, which is realistic enough to see that idealist models of Islamic banking have significant problems in terms of practicality and feasibility, but at the same time still maintain the interpretation of *riba* as interest.

It is possible to argue that the majority of Islamic bankers should be classified as pragmatists, prepared to balance practical realities with traditional Islamic principles. The result has been that these bankers and their *shari'ah* advisers have opted for a more pragmatic form of Islamic banking, interpreting relevant texts using an eclectic approach to the sources of Islamic law and principles of Islamic jurisprudence. Here the practical and feasible are given priority over the idealistic and impractical, even though this has led to a somewhat questionable outcome in terms of moving towards a so-called 'Islamic' banking and finance system.

The use of eclectic *ijtihad* resulting in a pragmatic approach will be discussed below in regard to *sukuk* structures. This pragmatic approach will be considered in contrast to the idealist approach.

3.3   HISTORY OF *SUKUK*

3.3.1   Origins of *Sukuk* in the Medieval Period

The Arabic word '*sukuk*' is the plural of the word '*sakk*', meaning 'certificate' or 'order of payment'.[38] Documentary evidence confirms the use of the word *sakk* in the early Islamic caliphates.[39] The Muslim societies of the pre-modern period used *sukuk* as forms of papers representing financial obligations originating from trade and other commercial activities.[40] In the earlier theoretical legal works, written instruments of credit were present. Such written instruments are encountered frequently in *genizah* documents.[41] *Genizah* documents are documents that were stored in the Middle Eastern mosques and synagogues, because the word 'God' was written either in Arabic or Hebrew and, therefore, the merchants were reluctant to destroy such documents.

The Cairo *genizah* documents contain fragments that indicate the existence of *sakk* in the twelfth century AD and these money orders are remarkably similar in form to modern cheques.[42] They stated the sum to be paid, the order, the date, and the name of the issuer.[43]

During the Middle Ages, a *sakk* was a written vow to pay for goods when they were delivered and it was used to avoid money having to be transported across dangerous terrain.[44] As a result, these *sukuk* were transported across several countries and spread throughout the world. The Jewish merchants from the Muslim world transmitted the concept and the term *sakk* to Europe.[45] An interesting outcome of the trade and transport of these *sukuk* is that it functioned as a source of inspiration for the modern day cheque. Although the cheque has a British background,[46] the modern Western word 'cheque' appears to have been derived from the Arabic word '*sakk*' as was actually practised by merchants in Damascus as a form a of cheque.[47]

3.3.2   Recent History of *Sukuk* in Islamic Capital Markets

Today *sukuk* are known as instruments of the Islamic capital markets. In modern day Islamic finance, *sukuk* refer to Islamic securities with rather distinctive features. One of the very first definitions of modern day *sukuk* was given in February 1988 during the fourth session of the Council of the Islamic *Fiqh* Academy in Jeddah. Resolution No. 30 (5/4) of the Council of the Islamic *Fiqh* Academy dealt with the matter. This resolution was on investment certificates and more specifically on *muqarada* bonds (also known as *mudaraba sukuk*), which is a specific form of *sukuk*. The Council defined these *sukuk* as:

> investment instruments which allocate the [*muqarada*] capital ([*mudaraba*]) by floating certificates, as an evidence of capital ownership, on the basis of shares of equal value, registered in the name of the owner, as joint owners of shares in the venture capital or whatever shape it may take, in proportion to (. . .) each one's share therein.[48]

This is arguably the first description of *sukuk* in present times. Shortly after this description, in 1990 one of the first *sukuk* was issued by Shell MDS in Malaysia.[49] After this issuance, there were no other active issuances by other *sukuk* issuers until the beginning of the twenty-first century.[50] From 2000 onwards, a number of institutions started issuing *sukuk* and the *sukuk* market took off from there.[51] The immense growth of the market required certainty in regard to *shari'ah*-related matters and standardization. Hence, the Accounting and Auditing Organisation for Islamic Financial Institutions (AAOIFI) issued its *Shari'ah* Standard No. 17 on 'Investment *Sukuk*' in May 2003, which became effective from 1 January 2004. This *Shari'ah* Standard provides a definition of *sukuk* in section 2 of the *Shari'ah* Standard. The AAOIFI defines investment *sukuk* as: 'certificates of equal value representing undivided shares in ownership of tangible assets, usufruct and services or (in the ownership of) the assets of particular projects or special investment activity'[52]

The AAOIFI *Shari'ah* Standard on *sukuk* describes fourteen different *sukuk* structures structured on the basis of Islamic financial contracts such as *musharaka, mudaraba, ijara, murabaha* and so on. Over the first decade of the twenty-first century the market has witnessed several *sukuk* issuances in different forms and structures. In 2007, the *sukuk* market reached its peak in terms of issuance volume.[53] The AAOIFI *Shari'ah* Standard No. 17 on *sukuk* also provides specific rules to safeguard the *shari'ah* compliance of each *sukuk* structure.

3.4   *SUKUK* STRUCTURES: PRAGMATIC AND IDEALIST APPROACHES

In the light of the prohibition of *riba* under the *shari'ah*, trading in pure debt instruments is forbidden. Hence, *sukuk* are structured to generate the same economic effects as conventional bonds, but in a *shari'ah*-compliant manner.[54] Each *sakk* represents an undivided interest in an asset.[55] *Sukuk* reflect participation in the underlying tangible assets, so that what is being traded is not merely a debt.[56] *Sukuk* are entitlements to rights in certain assets inclusive of some degree of ownership.[57] For a *sukuk* structure to comply with *shari'ah*, the underlying assets must themselves also comply with *shari'ah*, which means that they should be *halal*.[58]

In this section we will discuss *sukuk* structures and contextualize them in the broader discussion of the different approaches of Islamic finance. First, the *shari'ah* requirements for *sukuk* will be described to determine what the conditions are for a valid *sukuk* structure from a *shari'ah* perspective. Once the *shari'ah* framework is clarified, we will discuss how some *sukuk* structures were structured in practice. This will show that the *sukuk* practitioners developed several mechanisms that seemed necessary from a practical point of view adopting a pragmatic approach. We will place this pragmatic approach in contrast to the idealist approach.

3.4.1   *Shari'ah* Requirements for *Sukuk* Structures

The most important Islamic principle for *sukuk* transactions – and probably for Islamic finance as a whole – is the prohibition of *riba*. Two important aspects of the prohibition of *riba* will be discussed: paying or receiving interest and the forbidden *bay' al-dayn*. As mentioned above, according to the majority of the contemporary scholars the prohibition of *riba* includes a prohibition on all forms of interest. Since interest payments are forbidden under the *shari'ah*, the transaction must be structured such that no interest payments are present in the entire transaction. Contrary to conventional bonds where the periodic payments are interest payments, the source for the periodic payments of the *sukuk* must be the return on the underlying transaction.

In the AAOIFI definition we read that the *sukuk* certificates must represent ownership rights in the underlying assets. This is the result of the prohibition of *riba* which indirectly leads to a prohibition on trading in debt receivables (*bay' al-dayn*). Therefore, pure debt instruments are forbidden. Money must be used to create real economic value and the trade in claims and receivables is not allowed. Consequently, the presence of underlying tangible assets in the transaction is required. This means that the Special

Purpose Company (SPC) needs to hold underlying tangible assets in order to issue *sukuk*. In addition, the *sukuk* holders must hold some degree of ownership in the underlying tangible assets as a consequence of the prohibition on the *bay' al-dayn*.[59] This makes the *sukuk* tradable in secondary markets: when the *sukuk* are traded in secondary markets, what is being traded is not merely a debt claim, but rather an ownership right in a tangible asset.

3.4.2 *Sukuk* Structures: a Pragmatic Approach

Now that the *shari'ah* framework of *sukuk* transactions is clarified, three *sukuk* structures will be discussed in further detail. This will illustrate how these *sukuk* are structured in practice. First, the *sukuk al-ijara* will be discussed.

Sukuk al-ijara structure

The *sukuk al-ijara* structure is based on the contract of *ijara*.[60] An *ijara* contract allows the transfer of the usufruct of an asset in return for rental payment; as such, it is similar to a conventional lease contract.[61] Thus, the *sukuk* are based on the underlying tangible assets that the SPC has acquired rather than being debt securities, which is the case with the issuance of conventional bonds.[62] Instead, the *sukuk al-ijara* structure uses the leasing contract as the basis for the returns paid to investors, who are the beneficial owners of the underlying asset and as such benefit from the lease rentals as well as sharing in the risk.[63] Figure 3.1 illustrates the structure of *sukuk al-ijara*.

The structure commences with a party who is in need of financing, here referred to as the originator. The originator will establish an SPC, a separate legal entity with the sole purpose of facilitating this transaction. Next, the SPC purchases certain tangible assets from the originator at an agreed predetermined purchase price, which will be equal to the principal amount of the *sukuk*. In order to finance the purchase of the assets, the SPC issues *sukuk* to *sukuk* holders. These *sukuk* holders are investors looking for s*hari'ah*-compliant securities. The SPC uses the *sukuk* proceeds to pay the originator the purchase price of the tangible assets. The SPC will also declare a trust over the tangible assets and hold the assets as a trustee for the *sukuk* holders, who are the beneficiaries.

Next, the originator and the SPC will enter into a lease agreement for a fixed period of time. Under this lease agreement, the SPC (lessor) leases the assets back to the originator (lessee). Consequently, the SPC receives periodic rentals from the originator for the use of the underlying tangible assets. The SPC uses these amounts to pay the periodic return to the *sukuk*

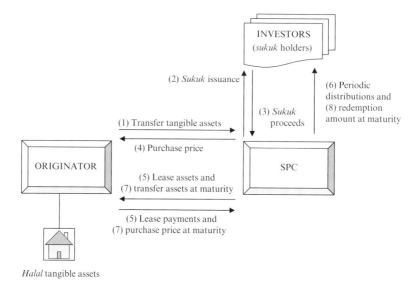

Source: Authors' own

Figure 3.1   Structure of sukuk al-ijara

holders, since they are entitled to these payments as the beneficial owners of the tangible assets.

The lease payments from the originator to the SPC, and the periodic payments from the SPC to the *sukuk* holders will continue until maturity date. At maturity date, the originator purchases the assets back from the SPC at a predetermined value pursuant to a purchase undertaking. The originator becomes the legal owner of the assets and pays a purchase price equal to the initial purchase price of the assets and, thus, also equal to the principal amount of the *sukuk*. Hence, the SPC can pay back to the *sukuk* holders their principal amount, which allows the *sukuk* certificates to be redeemed.

Although in a *sukuk al-ijara* structure the *sukuk* holders must acquire the ownership rights over the tangible assets from a *shari'ah* perspective, from a practical perspective this is often not possible due to legal impediments in most jurisdictions such as the impossibility to register the immovable assets in the name of thousands of *sukuk* holders. As a result, under the *sukuk al-ijara* structure the SPC holds the tangible assets in trust for the *sukuk* holders. This means that the legal ownership of the tangible assets will remain with the SPC, and the *sukuk* holders merely acquire the beneficial ownership of the underlying tangible assets.

In practice, however, more difficulties arose in meeting the ownership requirements of the *sukuk* holders. This is the first explication of the pragmatic approach of *sukuk* practitioners. Additional transfer taxes and restrictions on the disposal of governmental assets made it almost impossible for several originators even to transfer the title of the assets to the SPC.[64] As a result, in practice the legal ownership of the assets is not even transferred to the SPC. The *sukuk* holders are, consequently, one step further from the underlying tangible assets. The combination of the absence of transfer of legal ownership of the assets from the originator to the SPC with purchase undertakings and other forms of guarantees given by the originator, provided the SPC and, consequently, the *sukuk* holders recourse to the originator instead of recourse to the underlying tangible assets.[65] In the literature, this development has been referred to as a move from asset-backed *sukuk* to asset-based *sukuk*.[66]

Hybrid *sukuk* structure
Due to the significant growth of the market, *sukuk* issuance and trading have become important means of investment. However, the above described *sukuk al-ijara* structure limits the originator: the originator cannot issue *sukuk* if it does not have sufficient tangible assets. Thus, to meet the demands of investors, the hybrid *sukuk* emerged in the market.[67] In a hybrid *sukuk* structure, the underlying pool of assets can comprise an *istisna* contract, a *murabaha* contract as well as an *ijara* contract, which allows for a greater mobilization of funds.[68] Hence, the hybrid *sukuk* gives the possibilities to use financing contracts for refinancing means: it is a refinancing tool. It even shows similarities to a securitization structure, whereby debt receivables are sold to an SPC over which the SPC issues conventional bonds.

The structure involves the following steps. First of all, the originator transfers tangible assets with underlying *ijara* deals as well as *murabaha* and *istisna* deals to the SPC.[69] The SPC issues *sukuk* to the *sukuk* holders and receives *sukuk* proceeds from them, which are used to pay the originator.[70] The revenues realized with these *ijara* contracts, *murabaha* contracts and *istisna* contracts are paid through to the *sukuk* holders. At maturity date, the originator buys back the assets, consisting of tangible assets with *ijara* contracts, *murabaha* contracts and *istisna* contracts, from the SPC.[71] The *sukuk* holders receive fixed payment of return on the assets and the *sukuk* will be redeemed.[72] In essence, the hybrid *sukuk* concerns the same transaction as the *sukuk al-ijara* transaction. However, while in a *sukuk al-ijara* the SPC always owns tangible assets which are transferred from the originator to the SPC, in a hybrid *sukuk* there is not merely a transfer of tangible assets, but also of *ijara*, *murabaha* and

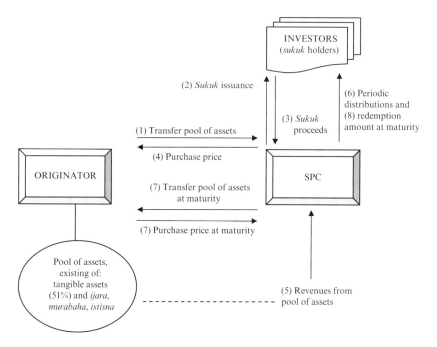

Figure 3.2   Structure of hybrid sukuk

istisna deals from the originator to the SPC. Figure 3.2 illustrates the hybrid *sukuk*.

With this structure, we witness the second explication of the pragmatic approach. Due to the growth of the market and the demand of issuers and investors for the product, the *sukuk* market seemed to deviate from the strict requirement of tangible assets in *sukuk* transactions.

As a result, at least 51 per cent of the pool in a hybrid *sukuk* must comprise of tangible assets. This refers to the presence of *ijara* contracts, because *murabaha* and *istisna* contracts cannot be traded in the secondary market as securitized instruments.[73] These contracts cannot be traded in the secondary market, because they create debt as the result of the *istisna*- and *murabaha*-based sale. Since the prohibition of *riba* does not allow the trade in debt receivables, at least 51 per cent of the pool in a hybrid *sukuk* must comprise *ijara*, because that means that there are underlying tangible assets in the transaction.

The *sukuk* market witnessed an even further deviation over time: in some structures even a minority of 30 per cent of tangible assets included in the pool of assets was accepted by the relevant *shari'ah* scholars.[74] Once again, the pragmatic approach towards the *shari'ah* framework is clearly evident in the mentality of the market.

Sukuk al-mudaraba structure

Sukuk al-mudaraba is structured through the *mudaraba* contract, which is a form of partnership. The structure commences, once again, with a party looking for *shari'ah*-compliant financing, the originator. The originator will establish an SPC and enter into a *mudaraba* contract with this SPC. Both the originator and the SPC will be the partners to the *mudaraba* contract. The originator will act as the managing partner, the entrepreneur of the *mudaraba* venture. As the *mudarib*, the managing partner will contribute his labour, skills and expertise. The SPC will act as the silent partner, the *rab al-mal* of the *mudaraba* venture. As the *rab al-mal*, the SPC contributes in the form of financial investment.

As the financing party to the *mudaraba*, the SPC will issue *sukuk* certificates to *sukuk* holders. The *sukuk* proceeds will be used to make the financial investment in the *mudaraba*. The SPC will declare a trust over all the units it is holding in the *mudaraba* in favour of the *sukuk* holders. Thus, *sukuk al-mudaraba* allows the pooling of investors' funds, with the *sukuk* holders having a common share of the *mudaraba* capital, so they are entitled to returns in proportion to their investment.[75] The profits of the *mudaraba* agreement will be paid to the *sukuk* holders according to an agreed percentage of the realized revenues.

The participation in the *mudaraba* will continue until maturity date. At maturity date, the managing partner will buy the units in the *mudaraba* from the *sukuk* holders through the SPC. The managing partner will pay an amount to the SPC to purchase the units in the *mudaraba*. That amount is used by the SPC to pay the *sukuk* holders their capital back, so that the *sukuk* certificates can be redeemed. Figure 3.3 gives a schematic overview of this structure.

The *sukuk al-mudaraba* structure is an equity-based *sukuk* structure where profits and losses are shared between the partners. Therefore, the periodic payments to the *sukuk* holders cannot be fixed returns; neither can their principal amount be guaranteed at maturity. However, in practice several instruments were used to fix the periodic returns over the *sukuk* and to guarantee the principal amount of the *sukuk* holders.[76] The periodic returns were often fixed returns: when the actual profits realized were less than the promised returns the originator provided for funding, while in the case of excess profits any surplus was for the originator as an incentive fee.[77] This limited the equity character of these securities, since the losses

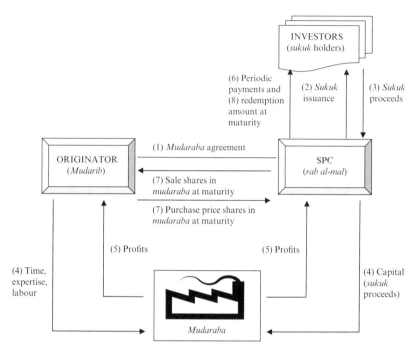

Source: Authors' own

Figure 3.3   Structure of sukuk al-mudaraba

were borne by the originator and the periodic returns to the *sukuk* holders were fixed, regardless of the performance of the underlying projects.

At maturity, pursuant to a purchase undertaking, the assets were bought back by the originator for a price equal to the principal amount of the *sukuk* holders. The purchase undertaking guaranteed the principal amount of the *sukuk* holders, regardless of the possible appreciation or deprecation of the assets.[78] These structural features practically turned the equity-based profit-and-loss-sharing arrangements into fixed-income instruments. Here we witness the third deviation from the s*hari'ah* framework as a result of the pragmatic approach in the *sukuk* market.

3.4.3   The AAOIFI Resolution: An Idealist Approach

The idealist approach towards *sukuk* structures is strongly present in the AAOIFI Resolution on *sukuk*. Before the issuance of the AAOIFI Resolution, Muhammad Taqi Usmani, a well-known *shari'ah* scholar, criticized the developments in the *sukuk* market in a paper on the contemporary application of *sukuk*.[79] He stated that 85 per cent of all the *sukuk* outstanding at that moment were not *shari'ah*-compliant.[80] The main target of his criticism was the equity-based *sukuk* structures – the *sukuk* issues based on *musharaka*, *mudaraba* and *wakala*.[81] He, nevertheless, also addressed some elements of *sukuk* issuances that were relevant in regard to the *sukuk al-ijara* structure and the hybrid *sukuk* structure.[82]

3.4.3.1   Usmani's critique

First, Usmani addressed the issue of the ownership rights of the *sukuk* holders. He mentioned that the presence of ownership rights in *sukuk* structures is the most distinguishing characteristic of *sukuk* when compared to conventional bonds.[83] Usmani noticed that the *sukuk* market had witnessed several structures in which there is doubt in regard to their representation of ownership rights, for example the *sukuk* merely offered the *sukuk* holders rights to returns.[84] Usmani emphasized that such *sukuk* structures cannot be *shari'ah*-compliant.[85] This point is relevant in regard to the *sukuk al-ijara* structure.

Usmani also addressed the occurrence of the hybrid *sukuk* structure in the *sukuk* market. In regard to this structure he noticed that the hybrid *sukuk* raised questions of *shari'ah*-compliance and has to be considered carefully, due to the presence of debts in the pool of assets.[86] According to Usmani, the presence of debts and receivables in the hybrid *sukuk* structure raises issues in regard to the forbidden *bay' al-dayn*, even if the percentage of the debts (as a result of the *murabaha* contracts) is considerably less than that of the tangible assets (linked to *ijara* contracts).[87] Thus, he not only addressed the development of hybrid *sukuk* structures where the tangible assets form a minority of 30 per cent of the pool of assets, but even questioned the *shari'ah*-compliance of hybrid *sukuk* structures where the pool of assets exists of a majority of 51 per cent of tangible assets.

In regard to the equity-based *sukuk* structures, Usmani criticized three elements in the contemporary application of these structures. First, he mentioned that the payment of any surplus as an incentive fee to the originating partner in the transaction is a mechanism that comes from conventional financing transactions and does not adhere to the Islamic finance concept, where the investor is taking more risks and, thus, must be rewarded for those risks taken.[88] The payment of any surplus to the originating partner is a form of fixing the return to the investors and limits profit-and-loss-sharing between them.[89] Furthermore, he criticized the payment of interest-free loans.[90] This mechanism is basically a form of fixing the periodic returns to the investors and, thus, the investors are not taking the risk that entitles them to a reward.[91] The third point that

Usmani condemned was the use of purchase undertakings at face value.[92] Through these purchase undertakings, the originating party was guaranteeing the principal amount of the *sukuk* holders and this is also not in line with the concept of profit-and-loss-sharing.[93]

An idealist approach towards the issuance of *sukuk* clearly resonates in the critique of Usmani. This is even more evident when he places his entire argument in the context of the higher purposes and objectives of Islamic economics.[94] Usmani emphasizes, for example, that the whole essence of equity-based transactions within Islamic finance is that it leads to equitable profit distribution, because the financer does not transfer all the risks to the borrower, and in the meantime the borrower does not only acquire all the benefits of the investment of the financer, but the profits are rather shared between them.[95]

3.4.3.2   AAOIFI Resolution

Shortly after the paper of Usmani, the AAOIFI Resolution was issued in February 2008.[96] The AAOIFI Resolution responded to the developments in the *sukuk* market and to Usmani's critique. It includes six rulings dealing with several s*hari'ah* issues raised. In its first ruling in regard to the ownership requirement, the AAOIFI resolution confirmed that *sukuk*, in order to be tradable, must be owned by the *sukuk* holders with all rights and obligations of ownership in the underlying tangible assets.[97] The AAOIFI, furthermore, rules that the manager issuing *sukuk* must certify the transfer of ownership of such assets in its books and must not keep them as his own assets, stressing that there must be a real transfer of assets.[98] As a result of this, the transfer of the beneficial ownership of the assets from the originator to the SPC is no longer sufficient, and one might even question the extent to which the transfer of merely beneficial ownership from the SPC to the *sukuk* holders is sufficient. Above we noticed that the transfer of legal ownership from the SPC to the *sukuk* holders, however, is almost impossible from a practical perspective.

In its second ruling, the AAOIFI Resolution mentioned that *sukuk*, in order to be tradable, must not represent receivables or debts at all.[99] Exceptions are made for cases where (a portfolio of) the assets of a financial entity that are sold includes unintentionally some debts that are incidental to the tangible assets present therein.[100] Thus, in all other cases the pool of assets cannot represent debts or receivables, not even when the debts represent a minority of the pool of assets of 49 per cent or even less.

In regard to the equity-based structures, the AAOIFI Resolution adopted two out of the three points mentioned by Usmani. First, the AAOIFI stated in the third ruling of the AAOIFI Resolution that it is not permissible to offer interest-free loans to the *sukuk* holders in case of shortfalls.[101] However, it is permissible to establish a reserve account for the purpose of covering such shortfalls.[102] The AAOIFI also permitted payments on account, so long as these payments are subject to final settlement at maturity date.[103] Second, the fourth ruling of the AAOIFI Resolution clarified that purchase undertakings according to which interests in the partnerships, that is in the *mudaraba*, *musharaka* or *wakala*, are bought back at nominal value are not permissible.[104] It is, however, permissible to offer a purchase undertaking according to which the originator can buy back the interests at their market value or at a price to be agreed upon at the moment of the sale.[105]

The AAOIFI Resolution clearly rules out several structural mechanisms that were developed in practice. Although an idealist approach towards the *shari'ah* framework is adopted in the Resolution, practical considerations are also taken into account and, therefore, several mechanisms are provided as alternatives such as the reserve account and payments on account in the equity-based structures. As a result, the idealist approach in the AAOIFI Resolution did not merely criticize contemporary practice by reference to the ideal structures from a *shari'ah* perspective, but it also provided some real alternatives showing the way forward to the market.

3.5   CONCLUSION

The discussion of the history of *sukuk* and its development showed that over the first decade of the twenty-first century, an imbalance was created in the *sukuk* market between an idealist approach to *sukuk* structures and the pragmatic approach that the *sukuk* practitioners have adapted in practice. The *shari'ah* framework of *sukuk*, furthermore, contextualized this imbalance. It will be interesting to see how the market will react to the criticism from the idealists towards the pragmatists' approach. In practice, most likely, a compromise of these two approaches will be the result. The difficulties associated with both the idealist and pragmatic approaches, however, does not perhaps justify the liberal approach that rejects *sukuk* entirely and argues that Islamic capital markets do not differ at all from the conventional capital markets. This is, because even when the pragmatic approach is adopted, certain conventional financial products such as credit default obligations or credit default swaps will be hard to realize in Islamic capital markets, if not impossible. One wonders if there is room in this debate for a more context-based *ijtihad*. Such *ijtihad* being less concerned with the outward 'form' of the structures will shift the focus towards *maslaha* and the underlying objectives of the *shari'ah*, such as fairness, justice and equity. In the future, this might provide a solution that will meet the needs of practitioners while adhering to the true spirit of the *shari'ah*.

NOTES

1. S.H. Nasr (2002), *The Heart of Islam: Enduring Values for Humanity*, New York: HarperOne, p. 123.
2. D. Pearl (1979), *A Textbook on Muslim Law*, London: Croom Helm, p. 1.
3. Notable exceptions are 'Izz b. Abd al-Salam's (d.660AH) and Shatabi's (d.790AH) attempts to understand the problem of *ijtihad* from a *maqasid* (objective) perspective without antagonizing the agreed-upon principles of *usul*. The Hanbali jurist Najm al-Din al-Tufi (d.716AH) is another exception. He went beyond any other jurist and declared that it is the *maslaha* (public interest) which should determine what is Islamic and what is not. Contrary to the generally accepted view, he argued that the *maslaha* could override even a clear text of the Qur'an or *Sunnah* in cases other than worship.
4. N.A. Saleh (1986), *Unlawful Gain and Legitimate Profit in Islamic Law: Riba, Gharar and Islamic Banking*, Cambridge: Cambridge University Press, pp. 13–14; M.A. El-Gamal (2006), *Islamic Finance: Law, Economics, and Practice*, Cambridge: Cambridge University Press, pp. 49–50.
5. Ibn Rushd (1996), *The Distinguished Jurist's Primer, Volume II: Bidayat al-Mujtahid wa Nihayat al-Muqtasid*, Reading: Garnet Publishing (translated by I.A.K. Nyazee), p. 158; Saleh (1986), pp. 13–14; El-Gamal (2006), pp. 49–50.
6. Ibn Rushd (1996), p. 158; Saleh (1986), pp. 13–14; El-Gamal (2006), pp. 49–50.
7. Qur'an 3:130.
8. Qur'an 2:275; Qur'an 2:276; Qur'an 2:277; Qur'an 2:278; Qur'an 2:279.
9. Qur'an 2:275, translation of the Qur'an by Yusufali, available at the Center for Muslim-Jewish Engagement, University of Southern California, <http://www.usc.edu/schools/college/crcc/engagement/resources/texts/muslim/quran/002.qmt.html>, accessed on 5 January 2010.
10. Ibn Rushd (1996), p. 158; Saleh (1986), p. 13.
11. Sahih Muslim, Book 10, Number 3853, translation of Sahih Muslim, available at the Center for Muslim-Jewish Engagement, University of Southern California, <http://www.usc.edu/schools/college/crcc/engagement/resources/texts/muslim/hadith/muslim/010.smt.html>, accessed on 5 January 2010.
12. Ibn Rushd (1996), p. 158; Saleh (1986), p. 13; A. Saeed, (1996) *Islamic Banking and Interest: A Study of the Prohibition of Riba and its Contemporary Interpretation*, Leiden: Brill, p. 32.
13. Ibn Rushd (1996), p. 158; Salch (1986), p. 13; Saeed (1996), p. 32.
14. U.F. Moghul and A.A. Ahmed (2003), 'Contractual forms in Islamic finance law and Islamic Investment Company of the Gulf (Bahamas) Ltd. v. Symphony Gems N.V. & Others: A first impression of Islamic finance', *Fordham International Law Journal*, **27**(1), p. 168.
15. Qur'an 4:29; 2:275.
16. A. Hanif (2008), 'Islamic finance – an overview', *International Energy Law Review*, 2008-1, p. 10.
17. D. Olson and T.A. Zoubi (2008), 'Using accounting ratios to distinguish between Islamic and conventional banks in the GCC region', *The International Journal of Accounting*, p. 47.
18. This element is particularly noticeable in Islamic financial contracts, such as the *musharaka* and the *mudaraba*. For an account of Islamic financial contracts, see M.T. Usmani (2002), *An Introduction to Islamic Finance* (Arab & Islamic Law Series), The Hague: Kluwer Law International; El-Gamal (2006); M. Ayub (2008), *Understanding*

Islamic Finance, Hoboken: John Wiley and Sons; H.S.F.A. Jabbar (2009), 'Sharia-compliant financial instruments: principles and practice', *Company Lawyer*, 2009-6, pp.176–88.

19. This is not the same as denying the time value of money. On this distinction, see M.A. El-Gamal (2000), *A Basic Guide to Contemporary Islamic Banking and Finance*, Indiana: ISNA.

20. Several *hadith* attest to this. On the interpretation of these *hadith*, see El-Gamal (2000); H.S.F.A. Jabbar (2009), 'Islamic finance: fundamental principles and key financial institutions', *Company Lawyer*, 2009-1, pp.23–32.

21. M.T. Usmani (2010), 'Principles of shariah governing Islamic investment funds', *Albalagh*, <http://www.albalagh.net/Islamic_economics/finance.shtml>, accessed on 1 January 2010.

22. With the exception of Malaysia, which allows debt claims to be traded (*bay' al-dayn*). See also A.H. Ismail (2003), 'A Malaysian view of sharia', *AJIF.org LLC* 2003, <http://www.ajif.org>, accessed on 5 November 2009; A. Thomas (2007), 'Malaysia's importance to the sukuk market: March 2007 report', *AJIF.org LLC* 2007, <http://www.ajif.org>, accessed on 5 November 2009; N.J. Adam and A. Thomas (2004), *Islamic Bonds: Your Guide to Issuing, Structuring and Investing in* Sukuk, London: Euromoney Books, pp.48–50; Securities Commission Shariah Advisory Council (2006), *Resolutions of the Securities Commission Shariah Advisory Council, Second Edition*, Kuala Lumpur: Securities Commission, p.19.

23. M.O. Farooq (2007), *Toward Defining and Understanding Riba: An Outline Essay*, <http://www.globalwebpost.com/farooqm/writings/islamic/intro_riba.doc>, accessed 25 May 2009, p.7.

24. Farooq (2007), p.14.

25. Farooq (2007), p.9.

26. Farooq (2007), p.7.

27. Farooq (2007), p.8.

28. Farooq (2007), pp.7–8.

29. Farooq (2007), p.15.

30. Some of these scholars are Muhammad Abduh, Rashid Rida, Abd al-Razzaq Sanshuri, Doualibi, Muhammad Asad and Fazlur Rahman.

31. Qur'an 2:90; 2:91.

32. M. Fadeel (2002), 'Legal Aspects of Islamic Finance', in: S. Archer and R.A.A. Karim (eds), *Islamic Finance: Innovation and Growth*, London: Euromoney Books and AAOIFI, p.91; IOSCO (2004), *Islamic Capital Market Fact Finding Report*, Malaysia: Islamic Capital Market Task Force, p.8.

33. S. Archer and R.A.A. Karim (2002), 'Introduction to Islamic finance', in: S. Archer and R.A.A. Karim (eds), p.3; IOSCO (2004), p.8.

34. Qur'an 2:219; 5:90.

35. Ayub (2008), p.112.

36. IOSCO (2004), p.8.

37. Hanif (2008), p.10.

38. M.A. Khan (2003), *Islamic Economics and Finance: A Glossary*, Routledge: London, p.163; S. Cakir and F. Raei (2007), *Sukuk vs. Eurobonds: Is There a Difference in Value-at-Risk?* (IMF Working Paper 07/237), Washington: International Monetary Fund, p.3.

39. Adam and Thomas (2004), p.43.

40. N.J. Adam and A. Thomas (2004), 'Islamic fixed-income securities: sukuk', in: S. Jaffar (ed.), *Islamic Asset Management: Forming the Future for Shari'a-Compliant Investment Strategies*, London: Euromoney Books, p.73; A. Thomas (2003), 'What are sukuk?', *AJIF.org LLC* 2003, <http://www.ajif.org>, accessed on 5 November 2009; Khan (2003), p.163.

41. A.L. Udovitch (1979), 'Bankers without banks: commerce, banking, and society in the Islamic world of the Middle Ages', in: Center for Medieval and Renaissance Studies,

UCLA (ed.), *The Dawn of Modern Banking*, New Haven & London: Yale University Press, pp. 268–74.

42. A.Z.J.B.J. Ha-Kohen, 'Cheques', *Taylor Schechter Collection*, Cambridge University Library, <http://www.lib.cam.ac.uk/Taylor-Schechter/exhibition.html>, accessed on 5 November 2009; *Genizah* document, 'T-S Ar.30.184', *Taylor Schechter Collection*, Cambridge University Library, <http://www.lib.cam.ac.uk/cgi-bin/GOLD/thumbs?class_mark=T-S_Ar.30.184>, accessed on 5 November 2009.

43. See: Ha-Kohen, *Taylor Schechter Collection*; *Genizah* document, 'T-S Ar.30.184', *Taylor Schechter Collection*. Some even suggest that the ancient Romans had used an early form of the cheque known as *praescriptiones* in the first century BC. During the third century AD, banks in Persia and other territories in the Persian Empire also issued letters of credit known as *sakk*. Hence, it is mentioned that the Arabic word '*sakk*' comes from the Persian language. See: StateMaster, *Encyclopedia: Cheque, NationMaster.com*, <http://www.statemaster.com/encyclopedia/Cheque#_note-Vallely>, accessed on 5 November 2009; A. Markels (2008), 'The glory that was Baghdad', *U.S. News*, 7 April 2008, <http://www.usnews.com/articles/news/religion/2008/04/07/the-glory-that-was-baghdad.html>, accessed on 5 November 2009; M. Wright (2009), 'Just write me a 'sakk'', *SundayMirror.co.uk*, 22 February 2009, <http://www.mirror.co.uk/sunday-mirror/2009/02/22/just-write-me-a-sakk-115875-21142872/>, accessed on 5 November 2009. However, the first evidence of *sakk* dates from the Middle Ages.

44. P. Vallely (2006), 'How Islamic inventors changed the world', *The Independent*, 11 March 2006, <http://www.independent.co.uk/news/science/how-islamic-inventors-changed-the-world-469452.html>, accessed on 5 November 2009.

45. F. Braudel (1973), *The Mediterranean and the Mediterranean World in the Age of Philip II, Volume II*, New York: William Collins Sons & Co., p. 817.

46. The cheque has a British background. English banks started using cheques around the seventeenth and eighteenth century in order to counteract the issuance monopoly of the Bank of England. See: P. de Vroede (1981), *De Cheque: de postcheque en de reischeque*, Antwerpen: Kluwer, p. 3; J.A.F. Geisweit van der Netten (1892), *De Cheque*, Utrecht: Utrechtsche Stoomdrukkerij, p. 5.

47. For more on this, see: G.W. Heck (2006), *Charlemagne, Muhammad, and the Arab roots of capitalism*, Berlin: Walter de Gruyter 2006, pp. 217–18; Udovitch (1979), pp. 268–74; A.L. Udovitch (1989), 'Trade', in: J.R. Strayer (ed.), *The Dictionary of the Middle Ages, Volume 12*, New York: Charles Scribner's Sons, pp. 105–108. The UK-based educational project and exhibition exploring the Muslim contributions to building the foundations of Modern Civilisation, called '1001 inventions: discover the Muslim heritage in our world', also confirmed that the word 'cheque' comes from '*sakk*'. See: 1001Inventions < http://www.1001inventions.com>, accessed on 5 November 2009; Vallely (2006), *The Independent*, 11 March 2006.

48. Resolution No. 30 (5/4) concerning 'Muqarada' Bonds and Investment Certificates, The Council of the Islamic *Fiqh* Academy, holding its Fourth Session in Jeddah, Kingdom of Saudi Arabia, from 18 to 23 Jumada Tahni 1408 AH (6–11 February 1988), in: International Islamic Fiqh Academy, *Resolutions and Recommendations of the Council of the Islamic Fiqh Academy 1985–2000*, Jeddah: Islamic Development Bank, Islamic Research and Training Institute & Islamic Fiqh Academy, 2000, pp. 61–2.

49. A.W. Dusuki (2009), 'Challenges of realizing *Maqasid al-Shari'ah* (objectives of shari'ah) in the Islamic capital market: special focus on equity-based *sukuk* structures', *ISRA Research Paper*, No. 05/2009, p. 8.

50. Dusuki (2009), p. 8.

51. R. Haneef (2009), 'From "asset-backed" to "asset-light" structures: the intricate history of *sukuk*', *ISRA International Journal of Islamic Finance*, **1**(1), pp. 103–26; Dusuki (2009), pp. 8–9.

52. Section 2 AAOIFI *Shari'ah* Standards No. 17 on Investment *Sukuk*.

53. The prevailing *sukuk* structures were the equity-based *sukuk* structures in 2007, see S.

Mokhtar (2009), 'A synthesis of shari'ah issues and market challenges in the application of *wa'd* in equity-based *sukuk*', *ISRA International Journal of Islamic Finance*, **1**(1), pp. 139–45; Dusuki (2009), pp. 8–10. From 2008 onwards, the *sukuk al-ijara* started to dominate the *sukuk* market due to a drop in equity-based *sukuk* structures as a result of a Resolution issued by the AAOIFI in 2008; see O. Salah (2010), 'Islamic finance: The impact of the AAOIFI Resolution on equity-based *sukuk* structures', *Law and Financial Markets Review*, **4**(5), September, pp. 507–17.

54. M. Ainley et al. (2007), *Islamic Finance in the UK: Regulation and Challenges*, London: Financial Services Authority, p. 24.

55. Adam and Thomas (2004), p. 42.

56. Z. Iqbal and A. Mirakhor (2006), *An Introduction to Islamic Finance: Theory and Practice* (Wiley Finance), Singapore: John Wiley & Sons (Asia), p. 177; L. Saqqaf (2006), 'Middle East debt: The new sukuks; Innovative structures are changing the face of Islamic bonds', *International Finance Law Review*, 2006–10, p. 19.

57. Allen & Overy (2003), *Allen & Overy Advises on Islamic First* (Internet Press Release), 12 August 2003.

58. T. Box and M. Asaria (2005), 'Islamic finance market turns to securitization', *International Finance Law Review*, 2005–7, p. 22; M.J.T. McMillen (2007), 'Contractual enforceability issues: sukuk and capital market development', *Chicago Journal of International Law*, 2006–2007, pp. 427–9.

59. A.H. Abdel-Khaleq and C.F. Richardson (2007), 'New horizons for Islamic securities: emerging trends in sukuk offerings', *Chicago Journal of International Law*, 2006–2007, pp. 418–19.

60. Iqbal and Mirakhor (2006), p. 182.

61. HM Revenue & Customs (2008), *Stamp Duty Land Tax: Commercial sukuk; Consultation Document, 26 June 2008*, London: HM Revenue & Customs, p. 20; HM Treasury (2007), *Government Sterling Sukuk Issuance: a consultation, November 2007*, London: United Kingdom Debt Management Office, p. 17.

62. HM Revenue & Customs (2008), p. 20; HM Treasury (2007), p. 17.

63. HM Revenue & Customs (2008), p. 20; HM Treasury (2007), p. 17.

64. Haneef (2009), p. 103–26.

65. Haneef (2009), p. 103–26.

66. Haneef (2009), p. 103–26.

67. In the literature, hybrid *sukuk* are also referred to as 'blended assets' *sukuk*, see Haneef (2009), pp. 103–26.

68. A.A. Tariq and H. Dar (2007), 'Risks of sukuk structures: implications for resource mobilization', *Thunderbird International Business Review*, 2007–2, p. 205; Dar Al Istithmar (2006), *Sukuk, An Introduction to the Underlying Principles and Structure, June 2006*, Oxford: Dar Al Istithmar Ltd, p. 31.

69. Dar Al Istithmar (2006), p. 33.

70. Dar Al Istithmar (2006), p. 33.

71. Dar Al Istithmar (2006), p. 33.

72. Dar Al Istithmar (2006), p. 33.

73. Tariq and Dar (2007), p. 205; Dar Al Istithmar (2006), p. 31.

74. Haneef (2009), pp. 103–26.

75. HM Treasury (2007), p. 19.

76. Salah (2010), pp. 507–17.

77. Salah (2010), pp. 507–17.

78. Salah (2010), pp. 507–17.

79. M.T. Usmani (2008), *Sukuk and their Contemporary Applications*, Bahrain: AAOIFI Shari'ah Council, <http://www.sukuk.me/library/education/MuftiTaqiSukukpaper.pdf>, accessed on 5 September 2010.

80. W. McSheehy (2008), 'Islamic bond scholars toughen rules on sukuk sales', *Bloomberg*, 13 March 2008; Arabian Business (2007), 'Most sukuk "not Islamic", body claims', *Reuters* 22 November 2007, <http://www.arabianbusiness.

com/504577-most-sukuk-not-islamic-say-scholars>, accessed on 5 September 2010;
M. Abbas (2008), 'Sukuk should be equity instruments', *Reuters*, 7 June 2008, <http://
gulfnews.com/business/investment/sukuk-should-be-equity-instruments-1.110624>,
accessed on 5 September 2010.
81. Usmani (2008), *Sukuk and their Contemporary Applications*, pp. 4–13.
82. Usmani (2008), *Sukuk and their Contemporary Applications*, pp. 3–4.
83. Usmani (2008), *Sukuk and their Contemporary Applications*, pp. 3–4.
84. Usmani (2008), *Sukuk and their Contemporary Applications*, pp. 3–4.
85. Usmani (2008), *Sukuk and their Contemporary Applications*, pp. 3–4.
86. Usmani (2008), *Sukuk and their Contemporary Applications*, pp. 3–4.
87. Usmani (2008), *Sukuk and their Contemporary Applications*, pp. 3–4.
88. Usmani (2008), *Sukuk and their Contemporary Applications*, pp. 5–7.
89. Usmani (2008), *Sukuk and their Contemporary Applications*, pp. 5–7.
90. Usmani (2008), *Sukuk and their Contemporary Applications*, pp. 7–8.
91. Usmani (2008), *Sukuk and their Contemporary Applications*, pp. 7–8.
92. Usmani (2008), *Sukuk and their Contemporary Applications*, pp. 8–13.
93. Usmani (2008), *Sukuk and their Contemporary Applications*, pp. 8–13.
94. Usmani (2008), *Sukuk and their Contemporary Applications*, pp. 13–14.
95. Usmani (2008), *Sukuk and their Contemporary Applications*, pp. 2–3.
96. AAOIFI Shari'ah Board (2008), *Resolutions on Sukuk, February 2008*, Bahrain:
     AAOIFI, <http://www.aaoifi.com/aaoifi_sb_sukuk_Feb2008_Eng.pdf>, accessed on
     5 September 2010.
97. Ruling 1 AAOIFI Shari'ah Board, *Resolutions on Sukuk* (2008).
98. Ruling 1 AAOIFI Shari'ah Board, *Resolutions on Sukuk* (2008).
99. Ruling 2 AAOIFI Shari'ah Board, *Resolutions on Sukuk* (2008).
100. Ruling 2 AAOIFI Shari'ah Board, *Resolutions on Sukuk* (2008).
101. Ruling 3 AAOIFI Shari'ah Board, *Resolutions on Sukuk* (2008).
102. Ruling 3 AAOIFI Shari'ah Board, *Resolutions on Sukuk* (2008).
103. Ruling 3 AAOIFI Shari'ah Board, *Resolutions on Sukuk* (2008).
104. Ruling 4 AAOIFI Shari'ah Board, *Resolutions on Sukuk* (2008).
105. Ruling 4 AAOIFI Shari'ah Board, *Resolutions on Sukuk* (2008).

4. A guide to Islamic finance principles and financial engineering

Munawar Iqbal

4.1 INTRODUCTION

Despite commendable progress in product development, there are many areas of financial transactions where suitable alternatives for modern conventional products have yet to be developed. Product development is one of the biggest challenges facing the Islamic Finance Industry (IFI). In the Islamic theory of contracts of exchange, the general rule is that of *permission*. Every contractual arrangement is permissible unless expressly prohibited by *shari'ah*, and the prohibitions are surprisingly very few.

Until now, Islamic financial products have essentially been based on classical modes developed centuries ago. While they may serve as useful guidelines, they may not serve the needs of modern financial markets which are becoming more and more sophisticated and competitive. In order to exploit the fast-changing market environment and to face increasing competition, financial engineering innovation is imperative. While it is possible to modify classical contracts to suit modern conditions, a much broader scope for financial engineering exists in developing new contracts. However, because of the requirement that every new product be compatible with *shari'ah*, anyone wishing to enter this arena needs to know the basic principles of the Islamic theory of contracts and the do's and don'ts of *shariah*. Explaining these is the purpose of this chapter.

Financial engineering means different things to different people. One of the meanings, which is the most relevant to this discussion, is 'it is the process of design, development and implementation of new innovative financial products, processes and the formulation of creative solutions to problems in finance'. Financial engineering may involve (i) adapting an old/existing financial structure to fulfil some new need, for example, to reduce risk; (ii) creating an entirely new structure to attract potential new investment; (iii) combining two or more existing contracts to create a new financial instrument for meeting special needs, as for example, in avoiding interest, which is not acceptable to most Muslim investors.

Financial engineering could be a simple exercise or very mathematically intensive if a number of risks and return profiles are to be considered before the new product can meet the market requirements. However, almost invariably it needs involvement of more than one specialization. In the field of Islamic finance an *inevitable* specialization is Islamic *shari'ah*. What is needed is not always a *shari'ah* expert, at least at the designing stage, but someone who has the minimum knowledge of the do's and don'ts of *shari'ah*. Once designed, the product may have to be vetted by a bona fide *shari'ah* scholar, but by that time 90 per cent of the work would have been completed.

In this chapter, I will make an attempt to derive a minimum (not the maximum) list of requirements so that all the participants in this new niche finance industry can understand the use of financial engineering in Islamic finance. The next section provides an introduction to the principles by reference to the two important sources that provide the theoretical foundation for Islamic finance as being determined by doctrinal principles traceable to Islam and as interpreted to suit changing conditions of human societies over the centuries. One thing that the reader will find in this discourse is that the core fundamentals have remained constant, while there is considerable freedom to change or adapt principles to changing conditions of societies. After that, in sections 4.3 and 4.4, the reader will find a simple guide to product design, which I dub the ten commandments of Islamic banking product design.

4.2 NEED AND SCOPE OF FINANCIAL ENGINEERING IN ISLAMIC FINANCE

In the last 40 years, a lot of progress has been made in the field of developing new financial products which are *shari'ah* compliant. However, the *new* Islamic financial products have essentially been limited to fine-tuning classical modes, such as *mudaraba, musharaka, ijara, bay al-murabaha*, and so on,[1] which were developed centuries ago. They were developed to meet the needs of those societies. While these contracts may serve as useful guidelines for contemporary Islamic contracts, there is no reason whatsoever to offer these restricted contracts only. In my view, this has sometimes been counterproductive to making advances appropriate to this stage of market development.

The end result of that fine-tuning has been that the ordinary investors can hardly distinguish between the so-called Islamic products and their conventional counterparts. Sceptics have labelled it 'old wine in new bottles'. While there could be a grain of truth in this criticism (and we should encourage professional evaluation) the fact of the matter is that theoretically there are *visible* differences among the two types of products. When it comes to practice, there are indeed many lapses. My approach is to criticize *all* departures from approved contracts to ensure their implementation in letter and spirit; but this criticism should be with the spirit of correcting the mistakes and not killing the experiment.

Credit must be given that in a very short span of time a lot of progress has been made. Forty years is not a long period in the development of the banking and finance industry. Modern conventional banking is at least 250 years old: the origin of banking could be traced back many centuries. The first banks were probably the religious temples of the ancient world, and were probably established in the third millennium BC. Banks probably predated the invention of money. Deposits initially consisted of grain and later other goods including agricultural products, and eventually precious metals such as gold, in the form of easy-to-carry compressed plates. Temples and palaces were the safest places to store gold as they were constantly attended and well built. As sacred places, temples presented an extra deterrent to would-be thieves. There are extant records of loans from the eighteenth century BC in Babylon, which were made by temple priests/ monks to merchants. By the time of Hammurabi's Code, banking was well enough developed to justify the promulgation of laws governing banking operations.[2]

Ancient Greece holds further evidence of banking. Greek temples, as well as private and civic entities, conducted financial transactions such as loans, deposits, currency exchange, and validation of coinage.[3] Historical records show that the Israelis at the time of the Prophet Moses had a completely functioning banking system which was based on interest. Reference to that can also be found in the Holy Qur'an. Let me quote only one verse:

$$\text{وَأَخْذِهِمُ الرِّبَا وَقَدْ نُهُوا عَنْهُ وَأَكْلِهِمْ أَمْوَالَ النَّاسِ بِالْبَاطِلِ وَأَعْتَدْنَا لِلْكَافِرِينَ مِنْهُمْ عَذَابًا أَلِيمًا}$$

That they took usury, though they were forbidden; and that they devoured men's substance wrongfully;- we have prepared for those among them who reject faith a grievous punishment. [4:161]

Having given the credit that was due, let me mention that financial markets today are becoming more and more sophisticated, and competitive. Traditional Islamic[4] products will simply not meet the modern requirements. In order to exploit the fast-changing market environment and face increasing competition, financial engineering and innovation is imperative. Financial needs of both individuals and businesses have changed, and there are pressing circumstances that call for financial engineering.

Based on explanations of financial innovation by conventional economists, taken collectively, the factors that stimulate financial engineering can be classified into ten categories:

1. opportunities to reduce some form of risk, such as credit risk or liquidity risk, or to reallocate risk from one market participant to another who is either less risk averse or willing to bear the risk at lower cost;
2. to reduce agency costs;
3. to reduce issuance costs;
4. tax asymmetries that can be exploited to produce tax savings for the issuer or for investors, or both, that are not offset by any added tax liabilities of the other;
5. for regulatory or legislative change;
6. to level volatility of interest rates;
7. to level volatility of prices and exchange rates;
8. for academic and other research that results in advances in financial theories or better understanding of the risk-return characteristics of existing classes of securities;
9. for accounting benefits (which may, and often do, have at best an ephemeral effect on shareholder wealth);
10. for technological advances and other factors.

In order to meet the above-mentioned needs, modern finance engineers have designed several new ways such as mortgages, options, derivatives, hedging, insurance pension plans, credit cards and so on. We must examine what needs are being fulfilled by these instruments. If the needs are genuine (conforming to Islamic contracts) then we must either adapt them for our purposes or invent Islamic alternatives for them. There is no reason whatsoever to be restricted only to the classical contracts. In the light of the fast-changing financial scene, a needs approach to financial engineering is desirable, of course within the known principles of Islamic finance. In the following sections we will attempt to provide necessary tools and principles for financial engineering in modern times.

4.2.1 Some Guiding Principles for *Shari'ah*-compliant Financial Engineering

The scope of financial engineering is very wide but certain basic principles need to be observed. In this section I mention some principles (along with their *shari'ah* justifications) that I consider to be the most important.

Principle of ease: the spirit of Islamic *shari'ah*
Checking contracts to ensure their *shari'ah* compatibility is of course necessary. However, in this process it must be kept in mind that the basic spirit of *shari'ah* is to make things easy for people subject to the proviso mentioned a few paragraphs later. There are a number of *nusus* (texts of Qur'an and *hadith*) that support this statement. For the sake of brevity, I quote only Qur'anic verse and one *hadith*:

$$ يُرِيدُ اللَّهُ بِكُمُ الْيُسْرَ وَلَا يُرِيدُ بِكُمُ الْعُسْرَ $$

Allah intends for you ease, and He does not want to make things difficult for you. [2:185][5]

$$ مَا خُيِّرَ رَسُولُ اللَّهِ صَلَّى اللَّهُ عَلَيْهِ وَسَلَّمَ بَيْنَ أَمْرَيْنِ إِلَّا أَخَذَ أَيْسَرَهُمَا عَنْ عَائِشَةَ رَضِيَ اللَّهُ عَنْهَا أَنَّهَا قَالَتْ $$
$$ مَا لَمْ يَكُنْ إِثْمًا فَإِنْ كَانَ إِثْمًا كَانَ أَبْعَدَ النَّاسِ مِنْهُ (بخاري) $$

Ayesha (R) stated that Prophet (SAW) always selected the easier of the two options if it did not involve any sin and if it did, then he stayed away from it.

The meaning is that among the *halal* (permitted) options, the *Sunnah* (the way of prophet) is always to choose the one which is easy for people. I must caution that one should be cautious not to misuse this principle. The rules and regulations which are clearly established by *nusus cannot* be tampered with on the pretext of seeking ease. While making the rules and regulations, the Law Giver has already taken care of the principle of ease. This is evident from the following text:

$$ لَا يُكَلِّفُ اللَّهُ نَفْسًا إِلَّا وُسْعَهَا $$

Allah does not burden anyone beyond one's ability (to fulfil it). [2:286 (part of the verse)]

The doctrine of maximizing human welfare
Seeking benefit and the repelling of harm for everyone (*maslaha*) is another well-recognized *shari'ah* guideline. This is known as the Principle of *maslaha*. It is something similar to the Principle of Utility of Jerry Bentham, who is considered to be the father of Utilitarianism. His student, John Stuart Mill, enshrined it as the Greatest Happiness Principle. It holds that one must always act so as *to produce the greatest happiness for the greatest number of people*. How does that compare with the Islamic doctrine of maximizing human welfare?

While emphasizing the importance of maximizing human welfare,

Muslim jurists have pointed out that, from a technical point of view, the principle of *maslaha* (public welfare) means the securing of the objectives of *shari'ah* rather than maximization of happiness *as seen by human beings*. This is so because quite often people themselves do not know what is good for them due to their limited knowledge and almost complete ignorance about the final consequences of their acts. The Holy Qur'an states this fact in the following verse:

وَعَسَى أَنْ تَكْرَهُوا شَيْئًا وَهُوَ خَيْرٌ لَكُمْ وَعَسَى أَنْ تُحِبُّوا شَيْئًا وَهُوَ شَرٌّ لَكُمْ وَاللَّهُ يَعْلَمُ وَأَنْتُمْ لَا تَعْلَمُونَ

> It could be that you dislike something, while (in fact) it is good for you; and it could be that you like something while (in fact) it could be bad for you. Allah knows, and you do not know. [2:216 (part of the verse)]

I could have given more examples to show how true this is, but I do not find any need for that because the readers must have noticed or even experienced it in their lives. The Creator, who has full and unlimited knowledge of everything past, present and future, knows what is best for His creations. He is also the most merciful. As such, He has enshrined the means of maximizing human welfare in this life as well as in the life hereafter in the basic principles of *shari'ah*.

When any new situation arises and one needs to engineer a financial solution for it, scholars have laid down the procedure and conditions to find out what the principle of *maslaha* demands. Shatabi has laid down three conditions.[6] Any rule adopted under *maslaha* must be in conformity with the overall objectives of *shari'ah*.

When the solution is presented to people, the general logic accepts it; it must fulfil some *genuine* need. Once something is accepted as *maslaha*, the next issue is to determine the means to achieve that *maslaha*. These means must also be compatible with *shari'ah*. A very useful technique in pursuit of *maslaha* is *istihsan*, which therefore deserves some elaboration.

Istihsan literally means preferring something over another. Technically, it has been defined in several ways. In essence, it refers to departure from a ruling based on previous analogy (*qiyas*) in a particular situation in favour of another ruling, which brings about ease.

Some people have criticized *istihsan* saying it amounts to moving away from a rule deduced through *qiyas* toward the personal opinion of a jurist. However, this is not in fact the case. In *istihsan*, a ruling is preferred to another based on stronger evidence, usually from texts (*nusus*) due to consensus (*ijma*) or to the doctrine of necessity, all of which have a sound basis in *shari'ah*. As Al-Sarakhsi explains,[7] *istihsan* is a way of looking at the consequences of the application of two legal rules and selection of the one that creates ease and facility. This is done by taking a lenient view of an act which would be considered a violation on a stricter interpretation of the action based on earlier *qiyas*. It may also mean, giving an exception to a general principle due to stronger evidence provided, the general principle from which exception is being granted was based on *qiyas* and not the primary sources. In the rules of Islamic jurisprudence, seeking benefit (*jalb al-manfa'*) and removing a harm (*raf al-haraj*) occupy very high positions. The following examples will make the purpose and import of *istihsan* clear.

In general, it is not allowed to sell anything that is not in one's possession at the time of the sale. But *bay al-salam*, a sale in which a well-described commodity is bought on the basis of advance payment, with delivery of the good postponed, is permitted on the basis of a *hadith*. The Prophet allowed such sales because of the need of the people, but laid down clear rules to protect the interests of both parties.[8]

The contract of *istisna* is a futures contract similar to *salam* which should have been prohibited for the same reason. However, it is permitted on the basis of consensus of contemporary jurists. In the contract of *ijara* (leasing) also, the usufruct which is the subject matter of the sale does not exist at the time of the contract. It is permitted on the basis of need.

The doctrine of general permissibility

Another relieving factor for financial engineers is what I call 'the doctrine of general permissibility', which is explained below: Islamic *Ahkam* (commandments) are broadly speaking of two kinds: (1) *ibadat* (worshipping) and (2) *muamalat* (dealing among human beings). The general rule in the field of worshipping is that an act is worship only when permitted by *shari'ah*. On the other hand, in the case of mutual dealings, the general principle is that everything is permitted unless clearly prohibited by the *shari'ah*. I call this the doctrine of general permissibility.

In theory of contracts, parties are free to agree on any terms as long as known Islamic rules and principles are not violated. Again there are many texts to establish this principle, but I quote only one Qur'anic verse and one *hadith*. In the Holy Qur'an Allah says:

يَسْأَلُونَكَ مَاذَا أُحِلَّ لَهُمْ قُلْ أُحِلَّ لَكُمُ الطَّيِّبَاتُ

They ask you (O Muhammad!) what is lawful for them? Say: 'Lawful unto you are all kinds of Halal (lawful) things'. [5:4 (part of the verse)][9]

The Prophet explained it and its general applicability when he said:

ٱلْمُسْلِمُونَ عَلَى شُرُوطِهِمْ إِلاَّ شَرْطًا حَرَّمَ حَلاَلاً أَوْ أَحَلَّ حَرَامًا (ترمذى)

> Muslims are free to determine the conditions for their contracts except any condition make something forbidden as permissible or something permissible as forbidden.

God, the most Merciful, has prohibited very few things. The approach usually taken of fitting a contract into the mould of one of the classical modes is not very fruitful. The correct approach in the light of the above *hadith* is to examine any contract to see if it involves any prohibition. If not, it should be allowed, whether or not it fits a particular classical cast. This will require a radical change in the attitude of Islamic jurists, who try to examine whether a contract is *mudaraba* and hence fulfils the conditions of the classical *mudaraba* contract, or whether it is *ijara* and hence complies with *ijara* conditions and so forth.

Most modern contracts are hybrids and involve departures from classical conditions. Those conditions were set by jurists suiting the conditions of their time. They can be changed in view of the changed circumstances. What is important is to examine that any contract does not violate any condition established in the basic sources of Islamic law. Within these limits, variations on classical contracts should be acceptable. As mentioned before, the prohibitions are very few. It will be useful to mention the most important of such prohibitions that are relevant for Islamic finance. These are outlined as briefly as possible.

The doctrine of necessity

This doctrine allows *temporary suspension* of normal law in case of dire need. The rule of removing harm applies here also. This doctrine is based on the Qur'anic verse:

إِنَّمَا حَرَّمَ عَلَيْكُمُ الْمَيْتَةَ وَالدَّمَ وَلَحْمَ الْخِنْزِيرِ وَمَا أُهِلَّ بِهِ لِغَيْرِ اللَّهِ فَمَنِ اضْطُرَّ غَيْرَ بَاغٍ وَلَا عَادٍ فَلَا

إِثْمَ عَلَيْهِ إِنَّ اللَّهَ غَفُورٌ رَحِيمٌ

> He has only prohibited for you carrion, blood, the flesh of swine and that upon which name of someone other than 'Allah' has been invoked. However, whoever is compelled by necessity, neither seeking pleasure nor transgressing, there is no sin on him. Verily, Allah is Most-Forgiving, Very-Merciful. [2:173]

This doctrine is often misused. Therefore, a word of caution is in order. The doctrine of necessity is meant to be used very sparingly. It is a rule to handle emergencies. Even in emergencies, it does not provide an automatic and unrestricted suspension of the law. First of all, it has to be determined that a situation has arisen where the doctrine can be invoked (the words in the verse mean compelling circumstances). While in individual cases, it is the individual's conscience which will determine this; in the case of public application, a ruling must be given by *shari'ah* scholars, in consultation with the experts of the concerned field. Secondly, the suspension of the normal law is not absolute. There are limits and conditions to be observed. The Qur'anic verse quoted above itself lays down two more conditions: (i) the user must accept the sanctity of the original law (implying a return to it as soon as possible) and in the meanwhile, (ii) using the exception to the minimum possible extent.

Prohibitions in the field of Islamic finance

In the following paragraphs, I mention the most important prohibitions in the field of finance. The list may not be exhaustive, but in my view, if the Islamic financial engineers can take care of them, 90 per cent of their job is done.

Prohibition of usury (riba)   That *riba* is prohibited in Islam is non-controversial. It is established by a number of verses of the Qur'an as well as *ahadith* of the Prophet.[10] But what does this term encompass? The word '*riba*' as a noun literally means in Arabic 'an increase', and as a root, it means the process of increasing. The prohibition of *riba* essentially implies that the fixing in advance of a positive return on a loan as a reward for waiting is not permitted by the *shari'ah*. According to a vast majority of jurists, bordering on true consensus, it makes no difference whether the return is big or small, fixed or variable or an absolute amount to be paid in advance or on maturity, or a gift or service to be received as a condition for the loan. It also makes no difference whether the loan was taken for consumption or business purposes.

Therefore, in its basic meaning *riba* can be defined as 'anything (big or small), pecuniary or non-pecuniary, in excess of the principal in a loan that must be paid by the borrower to the lender along with the principal as a *condition*,[11] (stipulated or by custom), of the loan or for an extension in its maturity'. Throughout history, there has been near consensus among Islamic jurists that bank interest is covered by this prohibition.

The prohibition of *riba* is so strict in Islam that: (i) giving or taking of interest is considered as declaring a war against God; (ii) not only the giver and taker but even the scribe of the *riba* deal is cursed; (iii) it is prohibited to take even an indirect benefit from the borrower such as riding his mule, sitting under the shade of his wall, or accepting a gift from him; (iv) means that could lead indirectly to taking *riba* are also prohibited. This last point needs further elaboration.

Islamic jurists have used the term *riba* in three senses; one basic and two subsidiary. The kind of *riba* described above is called *riba al-qard* (loan) or *riba al-nasa'*. It is also referred to as *riba al*-Qur'an as this is the kind of *riba* which is clearly mentioned in the Qur'an. Islam, however, wishes to eliminate not merely the exploitation that is intrinsic in the institution of interest, but also that which is inherent in all forms of dishonest and unjust exchanges in business transactions. Thus, the term *riba* has a more comprehensive meaning and is not merely restricted to loans. *Riba* may even surreptitiously enter into sales transactions.

Hence the two subsidiary meanings of *riba* relate to such transactions and fall into the category of *riba al-buyu* (*riba* on sales). The first of these is *riba al-nasi'ah*, which stands for the increase in lieu of delay or postponement of payment of a due debt. It may be mentioned that the debt may have arisen because of a loan contract, in which case it will be covered by *riba al-nasa'* mentioned above; or the debt may arise from a sales contract in which the payment has been deferred. A third kind of debt may arise as a compensation for certain rights. Examples of this are dower money due to a wife, or blood money as a compensation for an unintentional killing, if the payment is delayed for some reason. A modern-day example would be payments due in libel cases. *In all such cases, once the amount has been determined, the debtor cannot be asked for any increase if the payment is delayed.*

The second subsidiary meaning relates to *riba al-fadl,* which arises in the barter exchange of commodities. *Riba al-fadl* refers to the excess taken by one of the trading parties while trading in any of the six commodities mentioned in a well-known authentic *hadith* which says: 'Gold for gold, silver for silver, wheat for wheat, barley for barley, dates for dates and salt for salt, like for like, payment being made hand by hand. If anyone gives more or asks for more, he has dealt in riba. The receiver and giver are equally guilty.' (Muslim). Islamic jurists have over the centuries debated the question of whether *riba al-fadl* is confined only to these six items or whether it can be generalized through *qiyas* to include other commodities and if so, what reasoning (*illah*) should be used for this purpose.

Of the six commodities specified in the *hadith*, two (gold and silver) unmistakably represent commodity money used at that time. One of the basic characteristics of gold and silver is that they are monetary commodities. As a matter of fact, each of the six commodities mentioned in the *hadith* has been used as a medium of exchange at some time or another. Hence, it has been generally concluded that all commodities used as money enter the sweep of *riba al-fadl.*

The other four commodities specified in the *hadith* represent staple food items. There is a difference of opinion with respect to the rationale for the prohibition in this case. One opinion argues that since all four commodities are sold by weight or measure, therefore all items which are so saleable through weight or measure are subject to *riba al-fadl* (Hanafi, Hambali and Zaydi). A second opinion is that since all four items are edible, *riba al-fadl* is involved in all commodities which have the characteristic of edibility (Shafei and Hambali). A third opinion is that since these items are necessary for subsistence and are storable (without being spoilt) all items that sustain life and are storable are subject to *riba al-fadl* (Maliki).[12]

It must be mentioned that, economically speaking, it would be irrational to exchange one kilogram of wheat with one and a half kilograms of wheat in a spot exchange. Therefore, some *fuqaha'* have pointed out that *riba al-fadl* has been prohibited because if it was not prohibited, it could be used as a subterfuge for getting *riba al-nasi'ah.* It is not always possible to determine the scale of difference in the quality of two brands of the same kind and hence what should be the ratio of exchange in the case of a direct hand to hand transfer. It was therefore prescribed to sell the commodity of one quality on the market for money and then buy the same commodity of different quality from the market. In this way the true value of each can be determined and there is no scope for exploitation of one party by the other due to lack of knowledge.

The scope of *riba al-fadl* is much wider in a barter economy than in modern-day market economies. One important application in modern times is the trade in currencies. Currency exchange in Islamic systems is governed by the rules of *bay al-sarf* which require that exchange of currencies must be hand to hand (that is, no future trading) at the current market exchange rate with no increase within exchanging the same currency.

In the literature several reasons have been mentioned as the rationale behind the prohibition of *riba*. The most important among these relates to justice and equity between the parties. Islam emphasizes justice to all parties. A contract based on interest involves injustice to one of the parties, sometimes to the lender and sometimes to the borrower. Since the results of an investment cannot be predicted, equity demands that *both parties share in the risks* that are part of ordinary business to which money is lent. This has led to the derivation of a universal rule that '*Al-kharaju bi-al-daman*' which can be translated as 'gain is contingent upon assuming liability for loss'.[13]

Gharar   The second most important prohibition in exchange contracts is that of *gharar* trading. This prohibition is based on authentic *ahadith* of the Prophet. Reliable sources have reported through a number of the Prophet's companions that the Prophet has forbidden *gharar* trading.[14] Let us see what the term '*gharar*' encompasses.

Literally, *gharar* means to expose oneself or one's property to jeopardy unknowingly. In jurisprudential literature, *gharar* has been variously defined. Mainly, there are three views. First, *gharar* applies to cases of uncertainty, as in the case of not knowing whether something will take place or not. A second view holds that *gharar* applies trading of the unknown. Thus, according to Ibn Hazm, *gharar* in sales occurs when the purchaser does not know what he/she has bought and the seller does not know what he/she has sold. Third is a combination of the two opinions; *gharar* covers both the unknown and the doubtful, as exemplified by the definition proposed by Al-Sarakhsi which states that *gharar* obtains where consequences of a contract are not known. This is the view favoured by most jurists.

   Gharar has been one of the most difficult Islamic juristic terms to under-stand. Perhaps the best way to visualize its true scope and import is to list some examples. The most important categories are the following:

1. *Ignorance of the genus.* For example saying 'I will sell you 1 kilogram of apples for $5'. This involves *gharar* because it is not clear what type of apples are the subject of the sale.
2. *Ignorance of the species.* For example, saying 'I will sell you my pet for $100'. It is not known what the pet is.
3. *Ignorance of the attributes.* For example, saying 'I will sell you my car for $5000'. (However, if the object is available and offered for inspection with known defects declared then there is no *gharar.*)
4. *Ignorance of the quantity of the object.* For example, saying 'I will sell you a box of oranges for $20' without mentioning the type of oranges and the weight.
5. *Ignorance about price.* For example, saying 'I will sell you this dress for a week's salary'.
6. *Ignorance of the specific identity of the object.* For example, saying 'I will sell you one flat in this building for $50 000'.
7. *Ignorance of the time of payment in deferred sales.* For example, saying 'I will buy this house from you for $100 000 which I will pay when my farm is sold'.
8. *Inability/uncertainty to deliver the object.* For example, saying 'I will sell you the bird sitting on that tree or I will sell you my BMW which has been stolen when it is recovered for only $500'.
9. *Contracting on a non-existent object.* For example, saying 'I will sell you the harvest of my farm from the next crop'.
10. *Not being able to inspect the object.* For example, saying 'I will sell you the contents of this carton for $50 on an as is basis'.
11. *More than one option in a contract unless one is specifically chosen.* For example saying 'you can either take my car for $10 000 or my

boat for $15 000'. The sale would become valid only after you exercise your option and specifically choose what you are buying.
12. *Contingent sale.* For example, saying 'I will sell you my house if Peter rents his house to me'.

These examples are not exhaustive but they should be sufficient to give a fairly good idea of what the prohibition of *gharar* implies. In essence, *gharar* refers to acts and conditions in exchange contracts, the full implications of which are not clearly known to the parties. This is something very similar to *asymmetric information.* Lack of knowledge with respect to all implications of a contract vitiates against the principle of voluntary consent of all parties, which is a necessary condition in all contracts of exchange according to Islamic law. In other words, had the parties known the full implications of the contract, one (or both) of them may have preferred not to enter into that contract. In the presence of asymmetric information, the agreement of the parties cannot be considered as voluntary consent. *The objective of the prohibition of* gharar *is to minimize possibilities of post facto misunderstandings and conflicts between the contracting parties.*

Jurists make a distinction between two kinds of *gharar*: *gharar fahish* (substantial) and *gharar yaseer* (trivial). The first kind is prohibited while the second is tolerated, since this may be unavoidable without causing considerable damage to one of the parties with the possibility of post facto conflict. In many cases, it is simply not possible to reveal all information; not because the seller wants to hide anything, but because it is in the nature of the product. The buyer has to trust the seller. For example, the buyer of a built house has to take the word of the seller as to what kind of material is used in the foundations of the house. The seller obviously cannot dismantle the house to reveal the foundations to the buyer. His intention is not to hide essential information, but the nature of the subject matter of the contract is such that he cannot show it to the buyer. Therefore, such lack of knowledge does not violate contracts. The principle in such cases is that the seller must act as a trustworthy person. Penalties may be imposed *ex post* if it is proved otherwise.

In the literature, some other prohibited types of trade or conditions therein are also mentioned. For example, prohibition of selling something not owned are; *ghish* (cheating, for example adulteration); *tatfif* (giving less value than agreed), two mutually inconsistent contracts (conditions) bunched into one contract; *ikrah* (coercion); *ghaban* (fraud); *najash* (raising prices by false bids). But on closer examination one finds that these are covered by the prohibition of *gharar.*

However, one special prohibition within the category of *gharar* may be noted separately. That is *maisir* (gambling). This needs a separate mention because of its wide application in modern times and also because its prohibition is based on Qur'anic verses.

Maisir (gambling)   Islam prohibits all kinds of gambling and games of chance. This is based on clear texts in the Qur'an. For example:

يَٰٓأَيُّهَاالَّذِيْنَ اٰمَنُوْٓا اِنَّمَا الْخَمْرُ وَالْمَيْسِرُ وَالْأَنْصَابُ وَالْأَزْلَامُ رِجْسٌ مِّنْ عَمَلِ الشَّيْطٰنِ فَاجْتَنِبُوْهُ لَعَلَّكُمْ تُفْلِحُوْنَ

> O, you who believe! Intoxicants (all kinds of alcoholic drinks), and gambling, and al-ansab (animals that are sacrificed in the name of idols on their altars) and al-azlam (arrows thrown for seeking luck or decision) are an abomination of Satan's handiwork. So avoid that (abomination) in order that you may be successful. [Qur'an 5:90]

In order to understand the meaning of gambling, it is important to draw a distinction between pure games of chance and activities that deal with uncertainties of life and business activities and involve an element of chance and risk-taking. Not all types of chance and risk-taking are prohibited. Rather, as we will mention later, one of the distinguishing features of Islamic banking is risk-sharing between financiers and entrepreneurs. The type of risk-taking that is prohibited is the one that arises from uncertainties that are not part of everyday life. They arise from various types of 'games' that 'create' risk for those who choose to participate. These risks are unnecessary. They are unnecessary for the individual in the sense that if someone chooses not to participate in these 'games', they will face no such risk. They are also unnecessary for society in the sense that they do not add any economic value to the wealth of the society. It is this type of risk-taking that is the essence of gambling and is prohibited by Islam.

Devour not your property among yourself wrongly
The scope of 'do not devour your property among yourselves wrongfully' in verse 4:29 also includes all those activities that are declared illegal by the state and its various echelons, because *shari'ah* binds Muslims to obey the rulers except if they command anything that amounts to disobedience of Allah. Examples of these are bribery, smuggling, money laundering and so on. Furthermore, it also includes anything that violates the rights of contracting parties. All kinds of fraud, corruption, stealing, robbery, unauthorized possession of others' property and so on are thus prohibited. Ways of creating wealth that violate the rights of third parties and society at large are also prohibited due to the general Islamic rule *'la darara wa la dirar'*. This may be translated as 'do not harm anyone, nor let anyone harm you'.

This principle lays down that if anyone causes any harm to others, they

can claim compensation. Examples of this are creating pollution, obstruct-
ing common passage ways and other negative externalities, as well as
dishonouring anyone, infringements of copyrights and so on.

No pain no gain (*al-kharaju bil-daman*)
Islam does not encourage parasitic life. The following *hadith* establish
three more principles, one of which is that the right to profit is contingent
upon taking responsibility (for loss).

قَالَ رَسُولُ اللَّهِ ـ صلى الله عليه وسلم ـ « لاَ يَحِلُّ سَلَفٌ وَبَيْعٌ وَلاَ شَرْطَانِ فِى بَيْعٍ وَلاَ رِبْحُ مَا لَمْ تَضْمَنْ وَلاَ

بَيْعُ مَا لَيْسَ عِنْدَكَ (أبو داود)

> Prophet (SAW) said 'It is not allowed to combine a contract of loan with a con-
> tract of trade nor is it allowed to have two deals in one deal;[15] nor profit without
> taking responsibility (of loss) and do not sell that which you do not possess.'

One of the principles established by this *hadith* is 'No pain, no gain'. The
other principles mentioned in this *hadith* are discussed elsewhere in the
chapter.

Possibility of hybrid contracts
In modern financial applications, usually several contracts have to be
patched together in a single deal. Is that permissible from an Islamic
point of view? In principle, Islamic law should not have any objection
to the combination of contracts in view of the Doctrine of General
Permissibility. Then how is the *hadith* quoted above, which prohibits combining two deals in one, to be interpreted?

Scholars have explained that the Doctrine of General Permissibility
provides the overall framework, while the above-quoted *hadith* limits that
in certain cases in order to remove *gharar*, which as mentioned above is
prohibited in order to avoid any post-contract dispute. They point out
that since all rights and obligations created by contracts bunched together
are to be viewed as inseparable obligations, one has to see the end result
and apply the *shari'ah* rule to it. What is at dispute is not the validity of combination of contracts in principle. The concern is with the
nature and form of such a combination. Scholars draw attention to the
qualifying clause in the *hadith* that is the basis of the Doctrine of General
Permissibility. It states that all conditions mutually agreed are acceptable 'unless they make something forbidden as permissible or something
permissible as forbidden', and *gharar* is indeed prohibited.

Therefore, in order to check the validity of the overall deal emerging
from a combination of contracts, certain parameters need be established.

Some of these can be stated as follows: if there is an explicit text in the primary sources of Islamic law that certain types of contracts cannot be combined, for whatever reason, then any structure that involves such a combination becomes unacceptable. If analysed, the rationale of prohibiting such a combination can also be found. Some examples will help to clarify this parameter.

There is a *hadith* prohibiting combination of a loan contract with a sales contract. It is easy to understand the reason for this prohibition. If allowed, a lender may advance the loan on an interest-free basis in the loan part of the deal, but he can buy something at a cheaper price in the sale part of the deal. This amounts to *riba*; any benefit accruing to the lender, even indirectly, is *riba*.

Similarly the Prophet prohibited 'two deals in one'. Some scholars take this *hadith* as a general prohibition of combining contracts. However, actually it implies that if more than one option is offered, one must be chosen before the deal is finalized. For example, if two prices for a commodity are included in a contract, a lower price for cash and a higher price for credit, the contract is invalid. The buyer must choose one of the options and only that should form part of the contract. The rationale for this prohibition is that such a combination amounts to *gharar* in the combined contract, which is one of the prohibitions in business contracts.

The combination must not attempt to circumvent a prohibition: a product structured on the basis of a combination of contracts should not be intended to circumvent impermissible transactions. Such attempts are called *hiyal* (legal artifices) and are not allowed. For example: the Prophet has prohibited *bay al-inah*, which is a sale and buy-back arrangement. For example, A sells his house to B for a cash price of $500 000 and simultaneously buys it back from B at a credit price of $600 000. It is easy to see that the end result is exchange of $500 000 now for $600 000 later. This is nothing but *riba*. The 'selling' and 'buying back' of the house is inconsequential.

The combination must not involve contradictory contracts/conditions   Each type of contract has unique legal implications and obligations. Contracts which are mutually contradictory cannot be combined. If the legal consequences do not conflict with each other then there is no problem in combining them. For example, a collateral condition supports a loan contract and is hence acceptable. On the other hand, a condition in a marriage contract stipulating that the spouses will live apart, defeats the purpose of the contract and is hence not acceptable.

The combination must not involve contingent contracts   The Prophet (SAW) has prohibited a sale that is circumscribed with a condition (*bay wa shart*). If the combination is such that the execution of one contract is contingent upon another contract, such a combination is not permissible. An example of this would be, William saying to Peter that he will sell his house to him *provided* Stephen rents his house to William.

4.3 PROCESS OF DEVELOPING NEW PRODUCTS

The process of adaptation through *ijtihad* is well recognized in Islamic *fiqh* and has never stopped. However, its speed needs to be greatly enhanced. Classical contracts have been modified in a number of cases to meet current needs. One potent example is the initiation of Islamic banking on the basis of the *al-mudarib udarib* principle, which provides that a *mudarib* (agent) may himself appoint another agent to actually run the business. The principle of *al-mudarib udarib* essentially allows for sub-contracting. There is no reason to restrict it only to *mudaraba*. Contracts can also be designed using other modes in which the original contractee may arrange to fulfil the obligations under the contract through third parties. That the principle is acceptable from an Islamic point of view is not questionable.

Mudaraba accounts in Islamic banks provide a good example that conditions of classical contracts can be changed to the extent required as long as the general purpose is maintained. In *mudaraba* accounts of Islamic banks, usually withdrawal in and withdrawal from the account is allowed at any time.[16] This would not have been allowed in a classical *mudaraba* contract. Similarly, new depositors can enter general *mudaraba* deposits at any time. Therefore, the depositors (*rab al-mal*) are not the same at the time of profit distribution as at the time of the opening of the *mudaraba* accounts. This is also a departure from classical conditions. These departures have been accepted because of the need to fit the *mudaraba* contract to modern conditions while keeping its spirit.

Another important adaptation of classical contracts is the practice of *murabaha* in Islamic banking. It turned the classical *murabaha* contract, which was a two-party contract, into a financial intermediation instrument by involving a third party, a bank, which buys merchandise from a supplier at a cash price, upon a promise by a client to purchase the same from it at a higher credit price.

While it is possible to modify classical contracts to suit modern conditions, a much broader scope for financial engineering exists in developing new contracts. These contracts could be hybrids of old contracts or may be entirely new. The approach to examine any contract for *shari'ah* compatibility should not use the classical contracts as the reference point. The touchstone should rather be the checklist of do's and don'ts of business contracts.

4.4   CONCLUSION

In the light of the above discussion, I propose the following shortlist for financial engineers to check their contracts against. I believe that if their contracts pass this list, there is a 90 per cent chance that, when presented to *shari'ah* scholars for vetting, which is a required step, the contract will stand a very good chance of approval.

Ten Commandments for Islamic Financial Engineering

1.   Principle of Ease: the Spirit of Islamic *Shari'ah*
2.   The Doctrine of Maximizing Human Welfare
3.   The Doctrine of General Permissibility
4.   Principle of Relief (*Istihsan*)
5.   The Doctrine of Necessity
6.   Prohibition of *Riba*
7.   Prohibition of *Gharar* (Including the Special Case of Gambling)
8.   Prohibition of Selling Without Having Possession and Two Deals in One
9.   No Pain No Gain (*Al- Kharaju Bil-Daman*)
10. Permissibility of Hybrid Contracts and Rules Governing them

NOTES

1.   These terms are defined in other parts of the book.
2.   The word 'bank' reflects the origins of banking in temples. According to the famous passage from the New Testament, when Christ drove the money changers out of the Temple in Jerusalem, he overturned their tables [Matthew 21.12]. In Greece, bankers were known as *trapezitai*, a name derived from the tables where they sat. Similarly, the English word 'bank' comes from the Italian *'banca'*, for bench or counter.
3.   Cohen, Edward (1992), *Athenian Economy and Society: A Banking Perspective*, Princeton, NJ: Princeton University Press.
4.   Are *mudaraba, musharaka, ijara, bay al-murabaha* (sale on mark-up) Islamic products? Those who proclaim that should think again. *Mudaraba* is a pre-Islamic contract. Regarding *musharaka* (partnership) and *ijara* (leasing), is there a country in the world including non-Muslim countries where these contracts are *not* used? Similarly, deferred sale on mark-up is practised throughout the world. So where is the difference? In my view it is that Islamic scholars took these contracts and removed aspects/conditions that were not in line with Islamic injunctions. Therefore, I do not 'stamp' them as Islamic as if Muslims were their inventors. I prefer to label them *'shari'ah*-compliant'. Perhaps it is only semantics, but I think it is important to claim *only* what is due to Islamic scholars.

5. Throughout the chapter in references to the Holy Qur'an the first number in the bracket refers to the *surah* (chapter) number and the second to the *ayah* (verse) number.
6. Shatabi, *Muafaqat*, Vol. 2, p. 43.
7. Usul Al-Sarakhsi, Vol. 2, p. 200.
8. For details see Iqbal, Munawar and Philip Molyneux (2005), *Thirty Years of Islamic Banking: History, Performance and Prospects*, Basingstoke: Palgrave Macmillan.
9. This particular verse deals with food, but there is a general rule in Tafseer (the science of explanation of the Qur'an) that the principles expounded in a particular context generally carry over to other fields unless there is a clear indication restricting them only to that field.
10. See the International Institute of Islamic Economics (IIIE) website for a good collection of these.
11. Thus any excess given by the debtor of his/her own accord, and without the existence of a custom or habit that obliges him/her to give such excess is not considered as *riba*.
12. For further details of this discussion, see Chapra, Umer M. (1985), 'The role of the stock exchange in an Islamic economy: comments on the paper of Dr Mokhtar Metawally', *Journal of Research in Islamic Economics*, Summer, pp. 75–81.
13. Abu Dawud, Tirmidhi, Nasa'i, IbnMaja.
14. *Sahih* Muslim, annotated by Al-Nawawi (III/156); and Ibn Majah's Sunan (II/10), and Ibn Dawood's Sunan.
15. See explanation below.
16. Although sometimes with notice.

5. History of Islamic public finance: *gharar* and risk aversion

Murat Çizakça

5.1 INTRODUCTION

Gharar is usually examined in the literature from the perspective of modern Islamic private finance. In this article, I will focus on public finance and try to explain how this important concept found an application in history. It is a concept that has a long history, and was embedded in Islamic jurist work over centuries of comments and interpretations. To the West, this idea has come as a borrowed concept to mean risk as the word is roughly translated as uncertainty, which has come to modern economics and finance as a fundamental concept of relevance to associate risk with returns in contemporary finance literature.

In this chapter, I will first make an attempt to define the concept as it is available in Islamic legal literature before tracing its applications. In section 5.2 the reader will find an attempt to lay the foundation principles of *gharar* meaning uncertainty including lack of symmetry in information provision. Section 5.3 describes how this concept was an underlying theme in the Turkish government's effort to raise tax revenue. This is followed in section 5.4 by a description of the evolution of tax-farming, which led to the development of principles of the Islamic debt instrument. This chapter concludes in section 5.5.

5.2 THE MEANING OF *GHARAR*

The word '*gharar*' comes from the Arabic root verb '*Gharara/gharra*' meaning to expose oneself and one's property to destruction without being aware of it. Thus, it has been argued, the most important element of *gharar* is deception and feeding the victim with false information, which disguises the truth, *haqq*. The word '*gharar*' appears in the Qur'an 27 times. Whether the word is used in verb or noun form, it always basically refers to deception. The *ahadith* also reveal the same meaning. *Gharar* is mentioned 23 times in *Sahih Muslim.* These are either in verb or noun form. All the verb forms mean 'to deceive'. But it is possible to find other meanings for the noun form, such as 'danger'.[1]

Some jurists have also interpreted *gharar* as doubt over the existence of the subject matter of the contract. Al-Sarakhsi has defined *gharar* as any bargain in which the result and the legal consequences of it are hidden and unknown. Ibn Rushd considers a transaction of *gharar* as: the buyer suffers a loss due to a lack of knowledge concerning either the price or the non-existence of the subject matter. The essence of concern about *gharar* has been best summarized by the Prophet: '*La darar wa-la dirar*', meaning that 'there shall be no unfair loss, nor the causing of such loss'.[2]

Al-Dhareer has identified 14 different *gharar* types.[3] Two of these, 'ignorance of the quantity of the object' and 'contracting on a non-existent object' are the ones that are relevant for this chapter. Concerning the first, if an object is not in sight, knowledge of its quantity is a condition for its validity. This otherwise general opinion has been objected by Al-Sharnbelali, a Hanafite (legal school) jurist, who did not make the validity of sale conditional on knowledge of the quantity of the sold object.[4] As we will see, this has direct relevance for the history of Islamic public finance.

Concerning the second type, contracting on a non-existent object, normally the sale will be null and void if the sold object is not in existence at the time of the contract or if its future existence is uncertain in that it may or may not exist. But this does not mean that every non-existent item cannot be sold. This is because there are non-existent items whose sale implies no *gharar*, since the consequence of the sale is not hidden from view, for example, the sale of goods that are non-existent at the time of the contract but that are customarily certain to exist, or the sale of goods that will come into existence in succession.

Ibn Taymiyya has also supported this view. According to him, there is no evidence to prove that the sale of the non-existent item is impermissible. The essential point here is that the non-existent item cannot be sold not because it is non-existent, but because it involves *gharar*.[5]

Al-Dhareer has clarified the issue as follows: 'every non-existent object whose future existence is uncertain must not be sold, and every non-existent object whose future existence is normally ascertainable, may be sold.'[6] The term 'future existence normally ascertainable' is of crucial importance here. As it is well known, the Prophet had forbidden the sales of years, meaning that the fruits of an orchard are sold for more than one year to come. Naturally, this prohibition does not apply to commodities which will become available in the near future. While based upon this *hadith* Imam Shafi'i forbade the sale of the non-existent fruits, the Malikites, the Imamite Shiites (another legal school) and the leading

Hanafites have permitted it on account of necessity. Ibn Taymiyya and Ibn al-Qayyim have supported the Malikite (another legal school) and the Hanafite view and this is considered to be the acceptable opinion.[7]

Indeed, necessity is considered to be of paramount importance in determining whether a contract is a *gharar* contract. It has been pointed out that if people are in any need of such a contract, *gharar* will not affect it, even if it is exorbitant. This is based upon the *shari'ah* principle of *removal of hardship* on the strength of the verse: 'He made no hardship for you in religion'.[8] Therefore, Al-Dhareer has concluded that it is the Lawgiver's justice and mercy to permit contracts that people need even if they contain *gharar*.[9]

Characterization of a contract as *gharar* is influenced by differences in societies and times. It has been recognized that it is the society that confers such a characteristic on the contract.[10] We will now focus on the question of to what extent a powerful Islamic state in the past dealt with the problem of *gharar* while finding ways to secure financing for itself.

5.3   TAX COLLECTION AS THE SOURCE OF INVENTION

Referred to in the literature as tax-farming, the most widespread form of Ottoman tax collection during much of the fifteenth to the seventeenth centuries was the *iltizam*. While the origins of this system can be traced to medieval Egypt, it was widespread and found application from the Balkans to India.[11] The Roman empire also auctioned off tax collection to private individuals.

This was a method of tax collection through public auctions and worked as follows. In this system, the state delegated its right to collect taxes to an entrepreneur. Thus, taxes were actually collected by the private enterprise. The state chose the entrepreneur who would collect taxes on its behalf through competitive public auctions. The Ottoman tax collector, the *mültezim*, was basically a risk taker, an entrepreneur. He competed with others to be appointed as the designated tax-farmer. The competition was in the form of commitments. The entrepreneur who committed him/herself to pay the highest amount to the state was appointed as the *mültezim* to a specific tax-source, *muqata'a*. This authorized him/her to collect taxes from this tax source for a given period, usually from one to three years.

Whenever a tax-farmer committed him/herself to collect a certain amount of taxes from a tax source and promised to pay the state a certain amount, he/she took a calculated risk based upon previous records and experience. Consider, for instance, collection of customs from a given port. In this case, the state would organize an auction to determine who would become the *mültezim.* The state would take its decision simply by considering who has promised to pay the highest amount (in modern terms, an English auction). This highest bidder would then be issued documents, which would grant him/her the right to collect the pertinent taxes in the name of the state.

The tax-farmer would base his/her decision to make his/her bid on the estimated amount of numbers of ships that would use the port. Because the number of ships, the amount of goods they will bring and the amount of customs revenue to be collected are not known, obviously, there is *gharar* (uncertainty) here. If, despite this uncertainty, this institution has been allowed to operate for centuries in various Islamic societies, this was probably based upon the two criteria we have mentioned above.

First, consider the sale of things which are non-existent at the time of the contract but which are *customarily* certain to exist, or the *sale of things which will come into existence in succession.* Obviously, the piecemeal arrival of ships at the port throughout the year means a gradual coming to existence in succession. This pertains to Al-Dareer's conclusion that '*every non-existent object whose future existence is normally ascertainable, may be sold*'. There is no doubt that while the future existence of the amount of goods to be unloaded and taxed in the port continued to be uncertain, based upon customary previous experience, future existence was normally ascertainable.

The second criterion pertains to necessity. We have noted above that most schools permit contracts on account of necessity even though they may bear the element of *gharar.* The necessity in this case was due to the fact that all early modern states collected their revenues (taxes) in kind and had difficulty converting these to cash. This conversion was made by entrepreneurs through the system of tax-farming. For all pre-modern states, in the Islamic world as well as the West, this conversion was vitally important.[12]

We can therefore conclude that based upon this criterion of necessity, tax-farming was permitted in most Islamic states throughout history. We will now focus on how the system of tax-farming evolved within the framework of Ottoman public finance.

5.4   EVOLUTION OF OTTOMAN TAX-FARMING

As already mentioned above, the Ottoman tax-farmer, the *mültezim*, was a risk-taking entrepreneur. Indeed, he/she committed him/herself to collect a certain amount of revenue from a tax-source on the assumption that the tax source would be able to generate this amount. If he/she managed to collect an amount greater than committed to the state, he/she made a profit; otherwise he/she suffered a loss. A *mültezim* not able to fulfil his/her commitment could face confiscation and even imprisonment. The system was widespread; in the year 1527, 23 per cent of the total revenues of the European provinces and 19.75 per cent of the Asian provinces were collected in this way. As much as 80 per cent of the Egyptian revenues were also collected through the *iltizam* system.[13]

The *gharar* element appears to have emerged as two different types in this system. First, at the time of the auctions when the *mültezim* committed him/herself, the amount of revenue to be collected from the tax-source was not known. Second, the tenure of the tax-farmer was also not known. This meant that although the intended duration of his/her contract may have been, say, three years, the actual duration may have been much less, say a year only. This is because the state did not commit itself to any specific duration and was free to give the tax-farm to another tax-farmer at any time. Thus, the tax-farmer could never be sure to collect the amount he/she envisaged, both because of the uncertainty of supply and because of the uncertainty of his own tenure.[14]

These uncertainties, that is, *gharar* elements of the two types, eventually started to have an impact, and undesirable consequences for the Ottoman public finance began to emerge. To start with, tax-farmers facing uncertain tenures and wishing to start making a profit as soon as possible, felt the need to maximize revenue in the short term. This meant that producers were harassed by these tax-farmers. Moreover, overshadowed by such *gharar*, tax-farmers simply did not make any investments to improve the productivity of the taxsource they were controlling. These developments eventually led to certain improvements in the system. Each such improvement played a role in the evolution of the Ottoman public finance.

To start with, as the state felt an ever-increasing urgency to collect its revenue in the shortest possible time, it began to demand from the tax-farmers that they pay their commitments up front. This increased the *gharar* element even further. Meanwhile, commitments were also continuously increasing. Risks as well as capital committed rapidly surpassed the means of single entrepreneurs, and partnerships had to be formed. Tax-farms which were particularly lucrative could only be obtained by paying to the state the promised amount in cash and up front. But when tax-farmers refused or could not pay up front, the state relented and allowed them to pay in instalments.

Payment in instalments led to another problem – this time it was the state which was facing *gharar*. After all, the state had firm commitments to pay its military and wanted to make sure that the committed amount would actually be paid.[15] To ensure payment, it demanded surety from tax-farmers. A *kefil*, a person who agreed to stand as surety for the tax-farmer, had to be introduced.

It has been argued that since no one would normally assume the risks of being surety without something in return, the *kefil* must have been actually the silent partner, *rab-al-mal*, of the tax-farming partnership.[16] Since archival evidence does not give evidence of a uniform procedure regarding *kefil*s of failed tax-farming partnerships, this inconsistency has been explained by the changing liability structures of classical Islamic partnerships. Put differently, it has been argued that while *kefil*s of *mudaraba*-type tax-farm partnerships would only be held responsible for paying the amount of their initial investment (limited liability), *kefil*s of the *mufawada*-type partnerships assumed an unlimited liability and could be subject to confiscation or even imprisonment.[17]

In view of these relative liabilities, it seems reasonable to assume that while the *kefil*s must have preferred to associate themselves through *mudaraba*, the state must have preferred tax-farmers associated through *mufawada*. These arguments, which should be considered as hypotheses, can only be vindicated by analyzing actual contracts between tax-farmers and their *kefil*s, a task not yet attempted.[18]

The *kafala* system just described does not appear to have provided sufficiently reliable revenue to the state. This is only natural, for what the state could collect from the economy always depended on the economic conjuncture, which fluctuated. While competition among the tax-farmers in times of rapid economic growth led to ever-increasing revenues (auction prices) from the tax-farms, in times of stagnation, revenues fell. Consequently, despite the *kafala*, the *gharar* that the state faced was such that it decided to shift the entire *gharar* upon the shoulders of the tax-farmers and their partners. This led to the emergence of the so-called frozen tax-farms.

What the state needed was definitive revenue and it was prepared to make further concessions to tax-farmers in return. Put differently, the Ottoman state had become risk averse. This risk aversion took the form of transferring to the risk-taking entrepreneurs, the tax-farmers, the potential profits of their tax-farms in return for fixed annual payments. Thus, after guaranteeing the payment of a fixed revenue, the state was prepared to allow tax-farmers to collect any remaining revenue that could be collected from the tax-farm as long as the tax laws (rates) were not violated. It has been argued that, particularly in times of economic growth, the system of frozen tax-farms must have allowed tax-farmers to collect more and more revenue, a situation which must have led to financial decentralization, even re-feudalization of the Ottoman state.[19]

To sum up, the *iltizam* system had the following disadvantages: first, the unreliability of the tenure of the tax-farmer led to excessive exploitation of the tax source. Second, the system was risk laden both for the state and the tax-farmer. When the state became risk averse it tended to transfer risks upon the tax-farmer, a process which reduced the earnings of the state and allowed tax-farmers to reap the real benefits, leading to decentralization. Third, the system was slow in generating revenue.

5.4.1 The *Malikane* System

It is clear that with all these disadvantages, the Ottoman state would eventually be forced to improve its financial system. The crisis came with the second siege of Vienna in 1683, when a long war ensued, which lasted until 1699. This war resulted in a significant territorial loss for the first time.[20] Huge budget deficits were the result and there was an urgent need to increase revenue substantially at the shortest possible time. The solution was found in the *malikane* system introduced in 1695.

The new system reflects the ever-increasing risk aversion of the state and what it was prepared to do to mitigate its risks. In a nutshell, *malikâne* transferred to the entrepreneurs, *malikânecis*, the right to collect taxes from a given tax-farm for a life time, in return for a large lump sum payment made up front, *muajjalah*, combined with more modest and fixed annual payments, called *mal*. The state calculated a minimum rate for the *muajjalah* as two to ten times the annual average estimated profit of the tax source. These calculated amounts were then displayed on the doors of the Finance Ministry in Istanbul. The candidates then came and registered the actual *muajjalah* amounts they were prepared to pay. The highest bidder obtained the right to collect taxes from a certain tax source for the rest of his/her life.

It will be argued here that the *gharar* element must have reached new heights in this system. This is because the *malikânecis* were now asked to pay a very large amount up front on the assumption that they would be able to cover their expenses in the future. There were two different *gharar* elements here. First, the entrepreneurs had to guess how much tax they would collect, which would be a function of the economic conjuncture in the future, and second, they would have to assume that they would live a certain number of years. This was particularly important because *malikâne* did not entail a transfer of full property rights to the entrepreneur – it was made clear that the tax-farm could not be inherited by the entrepreneur's offspring and that it would be taken away from his/her family upon his/her death. These risks were somewhat mitigated by the possibility of selling the *malikâne* to third persons. But such sales were subject to a tax of 10 per cent of the original *muajjalah* amount paid.

The *malikânecis* could keep their tax-farms as long as they paid the annuities, *mal*, regularly. Thus, the state was once again minimizing its risks. Indeed, if the *malikânecis* failed to pay the annuity, they would lose their tax-farm. Consequently, the very large *muajjalah* paid up front constituted a strong surety for the regular payment of the annuities.

In short, in the *malikâne* system the risk aversion of the Ottoman state had reached the maximum and all the risks were transferred to the tax-farming entrepreneurs. In return for this risk minimization, the entrepreneurs were granted near complete property rights for as long as they lived. It has been argued that the *malikâne* system paved the way towards full private ownership for members of the Ottoman *askerî* class.[21]

The *malikâne* system achieved the following: first, the massive budget deficit of 262 217 191 *akçes* that occurred as a result of the disastrous military situation in 1692–93 was reduced to 63 560 888 *akçes* in 1689–99. This was followed by a substantial improvement, and in the year 1701 a budget surplus of 111 866 873 *akçes* was generated.[22] Second, it improved substantially the reliability of tax collection. Indeed, in the earlier *iltizam* system, in times of depression tax-farms remained unsold – a situation which must have led to a considerable loss of revenue for the state.

The sensitivity of *iltizam* to economic conjuncture was also demonstrated by tax-farmers, who failed to pay their debts to the state despite the sanctions. Both of these problems were solved by the *malikâne* system. The former was solved by selling the tax source on a life-term basis. Indeed, once sold this way, the state no longer had to worry about selling it at the next auction. The next auction did not take place until the *malikâneci* died. The problem of arrears was also solved by making the continuous possession of the *malikâne* conditional on the regular payment of the annuities.

5.5 CONCLUSION

In public finance not only the entrepreneur but also the state had to deal with the problem of *gharar*. As its power declined, the Ottoman state became increasingly risk averse. It tried to reduce the *gharar* it faced by shifting it onto the shoulders of the entrepreneurs who collected its taxes. It was able to do this by granting to tax-farmers improved property rights. This took the form of more secure and life-term property rights.

Seen strictly from the perspective of Islamic law, it is not clear if *gharar* existed in tax-farming contracts. If we consider *gharar*, as Buang does, as deception, then we reach the conclusion that tax-farming contracts did not contain an element of *gharar*. This is because these contracts did not deceive anybody. The system was transparent and the experiences of the previous tax-farmers were well known. If we consider *gharar,* however, as Sunusi and Al-Dhareer do, as uncertainty with respect to the quantity of the object and non-existence at the time of the contract, then we must reach the conclusion that tax-farming contracts contained *gharar.* If so, then they must have been permitted for centuries based upon necessity and custom. The truth can only be learned by studying the discussions and verdicts of the *ulama* from as early as the seventh century.

Meanwhile, economic history teaches us an important lesson that such sustained liberal interpretations of the *shari'ah* (Islamic jurisprudence) over the very long run can lead to serious harm. Islamic states/empires applied tax-farming for centuries and a path dependency developed as a result. The system was by no means perfect. Mehmet Genç has estimated that approximately 75 per cent of the revenues collected were kept by tax-farmers and their colleagues, with only 24 per cent actually accruing to the state.[23] Had a more strict interpretation of the *shari'ah* applied and tax-farming had not been permitted, Islamic states would have been forced to invent other more efficient and better *shari'ah*-compliant systems.

Ironically, this is what happened in the West and such a system was developed by medieval Europeans under the pressure of the Catholic Church, which had been applying a stringent prohibition of *riba.* The result was the development of the so-called Permanently Funded Public Debt. This was a *riba*-free, non-loan system and it allowed European governments to obtain huge amounts of cash from the public. It has been estimated that in the year 1509, the little European city-state Genoa was able to obtain from the public 6 440 000 ducats through this system, an amount equal to five times the revenue of the Ottoman Central Treasury for that year.[24] Thus, a more stringent interpretation of the *riba* prohibition by the Church allowed Europeans to develop a more efficient system of revenue collection. This is confirmed by an eminent European financial historian who concluded: 'Thus the responses to the prohibition of usury promoted rather than retarded European economic progress'.[25]

Moreover, it has been shown that this system also led Europe towards democracy.[26] The Ottoman state belatedly adopted a similar system to the European Permanently Funded Public Debt in 1774 after it suffered a crushing defeat and had to pay a huge war indemnity to Russia. This new system was called *esham.*[27] But that story is too long to be included in this chapter.

[Editors' Note: The editors note with gratitude the comment of an anonymous reviewer of the manuscript that the role of *sukuk* for public finance needs further work in Islamic finance. We agree with this remark. *Sukuk* issues by public authorities account for a third to a half, sometimes more, of the issues in some of the *sukuk* markets. Proponents of this security, including the World Bank, suggest its ideal fit for developing countries to tap public savings via sharing the income streams of public assets when they raise this type of security.

Public finance was accessed through *sukuk* issues in historical times, and yet there has been to date no serious attempt to document the details on how this new security has automatic sharing of risk of an investment through sharing in the income streams of assets escrowed to the fund providers in the SPC. So, with such asset transfers to the fund providers borrowers could not keep borrowing beyond an affordable ratio of assets to the funds borrowed. This instrument is ideally suited for governments to tap funds from domestic sources and it provides an automatic break by requiring assets to be set aside to be owned by the issuers. This is not the feature of conventional bond issues, which is the reason we have the Paris Club (for the delinquent governments with too much debt) and heavily-indebted governments. This topic requires a separate research effort at a future date.]

NOTES

1. Buang (2000), pp. 30–32.
2. Sunusi (1993), pp. 87–100.
3. Al-Dareer (1997), p. 11.
4. *Ibid.*, p. 28.
5. *Ibid.*, pp. 31–2.
6. *Ibid.*, p. 32.
7. *Ibid.*, p. 33.
8. V:157. *Ibid.*, p. 49.
9. *Ibid.*, p. 49.
10. *Ibid.*, p. 46.
11. See on this, Morimoto (1981); Çizakça (1996), pp. 136–8.
12. Hicks (1973), ch. 6.
13. Çizakça (1996), ch. V.
14. If the tax-farm was given to another *mültezim*, the first tax-farmer was naturally reimbursed.
15. Indeed, payments to the military constituted the bulk of the state expenditure. Vital services such as health and education were financed, organized and maintained by the *waqf* system. See on this, Çizakça (2000).
16. Çizakça (1996), ch. V.
17. *Ibid.*, p. 148.
18. It is possible to do this research among the 11 000 volumes of Istanbul Ottoman Court Registers, held in the office of the *Mufti* of Istanbul.
19. Çizakça (1996), pp. 144–5.
20. From 1300 to 1683 Ottoman armies did not suffer any major loss of territory. The only exception was the defeat suffered in 1402, when Tamerlane attacked Anatolia – a war between Turks.
21. Çizakça (1996), pp. 160–63. While civilians enjoyed property rights, as embodied in Islamic law, members of the *askerî* class did not.
22. Genç (1975), p. 236.

23.   In Çizakça (1996), p. 166.
24.   Çizakça forthcoming; Özvar (2006), p. 204, table 48.
25.   Munro (2003), p. 561.
26.   Macdonald (2006).
27.   Genç (1995).

REFERENCES

Al-Dareer, Siddiq Mohammad Al-Ameen (1997), 'Al-Gharar contracts and its effects on contemporary transactions', Islamic Development Bank, IRTI, Eminent Scholars' Lectures, no. 16, Jeddah.

Buang, Ahmad Hidayat (2000), *Studies in the Islamic Law of Contracts: The Prohibition of Gharar*, Kuala Lumpur: International Law Book Services.

Çizakça, Murat (1996), *A Comparative Evolution of Business Partnerships. The Islamic World and Europe, with Specific Reference to the Ottoman Archives*, Leiden, Netherlands: Brill.

Çizakça, Murat (2000), *A History of Philanthropic Foundations*, Istanbul: Bogazici University Press.

Çizakça, Murat (forthcoming), *Islamic Capitalism and Finance: Origins, Evolution and the Future*.

Genç, Mehmet (1975), 'Osmanlı Maliyesinde Malikane Sistemi', in O. Okyar (ed.), *Türkiye İktisat Tarihi Semineri*, Ankara: Hacettepe University Press.

Genç, Mehmet (1995), 'Esham', in *Islam Ansiklopedisi*, Ankara: Türkiye Diyanet Vakfı.

Hicks, John (1973), *A Theory of Economic History*, Oxford: Oxford University Press.

Macdonald, James (2006), *A Free Nation Deep in Debt, The Financial Roots of Democracy*, Princeton, NJ: University of Princeton Press.

Morimoto, Kosei (1981), *Fiscal Administration of Egypt in the Early Islamic Period*, Kyoto, Japan: Dohosha.

Munro, John (2003), 'The medieval origins of the financial revolution: usury, *rentes* and negotiability', *The International History Review*, **XXV** (3).

Özvar, Erol (2006), 'Osmanlı Devleti'nin Bütçe Harcamaları, 1509–1788', in Mehmet Genç and Erol Özvar (eds), *Osmanlı Maliyesi, Kurumlar ve Bütçeler*, İstanbul: Osmanlı Bankası Arşiv ve Araştırma Merkezi, chapter 1.

Sunusi, Mahmood M. (1993), 'Gharar', *IIUM Law Journal*, **3**(2), 87–100.

PART II

Regulations of *sukuk* markets

6. Regulatory lessons on *sukuk* financial products, an opinion

Peter Casey

6.1 INTRODUCTION

In this chapter, I consider the regulatory issues on *sukuk* securities from the point of my view of essentially secular financial services regulation. That is, I do not consider the question of what is, or is not, compliant with *shari'ah*, though I shall necessarily consider issues of *shari'ah* governance. This partly reflects my own background, but it also reflects the fact that the *sukuk* market is an international one, despite my location in Dubai as the regulator. *Sukuk* are originated, bought and listed in many countries of the world, including some (like the United States) where Muslims are a relatively small percentage of the population.

In many such countries, regulators for constitutional, political or practical reasons must approach *sukuk* from an essentially secular standpoint, and this chapter sets out some of the issues they will face. Questions relating to *shari'ah* permissibility are considered in other chapters. In dealing with the regulatory issues, I shall consider *sukuk* both as capital market instruments raising market conduct issues which bear on investor protection, and as instruments which may be held (or issued) by financial institutions, raising issues of their treatment for capital adequacy purposes. I shall consider first the *sukuk* market as it currently exists, and then possible developments of it. I shall concentrate on the corporate, rather than the sovereign, market, since that is where the main regulatory issues lie, but shall include within it the various government-related (but non-sovereign) issuers. I shall deal only minimally with the short-term (bill-like) *sukuk* issued by governments such as those in Bahrain and the Gambia.

6.2 THE CURRENT *SUKUK* MARKET

One important point to make by way of preamble is that the *sukuk* market is dominantly an institutional one. This is true of bond markets generally; in the US, for example, only 10 per cent of debt issues are held by individual investors, though the figures are higher for certain types, notably municipal bonds. There are exceptions such as in Italy, which has a strong and actively traded retail bond market. But these are indeed exceptions.

In the case of *sukuk*, none of the countries where *sukuk* are issued or listed has an active retail debt market, and the issues themselves clearly target institutional investors.[1] For example, the Nakheel *sukuk* debt issued in 2006 had a minimum investment of US$100 000, as did the issues from IIG (2007), Saad Group (also 2007), the Government of Indonesia (2009) and the International Finance Corporation (also 2009). This clearly indicates that institutional investors are the targets, and this is borne out in those cases for which it has been possible to review lists of initial subscribers.

The nature of the market has an important impact on the typical regulatory approach. In an institutional market, a regulator will expect the primary regulatory tool for the protection of investors to be disclosure. Furthermore, a regulator will expect that the investors in question are both able and willing to analyse relatively complex documentation, either in-house or with the aid of professional advisers. Disclosures may therefore be relatively long and technical, provided that they are accurate and complete. In a retail market, much more attention would be given to the clarity and comprehensibility of disclosures, especially disclosures of the associated risks. There might also be some element of product control, for example a requirement for the issue to have an external rating.

Again, in the current market *sukuk* are traded to only a very limited extent; partly because demand exceeds supply, there is a general pattern of their being held to maturity. Where they are traded, trading usually takes place over the counter (OTC), even where the *sukuk* are listed on an exchange. This means that the issues of clearing, settlement and market manipulation are less prominent in regulators' minds than they would be in, say, the equities market.

6.3   REGULATION IN THE CURRENT *SUKUK* MARKET

I shall discuss regulation in the current *sukuk* market before turning to ways in which that market may develop, and the regulatory implications. I shall deal at the end of the chapter with prudential issues when *sukuk* are held, or occasionally issued, by financial institutions.

6.3.1 Regulation and *Shari'ah* Issues

Having established the context of a primarily institutional market, I now address the regulation of that market.

I begin with the issue of *shari'ah* regulation, since it is a feature which distinguishes *sukuk* from any conventional instrument. Even a secular regulator will need to consider this issue to some extent, because any claim that an instrument is Islamic, even if signalled only through the use of terms like *sukuk*, is a representation to investors about something that may be important to them. Regulators should at least consider whether such a representation falls within their area of interest and, if so, what their attitude towards it should be.

Globally, different regulators have different views on this, ranging from an active avoidance of any religious issue to full control, typically through some form of *shari'ah* council.[2]

The first position would be typified by many Western regulators. In some instances they would consider that it would be unlawful for them to be involved in any way with religious matters, either because they had been given no express power to do so or because it would contravene a more general principle of the separation of secular and religious authority. An example of an authority taking such a position would be the Autorité des Marchés Financiers in France. In other cases, though the regulator might be able to claim the necessary authority, it may conclude that for political or regulatory reasons it does not wish to become involved. The UK Financial Services Authority (FSA) would be an example.

Some regulators which decline to become involved in *shari'ah* issues may consider that general principles relating, for example, to market disclosure would nevertheless oblige *sukuk* issuers to make disclosures about *shari'ah* compliance where these may be material to an investment decision. For example, the UK FSA said in 2007, 'The FSA is in no position to assess the suitability of the scholars consulted by Islamic firms. It does, however, want to see the basis on which an Islamic firm claims to be Sharia-compliant is communicated appropriately to the consumer.'[3] Others would not go so far, at least in the sense of being willing to take action against a firm which failed to make such disclosures.

At the other end of the spectrum are those jurisdictions in which the regulator effectively takes full control of *shari'ah* matters, by setting up a *shari'ah* council which is the ultimate authority as to what is, or is not, permissible in that jurisdiction. Examples would be those in Malaysia or the Sudan. A council may work directly or by overseeing the work of *shari'ah* advisers or boards in individual institutions; for practical reasons the latter model is more common in jurisdictions with a significant Islamic finance industry. If such a council has authority over both capital markets and other Islamic financial institutions, such as banks, it may be able to ensure consistency between the views taken by issuers and at least some major investors. Inevitably, however, its authority will be confined to the jurisdiction in which it is established. In particular, its rulings cannot bind investors in other jurisdictions. Thus there is a risk that it may approve *sukuk* structures which are shunned by investors in other markets with different traditions of jurisprudence.

The *shari'ah* council approach may also be difficult to apply, for political or practical reasons or both, in Muslim minority countries. For example, although India has the third largest Muslim population in the world, its politics is dominated at different times by either a resolutely secular party (Congress) or a clearly Hindu one (the BJP). It is difficult to imagine either being content to see a regulator establish a *shari'ah* council. In some other cases, for example in Europe, even if there were no ideological objections it might be difficult to find sufficient credible scholars within the jurisdiction.

The third approach, which has been taken by the DFSA (Dubai Financial Services Authority) is that of *shari'ah* systems regulation. The regulator requires any firm holding itself out as Islamic to have a properly constituted *Shari'ah* Supervisory Board (SSB), systems to implement the SSB's rulings, arrangements for *shari'ah* review and audit, and so on. It may also require disclosure about the SSB and associated matters. These arrangements are supervised, in a similar way to other systems and controls requirements, but the regulator does not itself intervene in the substance of *shari'ah* decisions. For a *sukuk* issuer the requirements will be more limited, but in this approach there would typically be a requirement for a *fatwa* from a properly constituted SSB, and for some relevant disclosures. This approach to *shari'ah* governance allows greater diversity, which may be more appropriate for an international centre, and is capable of being monitored by competent supervisors of any religion. It may in the longer term prove acceptable in Muslim minority jurisdictions which would have difficulties in establishing a *shari'ah* council within the regulator.

This chapter is not the place to discuss in detail the advantages and disadvantages of these approaches, which may depend on the circumstances of the particular jurisdiction, and will almost certainly not be driven dominantly by the *sukuk* market. Other markets, whether banking, insurance or collective investment funds, typically require a higher frequency of *shari'ah* decisions, and their needs are likely to drive the regime, except in those jurisdictions which see themselves only as capital markets intermediaries. The consequence of the diversity of approaches is, however, that in the country of issue and/or listing, a *sukuk* issuer may face any one of a wide range of s*hari'ah* governance requirements, ranging from none at all to sign-off by a *Shari'ah* Supervisory Board overseen by a national *shari'ah* council. The difference may, however, be less important than appear at first sight since in practical terms investors are likely to require some form of *shari'ah*-based approval, and market demand is thus likely to force the issuer to obtain a *fatwa* from an SSB or at least a respected *shari'ah* adviser. Even non-Muslim investors might require such an approval, as a mitigant for the risk that aspects of the structure may be challenged in a court on *shari'ah* grounds, with unpredictable consequences for the interests of all investors.

6.4   CURRENT *SUKUK* STRUCTURES

At present, most issues in the *sukuk* market, whatever their form, are structured to have a similar economic effect to conventional bonds. That is, assuming the instrument proceeds to term as planned, investors will receive their principal *plus* an additional return which is either fixed or determined by an external benchmark (e.g. LIBOR). None of the cash flows depends in any meaningful way on the performance of the underlying asset or business.

Guarantees of one kind or another are put in place to secure these returns. Typically, these guarantees can be called in the event of any default, offering the investors at least the option of exchanging their claim over the underlying assets for a claim against an obligor, usually the originator of the *sukuk*. They may also be callable in the event of certain external developments, for example a change in the relevant tax regime.

In addition, there are typically arrangements for a predictable stream of payments during the lifetime of the *sukuk*. These may, for example, be regarded as payments on account of the expected profits, in principle subject to a final reconciliation at the end of the *sukuk* period.

With both the ultimate guarantee and the interim payment arrangements in place, the *sukuk* become very close in economic effect to fixed or floating rate bonds, with the return dependent in practice only on the credit risk of one or more obligors. Published guidelines on *sukuk* structuring are typically around how to secure this economic effect in different situations, and within the limits of *shari'ah*.

For example, under a *mudaraba* contract, the *rab-al-maal* and the *mudarib* share any profits but (absent negligence or misconduct on the part of the *mudarib*) losses are borne by the *rab-al-maal* alone.[4] In practice, the risk of loss is often mitigated by a purchase undertaking granted by the originator in favour of the Special Purpose Company (SPC) which acts as the issuer. This undertaking may be triggered if the proceeds of the enterprise are insufficient to meet the promised payments to investors. Similarly, if the proceeds exceed the amount promised, the *mudarib* may receive most or all of the excess through a performance fee. Arrangements are put in place for predictable payments during the life of the *sukuk*, so that investors are not even subject to any timing risk.

Prior to 2008, it was also possible for the originator to grant an under-taking to repurchase the *mudaraba* assets at a price determined by a formula which effectively ensured that investors were all but certain to receive their principal *sukuk* investment and profit, subject only to the continuing solvency of the originator. Such a *sukuk* structure thus approximated very closely in its economic effects to a conventional bond. In February 2008, however, a statement by the *shari'ah* council of AAOIFI indicated that any repurchase undertaking must be referenced to the market value of the *mudaraba* assets at the time of the repurchase. It is interesting that the effect of this has been substantially to reduce the use of *mudaraba* as a basis for *sukuk*, mainly in favour of *ijara*, for which no such restriction exists. There has also been exploration in the literature, though relatively little in practice, of alternative structures such as *wakala* with, sometimes, the explicit aim of being able to delink the payments to investors from the actual performance of the underlying assets.

Thus it appears that those involved in the structuring of *sukuk* transactions are keen to replicate the economic effect of conventional bonds, in which a predetermined return to investors is effectively subject only to the credit risk of an ultimate obligor. They will use contractual structures which allow them to achieve this aim, choosing an appropriate primary contract and adding further structural elements typically based on *wa'd*.

6.4.1   Disclosures in the Current *Sukuk* Market

Where *sukuk* are structured so as to be economically similar to conventional bonds, the normal response of the regulator, subject to points made below, will be to require substantively similar disclosures, both initial and continuing. The disclosures will, however, need to reflect the fact that the actual issuer of the *sukuk* will normally be an SPC, while *sukuk* holders will actually depend for their return on an ultimate obligor, normally the originator of the transaction. Most of the business and financial disclosures will therefore need to be those of that obligor and its group, rather than of the issuer itself.

At initial offer stage, the key features that will distinguish *sukuk* disclosures will concern the nature of the securities on offer, and the rights attached to them. A regulator is likely to take the view that this requires full disclosure of the *sukuk* structure, including at least the substantive provisions of each of the relevant contracts. It is likely that regulators will give more attention to these disclosures in the future, following several high profile defaults or renegotiations of *sukuk*. Some aspects of these failures or near failures will be discussed below.

Where the market regulator accepts some responsibility for *shari'ah* issues, it will generally require some form of disclosure about the basis on which the claim of *shari'ah* compliance is made. Typically this will involve disclosing the details of the *shari'ah* board or other body that has issued a *fatwa* (an opinion expressed after serious discussion on points of law usually by learned person(s)). This will be necessary even where there is an over-arching *shari'ah* council, at least where there is an international market, because those investors to whom compliance is important will continue to want to evaluate the quality of the *shari'ah* approval. Often the *fatwa* itself will be included in the public documentation, though usually only in summary form.

There has been discussion about whether *sukuk* issuers should be obliged to go further, and publish the reasoning leading to the *fatwa* for each issue. The arguments for this are of two kinds. The more straightforward would see it as a means by which the *shari'ah* board of a potential investor can satisfy itself on the relevant *shari'ah* issues, thus reducing the risk that they will find unacceptable a novel structure which nevertheless has good *shari'ah* foundations. If this were the case, however, one might expect some issuers to be making such disclosures voluntarily, because it would help their marketing. Furthermore, substantial institutional investors would in practice be able to require this information, either publicly or privately.

The second, often unspoken, argument for disclosure is that it will force scholars to reason carefully before approving a structure, and will expose to external criticism some of the allegedly weaker structures in the market. In principle, such an approach should be possible. It would have some impact on costs, but this would be limited in relation to the other costs involved in structuring and marketing a *sukuk* issue. It would add to the length of the prospectus, and would be irrelevant to some readers, but again the impact of this should be limited. However, regulators will be a little reluctant to force disclosures that do not appear to be wanted by investors.

Turning from initial disclosures to the subsequent disclosures to the market, whether regular (like annual reports) or event-driven (like a major change in management), in the conventional bond market, these would naturally relate to the bond issuer. In a typical *sukuk* structure, it will be an SPC that acts as the issuer, but it is on the creditworthiness of an ultimate obligor, normally the originator, on which the investors depend for both principal and the offered return on it. In these circumstances, it is the obligor that should make continuous disclosures to the market. This is relatively straightforward. Note, however, that where there is a guarantee from another party, for example another group company, it may be appropriate to seek disclosures in relation to that company too. (An example of such a guarantee would be that given by Dubai World in respect of one of the *sukuk* issues made by its Nakheel subsidiary in Dubai.)

Having analysed most current *sukuk* as economically equivalent to conventional bonds, I need to qualify this somewhat. The underlying assets are not wholly irrelevant because, as I have suggested, the *sukuk* holders may have at least the option of exercising a claim over them as an alternative to making a claim against an obligor. The problems or potential problems of several *sukuk* issues, including East Cameron, The Investment Dar, SAAD Group and Nakheel have focused attention on the role of the underlying assets. The questions over underlying assets considered as security are fundamentally of three kinds: can the investors take effective control over them; would they want to; and do they understand the position?

Recent commentary has focused on the first of these, including the difficulty of securing and registering good title to assets in jurisdictions where foreign ownership may be restricted, or where the court system may be inadequate or inexperienced in these issues.[5]

The first of the three related Nakheel *sukuk* issues, made in 2006 and subsequently redeemed with full payment to the investors, illustrates some of the issues that might arise. The Offering Circular for this *sukuk* states that: 'The *Sukuk* Assets shall comprise of the leasehold rights for a term of 50 years over certain land, buildings and other property at Dubai Waterfront (the Property) (as more particularly described in *Sukuk Assets*).' The description referred to, and the associated valuation report, make clear that at least part of the land in question consists of manmade islands yet to be constructed. One Nakheel-related company, Nakheel Holdings-1, granted the issuing SPC a 50-year lease on these assets, and the SPC then leased them to another Nakheel-related company, Nakheel Holdings-2. It is clear that, had Nakheel Holdings-2 failed to meet its obligations under the lease, the ability of the SPC to take possession of the assets and lease them to another user would have been severely limited by the legal uncertainty of leasehold title to land which does not yet exist. This point did not, however, form part of the risk disclosures (and in practice has not been tested in court).

It is likely that regulators will in the future pay more attention to disclosures about the assets, the quality of any title to them, and the associated risks. However, the importance of this should not be overstated. Even if investors can take effective title to the assets, those assets may have limited use outside the business of the obligor which, in a default situation, is hardly likely to be enjoying great success. Even where the assets have an alternative use, as may be the case for land and buildings, it is unlikely that the investors will be in a good position to realize value from this, where the original obligor could not. The Nakheel case is, again, a good illustration. The assets formed (or were to form) part of a very large development by Nakheel, and it is hard to imagine circumstances in which another user could derive much better economic value from them than a Nakheel group company.

Thus where the structure of an issue allows investors the opportunity to trigger a purchase obligation, even if this leads to their becoming unsecured creditors of the obligor, this may well be economically better for them than trying to take possession of the assets. If a purchase obligation is triggered, and the obligor lacks the liquidity to satisfy the obligation immediately, the investors may have the ability to bring insolvency proceedings against it. This could well be a very potent legal threat. This is the reason, I believe, for a number of *sukuk* which were considered in danger of default being either redeemed in full or restructured.

There are exceptions. In the case of the East Cameron *sukuk*, whose assets were a stream of royalty payments from oil and gas wells, the *sukuk* holders asserted a right to this stream of royalties, ahead of any other creditors of the failed company. The judge hearing the case has so far appeared to back their claim.

The reasonable conclusion for a regulator, therefore, is that the assets, and the ability legally to assert a claim to them, are significant but probably not the dominant issue for investors; given the way current *sukuk* are structured, it is reasonable to suppose that investors acting rationally would be primarily interested in the counterparty risk of the obligor. Furthermore, in a mainly institutional market with substantial minimum investments it is reasonable to assume that most investors will have made this analysis for themselves and, given adequate disclosure, will be able to assess how much weight to put on the supporting assets.

6.4.2 *Sukuk* Structures: do Regulators have a Role?

The question is sometimes raised whether regulators should intervene in the market to force, or to discourage, the use of particular structures. Where the arguments for involvement are based on *shari'ah* permissibility, this is equivalent to the question already discussed about the regulator's role in *shari'ah* matters. But arguments are sometimes advanced based on either investor protection or the development of the market through standardization.

So far as investor protection is concerned, it is difficult to argue that there are any structures so inherently flawed that, in an institutional market, the interests of investors cannot be protected by disclosure. An institutional investor contributing in excess of $100 000 can be expected to devote time and legal resource to understanding the structure and, in any realistic situation, the success of the issue will almost certainly depend on there being some investors contributing large multiples of this sum. Their diligence on the structure will to some extent act as a proxy for other investors. In a retail market the arguments would be more complex; they are discussed later.

So far as market development is concerned, the arguments depend in part on how the role of the regulator is viewed in more general terms. Some regulators would consider, perhaps based on an explicit mandate given to them by the legislature, that market development is no part of their role and should be left to other agencies or to the market itself. Others would see it as a proper role which, often in the specific circumstances of the jurisdiction, only the regulator can play effectively.

If the regulator has a legitimate role, how might standardization of structures help? It may reduce transaction costs, by allowing originators to work from more or less standard templates. It may increase investor acceptance of *sukuk*, effectively lowering their transaction costs by reducing the effort they need to put into analysing structures and documentation. These gains, however, will be greater in the domestic than the international market, since major international investors will in any event be faced with products from many different markets. On the other hand, forced standardization may stifle innovation in what is currently a dynamic market.

It may well be that the best thing a regulator can do, where it has an appropriate mandate, is to facilitate standardization in areas where there is an emerging consensus, but not to force it, either positively or negatively. Standardization might then be achieved either through informal market practice or through the efforts of trade bodies whose standard documentation becomes widely, but voluntarily, adopted. This view is, however, subject to the remarks made below on retail markets.

6.4.3 A Note on Market Supervision

It is one thing to have regulation, in the sense of an appropriate legal regime and structures; it is another to ensure, through supervision, that the regime is observed and the structures work effectively.

In the current *sukuk* market, the issues of market supervision are relatively straightforward. Even where *sukuk* are listed, most trading takes place OTC so, as already noted, issues of clearing and settlement are minimal, and there is little opportunity for market manipulation. The practical issues that arise are mainly concerned with ensuring adequate continuing disclosure. This is to some extent a similar position to that pertaining in the conventional bond market. Because bonds are rather less sensitive than equities to commercial developments in the issuer entity, they are less traded, and their originators are perhaps less aware of the need for continuing disclosures. In addition, businesses may raise money through the bond (or *sukuk*) markets rather than the equity markets precisely because they do not want the dilution of control, and the corporate governance disciplines, that come from an equity issue. But those disciplines will normally include the institution of processes to assess what information needs to be released to the market and when. In a bond or *sukuk* issuer, those processes may well be less developed.

A further factor is that instruments which are listed but not traded usually produce little revenue for the exchange in question. The incentive for the exchange to enforce market disclosure requirements is therefore limited. Yet these so-called compliance listings have value for issuers precisely because they are a signal to the market that certain regulatory standards are being met. It is difficult to see how any listing authority can allow its name and reputation to be used to give such a signal, without taking reasonable steps to ensure that it is well-founded.

All these factors lead towards a position in which the regulator may need to take a more active role in ensuring that proper disclosures are made to the market than for an equity listing.

6.5 POSSIBLE DEVELOPMENTS IN THE *SUKUK* MARKET, AND THEIR IMPLICATIONS

In this section I shall deal with some possible changes in the *sukuk* market, and their regulatory implications. I shall cover: the extension of *sukuk* to the retail market; the possibility of new *sukuk* structures; longer-dated *sukuk*; and pressures for more investments to be traded on exchanges, or at least centrally cleared.

There are other possible developments in the market including, for example, increased governmental issuance of short-dated *sukuk*, and the use of different structures to continue to replicate conventional bonds. Some, however, would have minimal regulatory implications.

6.5.1   The Extension of *Sukuk* to the Retail Market

It has previously been noted that some countries, for example Italy, have established retail[6] bond markets. As regards *sukuk*, there have been some government issues aimed at retail investors, for example the 1 Malaysia 2010 issue in May of that year. That issue was based on Commodity *murabaha* and can only be resold via agent banks at fixed prices. It was also a government issue in the national currency and aimed at its own citizens. These factors taken together mean that it carries minimal risks to investors and (like any similar issues by other governments) raises minimal regulatory questions.

The situation would, however, be very different for a commercial issue (posing real counterparty risks), especially of a traded instrument whose market value might therefore vary. The French securities regulator, the Autorité des Marchés Financiers, called attention to the risks of conventional retail bonds in a press release of 28 May 2010.[7] It drew particular attention to the counterparty risks and to the risk that liquidity might be low or non-existent throughout the life of the bond. Its best practice guide for issuers[8] points out the need to address market risks, liquidity risks and counterparty risks in a clear, precise and non-misleading client document.

If these disclosures are challenging for a conventional bond, they are still more challenging for *sukuk*. In addition to the risks noted, there would surely need to be clear disclosures of the structure, the extent of any asset backing, and the basis on which *shari'ah* compliance is claimed. The assumption, reasonable in an institutional market, that investors can and will analyse a lengthy prospectus, and draw their own conclusions from the material presented, provided that it is complete and accurate, will not hold in a retail one.

It is not clear that there are straightforward answers to these disclosure issues. Where disclosure does not work, the normal regulatory alternatives are either product regulation – restricting by one means or another the *sukuk* that can be sold to retail investors – or suitability – requiring any purchase or sale to be on the basis of advice from a regulated intermediary, who is held responsible for the advice given.

It would be possible for a regulator to limit *sukuk* in the retail market to a limited number of structures. This would be more attractive than requiring the regulator to review prospectuses in detail, partly because of the amount of work involved and the risk that the limitations of any regulatory approval – in particular that it is not a guarantee against loss – may not be apparent. But to avoid abuse the structures would need to be precisely specified, including at least outlines of all the transaction documents involved. There would be frequent commercial pressures to circumvent the effect of the limitations, requiring continued vigilance by the regulator.

The suitability approach is at first sight more attractive, and is one which is relied upon in various areas of financial services. It does, however, require a high level of regulatory effort with supervisors of sufficient quality to be able to assess not only whether proper procedures have been followed, but whether they have led to well-founded and unbiased recommendations. This is easier said than done, and supervisors have been criticized in the past for failure to spot quite systematic mis-selling, despite having the appropriate rules in place and adequate access.

Another implicit assumption in an institutional market is that the investors are sufficiently knowledgeable and resourced to be able to assert their rights through the legal system, provided that this system is adequate in itself. This cannot be assumed in a retail market, though there may be alternatives through class actions or alternative structures such as ombudsman schemes. These alternatives are, however, likely to be quite uncertain in their effect until jurisprudence is better developed, and small investors would be unwise to rely too heavily on them.

In many jurisdictions, therefore, the development of a retail (non-governmental) *sukuk* market is problematic, at least until there is market convergence on a limited number of structures, which can become well-understood by investors, and perhaps the development of practical jurisprudence on areas affecting investors' rights.

6.5.2 The Possibility of New *Sukuk* Structures

Still more interesting regulatory issues will emerge if *sukuk* are launched in the future which have a greater element of asset or business risk. Conceptually, these might well be seen as better aligned with the principles of Islamic finance than many of the *sukuk* currently on the market. There are, however, important market issues here. In conventional markets, investors are used to taking either equity risk or credit risk. Although there are some intermediates in the market, for example some of the subordinated debt instruments issued by financial services firms, the markets for them are relatively small.

Sukuk can of course be structured to have equity-like characteristics, but there is limited incentive to do so since normal equity structures are acceptable within Islamic finance. They therefore need to offer something different. One fairly straightforward option would be to offer limited term equity-like financing. However, where an equity instrument can be traded, its holders already have an effective, and more flexible, right of exit under most circumstances. They also have a right of voice, the ability to vote in various formal business of the company.

This is a valuable right because the market for control – the ability to sell shares to a possible bidder for the company – helps to underpin the value of the equity. It is a little difficult to see how this right of voice might be preserved in full within a limited-term equity structure, but without it the *sukuk* holders would rationally require a greater share of the returns than normal shareholders to compensate. This, however, might be difficult to structure within the provisions of *shari'ah*. All this suggests that, whilst simple limited term equity-like *sukuk* could be structured fairly easily, they might struggle to find a market position which would work for both investors and businesses.

Thus to offer something other than credit risk and remain economically attractive, new forms of *sukuk* will probably need to tap, or develop, a market somewhere between debt and equity, on the scales of both risk and return. It is as yet unclear whether there is a substantial market of this kind potentially available. If such a market does exist, it may well be for specialist applications such as project finance. There may, for example, be attractions in separating the risk and return of a particular project from the overall risk and return of the sponsoring business, and in offering a limited term exposure to that project. These ideas are being explored particularly with an eye to infrastructure finance, where the existence (or creation) of tangible assets and the generally *shari'ah*-compliant nature of their uses makes Islamic finance a natural avenue to explore.

Others have suggested that instruments could emerge taking a different kind of business risk based, for example, on turnover or value added rather than profit.[9] This would take both regulators and investors into completely new territory (though developments in the conventional world suggest that there may be markets, such as film finance, where investors might wish to take a position based on gross revenues). It would almost certainly take some years for the risks to be well understood and for the new instruments to be robust against, for example, manipulation of the accounts. Investors may well require a significant risk premium as the price of investing in untested instruments. In addition, there are likely to be elements of *shari'ah* risk. It is highly unlikely that new instruments will use well-studied contract forms in well-tested combinations.

Scholars are therefore likely to take some time to become comfortable with them, and this will inhibit commercial entities from using them for important transactions. It is therefore likely that any new instruments will be adopted initially on a small scale and in niche situations. (This is not necessarily a counsel of despair. In insurance, the catastrophe bond concept was developed on an essentially theoretical basis, and then some major firms used it in non-critical applications before it became an accepted business form. It is, however, less clear whether similar success will be achieved by the conventional bond that provides its return to investors in the form of chocolates.)[10]

Should *hybrid* or entirely novel *sukuk* emerge, the regulatory disclosures will be challenging. As suggested above, it seems likely that the first such *sukuk* will combine elements of equity and debt-like risk, for example financing a project which will later be acquired by a known obligor. In such a case, one might expect that disclosures would be necessary about both the assets or project in question and that ultimate obligor. At prospectus level this need not be too difficult. There will, however, be issues in continuing disclosure. The easy course would be to specify a full set of disclosures for the project or assets and the obligor. This risks overburdening the markets with information but, more importantly, there is very little regulatory experience of requiring disclosures for a limited set of business assets. I suspect that the disclosures will initially be specified in very broad risk terms, and that only as experience is gained will they be specified more precisely. However, with limited experience in the market of making and enforcing the disclosures, there are bound to be some awkward teething troubles.

If the instruments are wholly new, the position will be somewhat different. It is difficult to discuss new instruments in the abstract, with very little idea of their characteristics. However, in such a case there are bound to be issues concerned with the initial prospectus disclosures. The risk disclosures are an obvious area that will need serious thought. There will also need to be financial disclosures which appropriately cover whatever is the basis of the return to investors, and the various factors that influence it. The decisions made in respect of initial disclosures will need to be carried over into continuing disclosures.

It should also be noted that new structures, and new bases for return, may create new opportunities for manipulation, or insider dealing, in any actively traded market. There is no reason to believe that these opportunities will be greater than in the conventional market – merely different. But market supervisors will need to be aware that different groups of people may have the opportunity for insider trading, and different information may be capable of moving the market.

6.5.3 Longer-dated *sukuk*

At present, *sukuk* are concentrated in medium tenors, typically five years. There are some shorter-dated issues, dominantly by governments, but few longer-dated ones, at least in the international markets. In 2010, the

International Islamic Financial Market (IIFM) analysed the *sukuk* issued in the international market between September 2001 and June 2009.[11] Of the 77 issues, it was able to identify fully that 60 had a maturity of five years. Eight were shorter, and only two had a maturity over ten years.[12] IIFM noted the contrast with the conventional market, where there is a full spectrum of maturities from three months to over 30 years.

More short-dated issues would be valuable in fostering the development of the Islamic finance industry, particularly in respect of its liquidity management, but these raise few questions from the standpoint of a financial markets regulator. The issues of prudential regulation will be covered below.

Longer-dated *sukuk* raise more interesting questions. There is a demand for longer-dated issues, particularly as longer-term investment products, such as some family *takaful* (insurance) offerings, develop. In the conventional world governments, including both the UK and the US, commonly issue bonds with tenors out to 30 years. In the corporate world, 7 to 10-year tenors are relatively common, and the US has its municipal bond market, in which tenors may go out as far as 50 years. What are the prospects for such offerings to be made more frequently in the *sukuk* market?

One issue is structural. For most issuers, a long-term *sukuk* would imply finding assets with an appropriate lifetime. While governments will commonly own infrastructure assets (roads, airports, and so on) with appropriate lifetimes, this will not always be the case for commercial entities, even some quasi-governmental ones. Furthermore, a long-term repurchase undertaking based on current value will transfer asset risk to the *sukuk* holders in a way that may not be acceptable in the market. Nevertheless, there should be some scope for the origination of tradable *sukuk* structured under *ijara* or *istisna* and based on long-term assets. Even if these would not cover the full range of tenors offered in the conventional market, there seems to be no inherent reason why 10 to 20-year *sukuk* would not be possible. It may be, however, that buyers will need to become more comfortable with *sukuk* as a concept before they will be willing to invest at these tenors.

In general, longer-term *sukuk* pose few novel regulatory issues. There is one, however, that is difficult and does merit discussion: continuing *shari'ah* compliance. In principle, there is clearly a risk that an issue which was compliant at the time of issue may become non-compliant later. For example, an impeccably compliant logistics firm may change its business model and move into arms manufacturing, or may take on substantial conventional (interest-bearing) debt. The longer the tenor of a *sukuk* issue, the greater is the risk that this will happen. In principle, some investors will have invested on the basis that the underlying activities, or the use of the assets, are and will remain *halal*. If it became known that this requirement had been breached, the effect might be a fall in the market value of the *sukuk* as Muslim investors divested. (Such a fall would, of course, also impact the interests of non-Muslim investors.) It has been suggested that the appropriate way to deal with this risk is to have some kind of *shari'ah* board engaged throughout the lifetime of the *sukuk* to monitor continuing compliance. This is an expensive solution to what may prove a limited risk. It would be likely to significantly inhibit the use of the *sukuk* market by firms which did not need an SSB for other purposes.

In such a situation, it may be that an action in tort by the *sukuk* holders offers the right remedy without imposing additional costs on all issuers. Such actions will, however, be easier in a common law than a civil law jurisdiction, and civil law jurisdictions may need to introduce specific provisions to permit them. It is unlikely that a business development sufficient in scale to affect compliance would go unnoticed and, indeed, a major development might need to be reported under continuous disclosure provisions. So *sukuk* holders would be aware that their interests had been impacted. The one disadvantage of this approach is that it might, in a marginal case, lead to a secular court needing to rule on an issue of what is, or is not, compliant. However, the SSB approach would also be likely eventually to lead to the courts, since it is unlikely that in a non-Islamic firm an SSB would have enough influence to prevent non-compliant business developments; the most they could do would be to blow the whistle for investors.

6.5.4 Exchange Trading and Central Clearing

There are currently strong pressures to bring onto market, or at least into central clearing, contracts which have previously been traded OTC. This derives from some of the failings observed during the global financial crisis, and is being pursued energetically by the G20 through the Financial Stability Board and the international standards setters. The focus is primarily on derivatives, including asset-backed securities. There is, however, some risk that *sukuk* will be caught up in this by inadvertence (because they fit a definition of asset-backed securities) and a somewhat greater one that the general pressures towards exchange trading and/or central clearing will eventually extend to the *sukuk* market.

Central clearing should not in itself raise any new issues. It is intended primarily to reduce the risks associated with the default of a major market counterparty. Trading on exchange or – next best – central reporting of trades has a different purpose: improved price discovery. Should this become general in the *sukuk* market, regulators will be bound to devote more attention to ensuring that reported prices are fair. This will mean both increased scrutiny against market manipulation and increased attention to market disclosure. The issues in this area have already been discussed; the material change would be in the weight placed on them by regulators.

6.6   PRUDENTIAL ISSUES

Where *sukuk* are held by financial institutions, whether conventional or Islamic, the regulator may need to specify how they should be treated in the capital adequacy calculations of those institutions. At the time of writing, the revisions to the Basel Accord in the light of the global financial crisis have not yet been completed. However, there is no reason to doubt that the basic structure of Basel II will survive, that is that there will remain a separation between trading and non-trading books, and that in both regimes there will be a basic approach with asset risk weightings assigned by regulators, and more advanced approaches in which internal models may be used subject to regulatory approval. There will also be patterns for supervisory intervention, and enhanced market disclosures.

The Basel model may, in some jurisdictions, be applied to some non-bank financial services firms. For insurance, the International Association of Insurance Supervisors is moving towards standards within a broadly similar structure, and this is paralleled in the European Solvency II regime, which may be taken up by non-European countries as the basis of their standards. The remainder of this section therefore assumes a risk-based capital regime broadly along Basel II or Solvency II lines. Within such a regime, how should *sukuk* be treated?

Fortunately, the standards produced by the Islamic Financial Services Board (IFSB) take us a long way towards answering this question. There are two relevant standards.[13] The earlier standard deals with market risk, where *sukuk* are held for trading, on a similar basis to conventional bonds and based on the credit rating and the residual term to maturity. As regards credit risk, the standard analyses this on the basis of the underlying contracts and any variations in the exposures over time (for example where an asset is being constructed under *istisna*). However, it implicitly assumes that the *sukuk* are fully asset-backed structures involving full transfer of legal ownership of the underlying assets.

The second standard covers those cases where *sukuk* are asset-based (that is where the ownership rights over the underlying asset may not reliably result in an effective right of possession in the case of default, and where recourse to the originator therefore provides the primary protection for investors). It also deals with 'pass-through' structures. Although the standards are aimed primarily at banks, the principles are transferable to other financial services regimes, including Solvency II-like regimes for insurance.

If new types of *sukuk* emerge, especially hybrid types, it cannot necessarily be assumed that any of the treatments defined in these standards will be applicable. The principles and form of the analysis should be transferable fairly readily to new *sukuk* types, but will require a material intellectual input from regulators. One of the lessons of recent years has been that financial institutions have strong incentives to engage in regulatory arbitrage, especially when it comes to capital adequacy. There will therefore need to be capital charges which properly reflect the risks involved, in an area where the analysis may not be trivial.

There are also capital adequacy issues where *sukuk* are issued by financial institutions, particularly with regard to whether the assets can be derecognized from the institution's balance sheet. These situations are relatively rare in practice, and are dealt with in the second IFSB standard. This also covers retained securitization exposures, including those arising from the provision of credit risk mitigants to a securitization transaction, and extension of a liquidity facility or credit enhancement. Again the principles are transferable to other contexts, but their application will require careful thought.

NOTES

1. There are a few exceptions issued by governments and aimed at their own citizens. However, these are generally structured so as to pose minimal investor protection risks.
2. See, for example, paragraph 2.3 of 'Analysis of The Application of IOSCO's Objectives and Principles of Securities Regulation for Islamic Securities Products', International Organization of Securities Commissions, September 2008.
3. 'Islamic finance in the UK: regulation and challenges', Financial Services Authority, 2007.
4. See, for example, '*shari'ah* Standard 13', Accounting and Auditing Organisation for Islamic Financial Institutions, May 2002.
5. See, for example, 'Sukuk it up', *The Economist*, 15 April 2010, available at: http://www.economist.com/businessfinance/displaystory.cfm?story_id=15908503.
6. The term 'retail' is here used somewhat loosely to include those investors, whether individual or corporate, who do not have both great investable assets and sophisticated knowledge of markets. It is not intended to reflect a specific dividing line in any jurisdiction's regime, but would certainly cover those often referred to as 'mass affluent'. References to a retail market are to direct investment by such people; indirect investment, for example through collective investment funds, would in general rank as institutional.
7. http://www.amf-france.org/documents/general/9445_1.pdf.
8. 'Guide de bonnes pratiques pour la commercialisation des emprunts obligataires auprès des clients non professionnels', Autorité des Marchés Financiers, October 2009, available at: http://www.amf-france.org/documents/general/9120_1.pdf.

9.   See, for example, *Takaful Islamic Insurance: Concepts and Regulatory Issues*, S. Archer, R.A.A. Karim and Nienhaus (2009), Singapore: Wiley Finance. Although the context is Islamic banking, the analysis could equally well be applied to *sukuk*.
10. *Financial Times*, 25 May 2010, available at: http://www.ft.com/cms/s/0/2a40a130-6802-11df-af6c-00144feab49a.html.
11. *International Islamic Financial Market, Sukuk Report*, February 2010, Central Bank of Malaysia. There are some inconsistencies in the data, but they do not materially affect the line of argument.
12. These were the issues by Tamweel, (US$220 million with 30-year tenor) and Munshaat Real Estate (US$390 million with roughly a 20-year tenor).
13. Capital Adequacy Standard for Institutions (other than Insurance Institutions) offering only Islamic Financial services, Islamic Financial Services Board, December 2005, Kuala Lumpur, Malaysia.

7. Regulation and supervision of *sukuk* industry in Bahrain

Sat Paul Parashar

7.1 INTRODUCTION

This chapter provides an overview of the regulatory and supervisory environment as in the Kingdom of Bahrain in 2010 for the regulation and supervision of the *sukuk* industry. The most distinguishing characteristic of the regulation and supervision in Bahrain is that, except for additional requirements of *shari'ah* compliance, the regulation and supervision is the same as is applicable to conventional finance institutions, and on a par with international standards for debt securities.

The financial services industry tends to be regulated all over the world. The reason for this is not hard to find. The financial sector serves as the most potent engine of economic and social development by letting the financial institutions undertake a money-multiplier function, transforming short-dated savings into long-term investments for economic activities that take a long time to create productive capacity for a given economy. It thus serves to transform maturities of short-term savings into long-term maturities of investments.

The financial sector is permitted the highest leverage compared to any other industry. It may have a deposit to equity ratio of 20:1, meaning 5 per cent equity with 95 per cent total assets. Its total assets to equity ratio may be 15:1, meaning that the money multiplier is 6.67 times. Under Basel-II, the risk-weighted assets may be 12.5 times that of risk-capital: the minimum 8 per cent risk-capital requirement of Tier-1 equity and Tier-2 non-equity translates into 12.5 times risk-weighted assets to risk-capital, although under Basel III this will shrink in the long-term future. High leverage of the financial sector signifies a high risk for the depositors if depositors preserve the 'on demand' return of deposits, a common feature of some 100 years of banking history. It is here that the relevance of good quality regulation and supervision comes in to rein in excessive risk-taking. Islamic finance has been a relatively new field compared to conventional finance. Bahrain has focused on the development of the Islamic finance industry as a priority area. It has actively led the development of Islamic finance products including *sukuk* (often mistakenly translated as Islamic bonds).

In Islamic finance, interest (*riba*) is prohibited in contemporary times. So how does the *sukuk* industry function? How is it regulated and supervised to ensure *shari'ah* compliance and at the same time foster its development? These questions have elicited much interest all over the globe and that is the prime focus of this chapter.

The remaining part of this chapter is organized under six sections. Section 7.2 presents the Bahrain *sukuk* industry in the broader context of the Bahrain economy and the financial sector. Section 7.3 highlights the priority Bahrain has attached to the development of Islamic finance and within that the *sukuk* industry. Section 7.4 discusses the structure and processes of regulation and supervision of the *sukuk* industry and the role of the Central Bank of Bahrain (CBB) as the single regulator of the Bahrain financial sector including the *sukuk* industry. The *sukuk* industry in Bahrain is also mandated to follow the Accounting and Auditing Organisation for Islamic Financial Institutions (AAOIFI) standards, including those on *sukuk*. Section 7.5 highlights the AAOIFI standards in respect of *sukuk* issues. Section 7.6 discusses issues of interest concerning regulation and supervision in Bahrain. The conclusion is given in section 7.7.

7.2   BAHRAIN FINANCIAL SECTOR AND *SUKUK* INDUSTRY

Bahrain is a relatively small economy. Its GDP size will rank it among the smallest economies: the 2009 national income was BD7.7 billion (US$20 billion). Bahrain has a well-developed and diversified financial sector, licensing a wide range of conventional and Islamic financial institutions and organizing such markets, including retail and wholesale banks, specialized banks, insurance companies, finance companies, investment advisors, money changers, insurance brokers, securities brokers and mutual funds. There is also a stock exchange, providing for listing and trading both conventional and Islamic financial instruments: see Table 7.1.

The financial services industry constitutes a leading sector of the Bahrain economy. It constitutes almost 27 per cent of the Bahrain GDP. As of March 2010, Bahrain had 406 financial institutions. Bahrain has always strived to be an international financial hub. Bahrain Vision 2030 continues to focus on the same. Table 7.1 provides a glimpse of the Bahrain financial services sector as of March 2010.

Table 7.1   Financial services sector of Bahrain (March 2010)

	No.	US$ billion
No. of financial institutions	406	
Banks	138	Assets/224.1
i) Retail	32	
ii) Wholesale	78	
iii) Rep office	28	
iv) Islamic included in above	27	Assets/24.7
Investment business	45	
Insurance	169	
Funds	2610	NAV/8.73
Listed companies	49	Mkt Cap/17.27
Listed bonds	13	Issue Size/3.25
Sukuk included in the above	9	Issue Size/2.97

Sources: Central Bank of Bahrain, Bahrain Stock Exchange

It shows that, of the 406 financial institutions in Bahrain as of 2010, 138 were banks and 169 insurance companies. Of the 138 banks, 32 were retail banks, 78 were wholesale banks and 28 were representative offices. The Islamic banks numbered 27. There were 45 investment businesses. There were 2610 funds licensed. The number of listed companies and bonds on the Bahrain Stock Exchange, BSE, were 49 and 13, respectively. It is interesting to note from Table 7.1 that the total assets of Islamic banks in Bahrain were only US$24.7 billion, while the total assets of all banks were US$224.1 billion. Thus, the total assets of Islamic banks constituted only 11 per cent of the total banking assets in Bahrain.

Another interesting observation that may be made from Table 7.1 is that the Bahrain financial sector is dominated by banks. While banks' total assets, as of 2010, were US$224.1 billion, the total market capitalization of companies listed on the BSE was US$17.27 billion; that is 7.7 per cent of the total banking assets. The issue size of total listed bonds including *sukuk* was US$3.25 billion, that is 1.4 per cent of the total banking assets and 18.8 per cent of the market capitalization of the listed companies. The issue size of total *sukuk* listed was US$2.97 billion, that is 91.4 per cent of the issue size of all the bonds including *sukuk* listed. Clearly, the *sukuk* and bond markets of Bahrain are quite small in relation to the banking and financial sector of Bahrain. But it is worth mentioning that *sukuk* constitutes the lion's share of the Bahrain debt market.

It is also worth noting that the share of domestic banking assets to total assets of the banking system has only been around 20 per cent. Bahrain is home to many international financial services groups and is also a leading off-shore regional financial centre.

7.3   ISLAMIC FINANCE, A PRIORITY FOCUS AREA

It is, however, important to note that Islamic finance has been a priority focus area in Bahrain. In recent years, Bahrain has rapidly become a global leader in Islamic finance, playing host to the largest concentration of Islamic financial institutions in the Middle East. The banking, insurance and funds industry comprise both conventional and Islamic institutions.

The growth of Islamic banking, in particular, has been remarkable, with total assets in this segment jumping from US$1.9 billion in 2000 to US$24.7 billion by 2010, an increase of over 12 times. The market share of Islamic banks correspondingly increased from 1.8 per cent of total banking assets in 2000 to 11 per cent in 2010. Islamic banks provide a variety of products, including *murabaha*, *ijara*, *mudaraba*, *musharaka*, *al-salam and istisna*, restricted and unrestricted investment accounts, syndications and other structures used in conventional finance, which have been appropriately modified to comply with *shari'ah* principles.

In addition to the numerous Islamic financial institutions active in its financial sector, Bahrain also plays host to a number of organizations central to the development of Islamic finance, such as the Accounting and Auditing Organisation for Islamic Financial Institutions (AAOIFI); Liquidity Management Centre (LMC); the International Islamic Financial Market (IIFM), and the Islamic International Rating Agency (IIRA). The Central Bank of Bahrain has also recently established a special fund to finance research, education and training in Islamic finance (the Waqf Fund).

7.4   CENTRAL BANK OF BAHRAIN, SINGLE REGULATOR

The Central Bank of Bahrain (CBB) is responsible for regulating and supervising the whole of Bahrain's financial sector. Prior to the creation of the CBB in 2006, the Bahrain Monetary Agency (BMA) had acted as the sole regulatory authority for the Bahrain financial sector. The BMA was responsible, since its establishment in 1973, for regulating the Bahrain banking sector, and was subsequently given responsibility in 2002 to also regulate Bahrain's insurance sector and capital markets.

7.4.1 Capital Markets Supervision Directorate, Bahrain's Capital Market Regulator

The Capital Markets Supervision Directorate (CMSD) of the CBB is the supervisor and regulator of Bahrain's capital markets, including the equity and debt markets. The CMSD's main objective is to maintain a transparent, fair and efficient capital market for ensuring investor protection, thereby protecting Bahrain's integrity and reputation as the region's leading financial centre. The functions of the CSMD include:

- regulating and supervising licensed exchanges, clearing houses and central depositories;
- regulating and supervising licensees that are members of licensed exchanges, clearing houses and central depositories, with respect to their activities on those exchanges;
- approving the listing and/or public offerings of securities;
- undertaking market surveillance, investigations and enforcement; and
- undertaking investors education initiatives.

In pursuing its mandate, the CMSD strives to comply with all relevant international standards, in particular those of the International Organization of Securities Commissions (IOSCO). Bahrain has become a signatory to the IOSCO MMOU concerning consultation and cooperation and the exchange of information since 2008.

7.4.2 CBB Rulebook

The CBB has published its regulatory requirements in the form of a Rulebook. The CBB Rulebook is divided into separate volumes, each focusing on a particular category of licensee or industry sector, as follows:

- volume 1: conventional banks;
- volume 2: Islamic banks;
- volume 3: insurance licensees;
- volume 4: investment firm licensees;
- volume 5: specialized licensees;
- volume 6: capital markets.

Volumes 5 and 6 are currently under development. The CBB is currently working on developing volume 6 of the CBB Rulebook which, when completed, will update and consolidate existing regulations relating to capital markets, into a single, comprehensive and structured publication. This project has commenced with new modules having been issued during 2008.

7.4.3   Existing Bahrain Capital Market Regulations

The existing capital market regulations of Bahrain comprise:

- CBB Debt Securities Regulation;
- CBB Disclosure Standards;
- Guidelines on Insiders;
- Ministerial Order-Money Laundering;
- Collective Investment Schemes Regulation;
- Dissemination of Listed Companies' Financial Statements; and
- Board of Directors' Meetings.

The existing capital market regulations are thus fairly developed and comprehensive, and are fashioned along international best practices to be implemented.

7.4.4   Regulation of Stock Exchanges

The BSE has the status of a licensed stock exchange under the CBB and the Financial Institutions Law 2006, and is subject to the regulatory and supervisory oversight of the CBB.

The regulation of the BSE by the CBB focuses on:

- strong governance, financial resources and risk management systems, to reduce systemic risks and prevent defaults and market disruptions;
- an efficient trading, clearing and settlement system that is bench-marked against international best practices; and
- an effective discharge of delegated market surveillance responsibilities by the BSE, to ensure fair, transparent and efficient secondary markets.

A new multi-asset exchange, The Bahrain Financial Exchange (BFX), is expected to start functioning from the last quarter of 2010.

7.4.5   Supervision of Brokerage Firms

The CBB's supervision of brokerage firms consists of on-site inspections and off-site supervision. The purpose of the CBB's supervision and monitoring is to ensure compliance by the brokerage firms with CBB requirements applicable to investment firms, contained in volume 4 of the CBB Rulebook, which provides rules for capital adequacy requirements, risk management requirements, business conduct rules, principles of business, client asset rules, accounting standards, reporting requirements and other prudential requirements.

7.4.6 Regulation of Public Offerings and Initial Listings

The CBB acts as the listing authority. It also reviews prospectuses for initial and public offerings, as well as rights offerings, of securities. The CBB's Disclosure Standards provide for timely, comprehensive and specific disclosure requirements and conditions applicable to public offerings and initial listings; contents of the prospectus; ongoing financial reporting requirements; and continuous disclosure of material events and developments.

7.4.7 Investors' Education and Alerts

CMSD also supports investor education programmes, for instance, through the distribution of brochures, and presentations to schools and universities. It also supports the work of the Compliance Directorate of the CBB, which is mandated to combat financial crime, in identifying any attempts to defraud investors.

7.4.8 CBB Debt Securities (Including *Sukuk*) Guidelines

The existing guidelines for the issuing, offering and listing of debt securities in Bahrain were issued in 2004 and contain ten chapters and two appendices, as follows:

- chapter 1: Preliminary;
- chapter 2: Issuance of debt securities;
- chapter 3: Prospectus requirements;
- chapter 4: Public offering and announcement;
- chapter 5: Allotments, certificates and registrars;
- chapter 6: Protection of debt holders' interests;
- chapter 7: Listing and dealing;
- chapter 8: Ongoing obligations;
- chapter 9: Suspension of dealing and delisting;
- chapter 10: Fees and charges;
- appendix 1: Contents of the prospectus & appendix II: List of information (for approval and post-approval).

It is interesting to note that the CBB debt securities guidelines, as sketched above, set out the basic conditions that have to be met as a prerequisite to the issuance, offering and listing of all debt securities including *sukuk*. They apply to every method of issuance, offering and listing and to both new applicants and existing listed issuers, except where otherwise stated.

7.4.9   Additional Requirements in Respect of Islamic Private Debt Securities

The CBB debt securities guidelines, however, provide additional requirements in respect of Islamic private debt securities that the issuer must appoint either an independent *shari'ah* advisor or committee approved by the BMA or an Islamic Bank or a licensed Institution approved by BMA to advise on all aspects of the Islamic private debt securities.

7.5   AAOIFI STANDARDS FOR *SUKUK*

'In November 2007, Sheikh Mohammad Taqi Usmani sent shockwaves throughout the global ICM when he declared 85 per cent of *sukuk* from GCC are not *halal* [not compliant]' (Thomas, 2009). AAOIFI subsequently issued advice to 'Islamic financial institutions and *shari'ah* supervisory boards to adhere to the following matters when issuing *sukuk*.

First: *sukuk*, to be tradable, must be owned by *sukuk* holders, with all rights and obligations of ownership, in real assets, whether tangible, usufructs or services, capable of being owned and sold legally as well as in accordance with the rules of *shari'ah*, in accordance with Articles (2) and (5/1/2) of the AAOIFI *Shari'ah* Standard 17 on Investment *Sukuk*. The manager issuing *sukuk* must certify the transfer of ownership of such assets in its *sukuk* books, and must not keep them as his/her own assets.

Second: *sukuk*, to be tradable, must not represent receivables or debts, except in the case of a trading or financial entity selling all its assets, or a portfolio with a standing financial obligation, in which some debts, incidental to physical assets or usufruct, were included unintentionally, in accordance with the guidelines mentioned in AAOIFI *Shari'ah* Standard (21) on Financial Papers.

Third: it is not permissible for the manager of *sukuk*, whether the manager acts as *mudarib* (investment manager) or *sharik* (partner), or *wakil* (agent) for investment, to undertake to offer loans to *sukuk* holders, when actual earnings fall short of expected earnings. It is permissible, however, to establish a reserve account for the purpose of covering such shortfalls to the extent possible, provided the same is mentioned in the prospectus. It is not objectionable to distribute expected earnings, on account, in accordance with Article (8/8) of the AAOIFI *Shari'ah* Standard (13) on *mudaraba*, or to obtaining project financing on account of the *sukuk* holders.

Fourth: it is not permissible for the *mudarib* (investment manager), *sharik* (partner), or *wakil* (agent) to undertake to re-purchase the assets from *sukuk* holders or from one who holds them, for its nominal value, when the *sukuk* are extinguished, at the end of its maturity. It is, however, permissible to undertake the purchase on the basis of the net value of assets, its market value, fair value or a price to be agreed, at the time of their actual purchase, in accordance with Article (3/1/6/2) of AAOIFI *Shari'ah* Standard (12) on *sharikah* (*musharaka*) and Modern Corporations, and Articles (2/2/1) and (2/2/2) of the AAOIFI *Shari'ah* Standard (5) on Guarantees. It is known that a *sukuk* manager is a guarantor of the capital, at its nominal value, in case of his/her negligent acts or omissions or his/her non-compliance with the investor's conditions, whether the manager is a *mudarib* (investment manager), *sharik* (partner) or *wakil* (agent) for investments.

In case the assets of *sukuk* of *al-musharaka*, *mudaraba* or *wakala* for investment are of lesser value than the leased assets of Lease to Own contracts (*ijara muntahia bittamleek*), then it is permissible for the *sukuk* manager to undertake to purchase those assets – at the time the *sukuk* are extinguished – for the remaining rental value of the remaining assets; since it actually represents its net value.

Fifth: it is permissible for a lessee in a *sukuk al-ijara* to undertake to purchase the leased assets when the *sukuk* are extinguished for its nominal value, provided the lessee is not also a partner, *mudarib*, or investment agent.

Sixth: *Shari'ah* Supervisory Boards should not limit their role to the issuance of *fatwa* (an opinion expressed after careful deliberations by scholar(s)) on the permissibility of the structure of *sukuk*. All relevant contracts and documents related to the actual transaction must be carefully reviewed by the boards, and then they should oversee the actual means of implementation, and then make sure that the operation complies, at every stage, with *shari'ah* guidelines and requirements as specified in the *Shari'ah* Standards. The investment of *sukuk* proceeds and the conversion of the proceeds into assets, using one of the *shari'ah*-compliant methods of investments, must conform to Article (5/1/8/5) of the AAOIFI *Shari'ah* Standard (17).

Furthermore, the *Shari'ah* Board advised Islamic Financial Institutions to decrease their involvements in debt-related operations and to increase true partnerships based on profit and loss sharing in order to achieve the objectives of the *shari'ah*. It is important to note that in at least eight countries, AAOIFI standards are mandatory.

'As a result, issuers, including Islamic banks, are beginning to move from asset-based *sukuk*, to more asset-backed *sukuk*. This has amongst others, contributed to the fall in the value of *sukuk* outstanding while the spreads widened.' (Thomas, 2009)

In July 2010, AAOIFI issued new accounting standards on investments in *sukuk*, shares and similar instruments. Under these new accounting standards Islamic financial institutions are required to segregate their investments between debt-type and equity-type instruments. The segregation depends on characteristics of the investment instruments and purposes of the investments. Accounting treatments and disclosures that Islamic financial institutions have to carry out are to be based on this segregation.

7.6   ISSUES OF INTEREST ON *SUKUK* REGULATION AND SUPERVISION

Does CBB as a single financial sector regulatory agency represent the best practice for regulation of the *sukuk* industry? This may be one of the issues that are of great interest. Are single or multiple regulatory agencies the best practice? This question has been long debated. The recent global financial crisis has added new vigour to this debate. The conflict of interest has been the most common argument against the single regulator. It is argued that while development of banking encourages increasing intermediation, the development of capital markets needs increasing disintermediation. That presents a source of conflict for the single regulator. Separate regulatory agencies for banking and capital markets may therefore avoid such a conflict of interest.

The main argument against multiple regulatory agencies has been that these may lead to creating disconnected 'silos', with loss of an integrated and comprehensive approach to given issues. This is because banking institutions and capital markets tend to be interconnected and interdependent. Further, multiple agencies tend to create additional costs in infrastructure and administration. A single regulator, particularly for a country with a dominant banking sector and a small capital market like Bahrain, may be therefore more suitable. One may use the same argument to assert that countries like Bahrain, having small capital markets, need a separate regulator to give a greater push to capital markets and the *sukuk* industry.

'Does a single set of debt securities guidelines represent the best practice for regulation of the *sukuk* industry?' may be another issue of interest to consider. Again the argument for the single regulator, above, may be valid for having a single set of regulatory guidelines for all debt securities including *sukuk*.

The Governor of the CBB was asked during an interview in July 2010, 'Do you think that there is a case for the development of a specific set of regulations for Islamic financial institutions?' His response provides a very informative perspective in this matter. To quote, he said:

> Islamic banking and other Islamic financial services are generally under the same kind of scrutiny as conventional institutions. We don't have different Islamic banking regulatory standards in terms of corporate governance, Basel II and capital requirements. It happens that the way Islamic banks structure their deals is slightly different from how they are done in the conventional sector. However, in all other areas of banking regulations the Islamic banks have to comply. After all, it is still banking and Islamic institutions are dealing with clients, . . . I think that is why the Islamic banking sector in general, not only in Bahrain, has been able to fit in with so many different regulatory authorities and has been able to become a growing and integral part of international banking services.

7.7 CONCLUSION

Bahrain is a relatively small economy. The financial services sector constitutes a leading sector of the economy, and serves a wide area across the world, such as any international financial centre does. The financial sector of Bahrain has been well-developed and diversified, consisting of a wide range of conventional and Islamic financial institutions and markets, including retail and wholesale banks, specialized banks, insurance companies, finance companies, investment advisors, money changers, insurance brokers, securities brokers and mutual funds.

Banking constitutes the dominant segment within the financial services industry. The banking landscape is dominated by foreign banks. Domestic banking assets constitute about 20 per cent of the total banking assets. Bahrain's capital and debt markets are quite small. As of 2010, total market capitalization of companies listed on the exchange was about 7.7 per cent of the total banking assets. The issue size of listed bonds and *sukuk* is about 1.4 per cent of the total banking assets.

In recent years, Bahrain has rapidly become a global leader, along with Malaysia, in Islamic finance, playing host to the largest concentration of Islamic financial institutions in the Middle East. The banking, insurance and funds industry comprise both conventional and Islamic institutions.

The growth of Islamic banking in particular has been remarkable, with total assets in this segment multiplying twelve-fold in 20 years. The market share of Islamic banks correspondingly increased from 1.8 per cent of total banking assets in 2000 to 11 per cent in 2010. Interestingly, *sukuk* constituted about 91 per cent of the listed debt securities.

Bahrain also plays host to a number of organizations central to the development of Islamic finance, such as the Accounting and Auditing Organization for Islamic Financial Institutions (AAOIFI); Liquidity Management Centre (LMC); the International Islamic Financial Market (IIFM), and the Islamic International Rating Agency (IIRA). The Central Bank of Bahrain has also recently established a special fund to finance research, education and training in Islamic finance (the *Waqf* Fund).

It may be noted that in terms of regulatory and supervisory standards, in general, and *sukuk*, in particular, Bahrain is a clear leader. A distinguishing characteristic of the Bahrain financial regulatory regime is that it treats conventional and Islamic finance institutions on a par. Except for additional *shari'ah* compliance requirements for Islamic finance products and institutions, there is hardly any difference.

REFERENCES

Thomas, Abdulkader (2009), *Interest in Islamic Economics: Understanding Riba*, New York: Routledge.
www.aaoifi.com
www.bahrainstock.com
www.cbb.gov.bh

8. Securitization issues and Islamic financial products with reference to *sukuk*

Michael T. Skully

8.1 INTRODUCTION

Securitization is the creating and sale of new, usually liquid, financial assets backed by the security of other existing, usually illiquid, assets. It is through the shifting of risks and cash flow streams that otherwise illiquid assets owned by a firm become marketable. Conventional modern securitization involves the creation of a portfolio of homogeneous assets with identifiable cash flows. This portfolio is then sold to a credit-enhanced, Special Purpose Company (SPC). The SPC in turn raises the required funds through the sale of its own securities, which represents an interest in these assets. As this structuring is so important to its success, this activity is also known as structured finance.

Islamic securitization is effectively conventional securitization modified to accommodate *shari'ah* principles and results in the creation of a financial asset known as *sukuk*. A *sukuk* is sometimes also referred to in the popular press as an Islamic bond, but this would be a mis-representation. A more appropriate term is a *shari'ah-compliant investment certificate.* The difference, unlike a conventional debt instrument, is that a *sukuk* should be used to fund a specific investment rather than for general use. The income arising from profits (not interest) earned by the *sukuk* holders should also be related to the purpose of this funding, thus connecting the *real assets securitized* with their associated risk and return. A positive return is provided only when the underlying activity is profitable. These assets and their use must also be acceptable *shari'ah* activities. Finally, the *sukuk* represents a real transfer of the proportional ownership in these underlying assets, and the assets themselves and their use must be *shari'ah* compliant (IFSB, 2009, p. 3). Hence, there are significant fundamental differences in the contractual terms of this instrument, which has been offered since 1990.

This chapter first explains the process of securitization. This is followed by a discussion of the types of assets securitized, business risk mitigation and liquidity support utilized, and the need for a *shari'ah* advisor. Consideration is then given to the advantages and disadvantages of this approach. Finally, the chapter considers the future prospects for Islamic securitization.

8.2   TYPES OF ASSETS SECURITIZED

The key difference in Islamic and conventional securitization is that while the latter securitizes future cash flows, the former deals with the ownership of income-earning, tangible assets. The assets themselves as well as their use must also be acceptable under *shari'ah*. This difference means that Islamic securitization structures may be divided into two parts: those where the underlying assets are financial and those based on real assets. The financial asset-based products entail the sale of receivables, such as Islamic debt securitization (represented by the Malaysian IDPS Sukuk), and are sometimes called Islamic bonds (Pahlavi and Gintzburger, 2009, p. 271). Those that involve the sale of real assets typically follow an *ijara* (leasing) style of sale and lease back agreement and are sometimes called Global *sukuk*. In 2008, however, Sheik Taqi Usmani announced that most existing financial asset-based *sukuk* did not comply with Islamic standards. As a result, this chapter concentrates mainly on the *ijara* approach but later suggests some further risk mitigation measures that might also be applicable to a *musharaka* (share-like) structure.

With an *ijara sukuk*, or sale and lease back *sukuk*, the fundraiser typically sells specific real assets to an SPC (Special Purpose Company) for the value of the de facto finance provided and then leases them back. The lease payments to the SPC can then be fixed or adjusted by a specific index. The assets could also be rented to a third party. While the rent may be fixed, the income produced under the securitization must be derived from underlying activities and not simply a de facto interest. It is therefore not the deferred payment rent receivables that should be transferred, but rather the ownership of the underlying asset.

These *ijara* arrangements can be structured simply as rental agreements or as an *ijara-wa-iqtina* (rent to own) where the prior lease payments count as part of the purchase price, or that the asset is repurchased in full over the life of the underlying lease. It involves no initial down payment. Alternatively, there may be a purchase undertaking, which is to repurchase the assets for an amount equal to the principal due.

8.3   RISK MITIGATION AND LIQUIDITY SUPPORT

As with conventional securitization, the *sukuk* structure would normally seek a range of means to reduce investor exposure to business risk of the venture as well as its liquidity position. As mentioned previously, these measures must be *shari'ah* compliant themselves as well as not change the nature of the overall transaction. As Jomadar (2007) explained, 'Islamic securitisation must confer on investors clearly identifiable rights and obligations in securitised assets in order to ensure direct participation in any distribution of risk and reward between lenders and borrowers with limited risk mitigation and (or) indemnification through credit enhancement.'

Perhaps the most straightforward enhancement is where the assets' seller leaves part of the proceeds with a trustee. Then these funds could be used to address potential problems the SPC might experience. The most obvious is liquidity risk. Usually lease payments are expected on a certain date so that the certificate holders can be paid. Where the payment is late or insufficient, the retained funds are therefore available and are then replenished when the expected payment is received. If the lease works properly, the funds will be returned to the seller at the end of the contract. A standby third party letter of credit facility for the SPC will address this problem. Alternatively a withholding approach can be taken with a reserve account or first loss pool whereby again part of the purchase price is retained to offset any initial losses experienced.

Normal securitizations may also use third party credit enhancements to mitigate the investor's credit risk exposure. Similarly, Islamic securitization can do this, but only up to a point. As Kamil (2008, p. 27) explains, '*Sukuk* issuers are allowed to apply third party guarantees on the capital invested under the principles of *musharaka* and *muquradah/mudaraba*'. These guarantees, however, can only cover those losses that are due to the managing partner's negligence. They cannot cover the full business, or really the credit risk, exposure. Collateral can similarly be taken to cover potential possible gross negligence, but again not general business risk. The Accounting and Auditing Organisation for Islamic Financial Institutions (AAOIFI) *shari'ah* Committee's February 2008 rulings on *sukuk* also preclude a full guarantee of the principal which has no regard of the venture's profits or losses, but can guarantee to repurchase at their net asset or fair market value. This can be done by the issuer or, more likely, a third party. Insurance coverage against damage would also be expected via a *takaful* policy.

Another effective mitigation of concern is the status of the effective borrower itself. Where the credit quality is high, the above measures are much less empirical. It is therefore not surprising that government agencies were important in many early Islamic securitizations. Investors then did not need to consider the risk of the underlying assets and associated contracts; they simply looked to the government's status as a sovereign risk.

A further risk reduction tool is the use of multiple classes of securities, known as tranching and subordination. This mechanism is possible where parts of an asset rather than the full ownership are involved in the securitization's sale, lease back and repurchase, making the ownership of the asset divided between two parts or tranches. The SPC holding the senior tranche would have first entitlement to any payments or sales proceeds and so limits its potential loss: this requires careful study as this could make contracts less risky. The other junior or subordinate tranche holder would have to wait until the senior tranche payments were made. It is not uncommon for the de facto borrower or organizer to hold the subordinate tranche, but care must be taken in creating such structures. Otherwise *shari'ah* compliance problems might result.

Most projects will mitigate a range of business risks thorough contractual agreements relating to non-performance. Where a de facto borrower fails to deliver or its subcontractors do not perform, standby arrangements can be instigated. Such was the case in the East Cameron Gas *sukuk* default. While the SPC was shown to have real ownership of the drill site, they might have had difficulty operating it without back-up contracts. While this did not utilize an *ijara* contracting, the latter arrangement may have faced the same problems where a new facility was being leased. Such replacements for non-performance must be clearly specified in the various service contracts.

Turning to liquidity risk, this term requires further discussion, as the underlying *sukuk* structure is critical. With an asset-based transaction (as opposed to asset-backed) like an *ijara sukuk*, there is no problem where the provider is the buyer. With an asset-backed transaction where the *sukuk* SPC holds financial rather than real assets, these instruments must sell only at their par or face value; otherwise they may be viewed as involving de facto interest payments. As it is unlikely that the asset will sell at par when the borrower is in crisis, liquidity will be a problem. This yet again explains the desire for real asset-based transactions. While a mix of 51 per cent real and 49 per cent financial assets – as allowed under current regulations – would allow the instruments to trade at below or above face value, such a hybrid approach would seem very much against the spirit of the *shari'ah* rulings.

8.4   THE NEED FOR A *SHARI'AH* ADVISOR

As mentioned previously, unlike conventional securitization, Islamic securitization requires a *shari'ah* advisor, typically via a *Shari'ah* Supervisory

Board. This board consists of a few *shari'ah* experts, and is responsible for ensuring that the initial contracts and other documents associated with the issue and its related assets are *shari'ah* compliant. As Norman (2005) warns, 'there is much more to establishing a *shari'ah* compliant securitisation transaction than a simple rewording of conventional transaction documentation'.

This is important, as a *shari'ah*-compliant securitization should not be done without fulfilling the requirements of AAOIFI standards 13 and 17. These include special disclosure requirements in respect of the parties involved with making any guarantees and their nature as well as any contractual relationship between the issuer, *sukuk* manager, and the investors. The objective is one of full transparency (no asymmetric information) in respect to the parties' rights and obligations.

The advisor must first verify that the underlying assets to be securitized and their related returns are themselves *shari'ah* compliant. The overall structure and related contracts associated with the process are then scrutinized and approved. All credit enhancements, liquidity support, or prepayment risk mitigation must be carefully constructed. Lastly, the advisor must monitor the subsequent operations during the contract, ensuring that they, as well as the contract's completion, are all conducted appropriately. This involves formal reporting in each instance at the start and finish as well as annually during the operational phase.

8.5   ADVANTAGES OF SECURITIZATION

Securitization has proved very useful in modern finance, at least until the global financial crisis, for conventional banks, and most of these same advantages could seemingly be applied to Islamic banks, too. These include improved earnings and return on equity; enhanced credit, liquidity and other risk management; diversify balance sheet funding sources and so less need for deposit raising; and potentially lower cost of funding.

The improved earnings and return on capital is a function of many factors. As discussed below, if securitization takes assets off a bank's balance sheet, then there is less need for regulatory capital to support it. If the bank earns the same revenue as before but with less capital, then its return on equity increases, as does its return on assets. Similarly, where the securitized assets process results in fee income, these fees may also increase the bank's earnings. Lower risk exposure may similarly improve its earnings quality as well.

Improved risk management is a function of many factors. At the basic level, to the extent that the underlying assets that are securitized are largely illiquid, then their securitization reduces illiquidity risk on the bank's balance sheet. Their conversion to cash similarly increases bank liquidity and improves the bank's liquidity and leverage ratios. Their sale also removes any business risk that such assets might have entailed, particularly in respect to any over-exposure to a specific industry, geographic location, business or asset type. It may also help to reduce any maturity mis-matches between assets and liabilities.

Improved fundraising is a main attraction of securitization for developed country commercial banks as their increased access to the capital markets via this process reduces their deposit raising. While this could be an advantage, many developing country banks actually have a surplus rather than a shortage of deposit funding. To the extent that Islamic banks are in a similar position, they would be much less attracted to securitization. As Zaidi (2007) explains, 'securitization has not been used by Islamic banks because of a lack of demand' caused by their under-leveraged balance sheets.

The lower cost of Islamic funding is a function of its simpler asset structure and therefore added value for potential investors. Transactions normally involve just one asset class, typically with an extensive previous performance history on which the potential risk exposure can be assessed. So where an investor would have had to access to the bank's entire business risk when investing in a more general participation certificate, an asset-specific *sukuk* removes this task. The *sukuk*'s bankruptcy remote status means that only its underlying assets and support arrangements need consideration. So investors might similarly be attracted to the *sukuk* as it may allow them to diversify directly into specific asset classes, geographic locations or risk classes without having to pay a third party for such services.

8.6   DISADVANTAGES OF SECURITIZATION

While Islamic securitization has its advantages, it is not without its disadvantages. These include problems with credit rating agencies, liquidity, taxation, regulatory risk, human resource constraints, default procedures, and non-Muslim jurisdictions.

Credit rating agencies are still rather recent additions to Islamic finance. As a result, even the so-called Muslim agencies seem overly influenced by approaches of conventional rating agencies. This is because the latter's models seemed unable to incorporate the unique features of Islamic financial products into their calculations. So where one might expect that the real ownership transfer of the underlying assets might result in a lower credit risk than simply holding them as collateral, this does not seem as yet well appreciated, even by Islamic-focused rating agents.

A main attraction of conventional securitization is its creation of a highly liquid asset class. Unfortunately, the *sukuk's* actual liquidity must be questioned. Most purchasers take a buy and hold to maturity approach to investment, resulting in very limited secondary trading. According to Standard & Poor's (2010, p.4), 'the *sukuk* market's small size and limited liquidity is a challenge to its future growth. Islamic institutional investors are still mainly in their development phase and their poor understanding compared to conventional institutional investors also limits them as a potential purchasers'. Also, the lack of an international standard in respect to *shari'ah* compliance tends to fragment any attempts at a global market and similarly inhibits cross-border competition and therefore greater secondary market development.

Taxation may also be a significant risk depending on the actual jurisdiction of the underlying assets, the SPC, and end investor. In terms of the underlying assets, for example, the transfer of real assets may have ramifications across different jurisdictions, particularly in non-Muslim countries. Stamp duty may result unless specifically exempted, like in the UK, and greatly increase the costs entailed. Similarly, goods and services or value added taxes as well as capital gains taxes might also be applied. There are many problems in using *sukuk* in other jurisdictions. As Jung (2010) notes in respect to Korea,

> under current law, a *sukuk* bond would be subject to a variety of taxes, including value-added tax and an acquisition tax, on what is considered a transaction dealing with tangible assets. These additional taxes would raise the financial costs of *sukuk* bonds by 1.5 to 3.4 per cent percentage points above that of conventional bonds, making them unattractive to investors.

Regulator risk applies to Islamic securitization just as any other financial transaction. The arrangements are made to reflect the current policies, but these policies may change. Unless exempted (by grandfathering) the value of existing instruments may be greatly reduced. Furthermore, it is not just a function of banking, tax and all the other potential regulatory changes of conventional finance but also the risk that Islamic perceptions of specific transactions might also change. As Standard & Poor's (2010) noted, 'differing interpretations of Sharia law appear to have resulted in the fragmentation and lack of integration of the market for Islamic financial products'. The AAOIFI's *shari'ah* disapproval on most Malaysian debt-related *sukuk* issues is a strong reminder of the potential impact of regulatory change. Similarly, the Islamic application of conventional regulatory change, like the Basel III, may cause even more problems for both originators and investors.

Human resource limitations are yet another problem facing Islamic finance. Much of the regulatory risk reflects poor knowledge levels concerning Islamic finance. While Islamic finance has been active for some decades, the knowledge levels among finance professionals, institutional investors, potential fund raisers, and even academics could still be improved. Many jurisdictions claim that such staffing shortages remain a major obstacle in the industry's future development.

Default is something that no investor would wish to experience, but there is more uncertainty about a *sukuk* holder's position should the underlying issuer default on the transaction. The legal position might be well covered in a multitude of documentation, but the contracts' actual meaning cannot be certain until they have been proven in the courts. The irony is that as *sukuk* defaults have been few, there is only limited case law from which to offer a realistic opinion on the actual outcome. More failures, while hardly desirable, will help address this current lack of clarity. The use of English rather than local law as the localization of these matters may continue such problems locally in the future. Where, as often is the case, the jurisdiction for any disputes is different from that of where the underlying assets are located, there are many difficulties in obtaining the local enforcement of the foreign court's judgment.

While there might appear considerable merit in adopting a cross-country approach to Islamic securitization and in establishing a common set of documentation and contract requirements, the underlying nature of these transactions makes this difficult. Perhaps the key problem is related to the transfer of property. With an *ijara* structure, for example, one simply sells the soon-to-be-leased assets to the SPC and then arranges for their resale when the *sukuk* structure is to be redeemed. The problem is that there are considerable differences, not just between countries, but also often between different states within the same country. The most obvious is the ability to transfer title to the underlying assets.

Where these assets involve property, as is often the case, legislation may work against the transfer. Many countries, for example, have restrictions on the sale of land to foreigners. This might entail a total prohibition or prior government approval. The latter makes the transaction possible but may still result in potential problems if these assets are later sold to a third party. Depending on how foreign ownership is construed, it could even limit the potential ownership of the *sukuk* itself to local nationals. Even if the law allows foreign ownership, the position in practice might be quite different. Delays in transfers for any reason will potentially impact the end value received. Such a problem could be minimized by not legally transferring the title to the SPC but rather the SPC appointing the issuer to hold it as its agent. The ownership risk of course remains transferred all the same.

Non-Muslim jurisdiction presents even more problems. The UK and Singapore, for example, have moved to address many of the taxation and legal issues, but there is still much work to be done elsewhere, and this is hampered by human resource limitations. As the UK's Islamic Finance Council has warned, 'a shortage of skilled Islamic scholars and banking officials versed in *Shari'ah* compliant finance is hampering the industry's ability to develop global standards' (el Baltaji, 2010).

8.7   FUTURE PROSPECTS

As with many Islamic products, Islamic securitization itself is perhaps not completely new, as Ali (2008) notes, 'elements and features of securitisation were well documented in many classical and medieval *fiqh* [juristic] manuals and books'. Its modern development, however, is still relatively recent. The earliest potential example, again accordingly to Ali (2008), is that of the RM125 million Shell MDS Islamic Private Debt Securities issue of 1990. Others might suggest Caravan-I, a Saudi Arabia automotive backed *sukuk*, in 2004 as the first asset-backed issue. Regardless of the earliest instrument, most writers would agree that *sukuk* is still in its relatively early stages of development. It is attracting considerable attention not just within Muslim capital markets but also in Western ones. Its potential as a vehicle for infrastructure finance is particularly attractive and should receive considerable attention accordingly.

The key to its future growth is one of resolving the current cross-country differences in respect to regulatory and legal treatment. One cannot help but support the Islamic Finance and Global Financial Stability Report, which calls for the 'harmonisation of prudential standards and the development of innovative, diversified and universally-acceptable Islamic financial instruments across jurisdictions' (IFSB-IDB-IRTS, 2010). This was viewed as essential given the 'varying interpretations of *shari'ah* in key issues in different countries of markets' and the added complexity this entails with cross-border transactions.

NOTE

1. The author acknowledges the kind assistance of Saad Azmat and Nicky Duncan as well as comments from the delegates to the International Symposium on *Sukuk* Securities in Dubai on an earlier draft of this chapter.

BIBLIOGRAPHY

Ahmad, Abdel-Rahman (n.d.), 'Islamic modes of finance and the role of sukuk', *QFinance*.

Al-Salem, Fouad (2009), 'Islamic financial product innovation', *International Journal of Islamic and Middle Eastern Finance and Management*, **2**(3), 187–200.

Alayyed, Nidal (2010), 'Islamic securitization needs more thought', accessed 7 April at Ezine@articles http://ezinearticles.com.

Ali, E.R.A.E. (2008), 'Issues in Islamic debt securitisation', in M.D. Bakar and E.R.A.E. Ali (eds), *Essential Readings in Islamic Finance*, Kuala Lumpur: Centre for Research and Training, pp. 443–93.

Badri, Andri Aidham (2008), 'Overview of legal considerations in documentation of sukuk', in *Malaysian Sukuk Market Handbook: Your Guide to the Malaysian Islamic Capital Market*, Kuala Lumpur: RAM Rating Services, pp. 79–91.

el Baltaji, Dana (2010), 'Islamic finance faces hurdle, lacks expertise, UK body says', *Bloomberg Business Week*, 27 April.

Hales, Alice (2005), 'Asset backed securities: tapping surplus liquidity', *Islamic Finance*, Autumn, pp. 4–6.

Howladar, Khalid (2007), *ABANA Review*, 27 August.

IFSB-IDB-IRTS (2010), *Islamic Finance and Global Financial Stability Report 2010*, Kuala Lumpur: Islamic Financial Services Board, April.

Islamic Financial Services Board (IFSB) (2009), 'Capital adequacy requirements for sukuk, securisations and real estate investment', January.

Jobst, Andreas A. (2007), 'The economics of Islamic finance and securitization', International Monetary Fund working paper WP/07/117.

Jomadar, Bushan K. (2007), 'Islamic finance and securitisation: Manmade tale or reality', University of Westminister, School of Law Islamic Law and Law of the Muslim World paper no. 8–18, London.

Jung, Ha-won (2010), 'Islamic bonds stuck in limbo', *JoongAng Daily*, 20 April.

Kamil, Wan Abudul Rahim (2008), 'Introduction to Sukuk', in *Malaysian Sukuk Market Handbook: Your Guide to the Malaysian Islamic Capital Market*, Kuala Lumpur: RAM Rating Services, pp. 21–52.

Mirakhor, Abbas (2009), 'The recent crisis: lessons for Islamic finance', IFSB 2nd Public Lecture on Financial Policy and Stability, Kuala Lumpur, Malaysia.

Norman, Trevor (2005), 'Securitisation structures within an Islamic framework', *ISR*, July, 2–5.

Ossa, Felipe (2009), 'Asset backed sukuk: some drama but not action', *Asset Securitisation Report*, 2 October.

Pahlavi, Razi and Anne-Sophie Gintzburger (2009), 'Equity-based, asset-based and asset-backed transactional structures in Shari'a compliant financing: reflections on the current financial crisis', *Economic Papers*, **28**(3), 270–78.

Parker, Mushtak (2006), 'Prospects for Islamic securitisation bright', *Arab News*, 3 July.

Standard & Poor's (2007), 'New issue: East Cameron Gas Co.', *Standard & Poor's Ratings Direct.*

Tariq, Ali Arsalan (2004), 'Managing financial risk of sukuk structures', Master of Science degree thesis, Loughborough University, UK.

Van de Graaff, Sonya and Brian Gallogly (2008), 'Opportunities in the Islamic finance market', *International Securitization & Finance Report*, **11**(22), 2:20–23.

Westlaw Business (2009), 'Islamic finance terms: sukuk ijara, a securitization by any other name', *Thomson Reuters*, 9 July.

Zaidi, Jamal Abbas (2007), 'Overcoming barriers to liquidity: commoditization, sukuk, promoting issuance and a secondary market', paper presented to the Islamic Finance and Investment World Europe, 25–28 June.

APPENDIX A: EAST CAMERON GAS *SUKUK*

East Cameron Partners used a securitization structure, the East Cameron Gas *Sukuk* in 2006, to help the Texas-based company finance the development of a gas field in Louisiana. The gas exploration and production company effectively sold 89.68 per cent of its royalty rights to the proceeds of the production from two of its offshore natural gas leases in the Gulf of Mexico for a specified period, to an SPC formed for this purpose. This purchaser SPC, based in Delaware, was in turn fully owned by an issuer SPC in the Cayman Islands (due to withholding tax and regulatory reasons) which actually raised the USD165.67 million in investment trust certificate *sukuk*. The funding *sukuk* were to be repaid from the gas sales. The deal, arranged by Merrill Lynch and Bemo Securitisation SAL, was the first S&P-rated Islamic securitization issue and also received the *Euromoney* award of the 'Most Innovative Islamic Finance Deal of the Year' and *Islamic Finance News*' 'Best Structured Finance Deal of the Year'.

The purchase SPC was entitled to proceeds from the sale of a specific portion of the production until such time as a total of 63 million MMBtu of hydrocarbons were delivered. In the meantime, the *sukuk* certificate holders were protected against loss through a variety of risk mitigation measures similar in most part to a conventional securitization deal. These include the use of an escrow account, reserve account, and a subordination account as well as price protection on the end gas sales.

The escrow account, common in securitization deals, simply means the seller – East Cameron in this instance – not receiving their entire proceeds. Instead, an amount, US$38.12 in this instance, is placed in a special earn-out account. It is paid out gradually to the seller as certain of its specified performance obligations are fulfilled. The money is withheld until the seller is given an added incentive to deliver what was promised to the SPC investors.

The reserve account is similarly a withholding of the proceeds, here US$9.5 million, that are held on SPC's behalf, which is the equivalent of six months of return and expenses. Failure to perform by the seller will see these funds paid to the SPC.

The subordination account involved US$3 million, where 50 per cent of the royalties paid to other royalty holders will be pledged until this amount is achieved. The funds would then stay at that level and be held until the SPC is fully repaid.

The final measure involved arranging price protection so that the purchaser SPC would not suffer should the natural gas price significantly fall in price. This involved US$4.05 million being used for a commodity hedge agreement (effectively cap and collar options).

Besides these financial measures, other risk mitigation efforts included arrangements for a specific back-up contractor operator to assume operations should the seller experience problems producing the desired gas; external verification of the reserves by a third party expert; appropriate insurance against natural disasters; and gas price forecasts confirmed by a third party expert.

From a *shari'ah* viewpoint, the transaction was considered a *musharaka sukuk* with the venturing parties East Cameron and the issuer SPC. The underlying business was appropriate and its purchase on a true sale basis. The purchase and issuer SPC arrangements were also considered appropriate as the former's underlying risk and reward arrangements was passed on to the issuer SPC certificate holders. The hedge, as it involved commodities (natural gas) and was of true commercial value rather than speculation, was also acceptable. These matters of course were all subjected to an evaluation by a *shari'ah* expert and formally approved.

Sadly, from a financial viewpoint, this investment proved unsuccessful, with East Cameron defaulting on its obligations. When it filed for protection under Chapter 11 in the US courts, it claimed that the facility was effectively a secured loan rather than a transfer of assets and so could be restructured as part of any settlement. The SPC won with the true sale recognized. This meant the SPC could obtain additional funding to ensure the actual gas production and sales continued and hopefully its investors will recoup their investment in due course.

PART III

Sukuk markets and industry practices

9. Stylized facts about Islamic *sukuk* markets

Nasser H. Saidi

9.1 STYLIZED FACTS ABOUT ISLAMIC FINANCE AND THE *SUKUK* MARKET

The global market for Islamic financial services, as measured by *shari'ah*-compliant assets, is estimated by IFSL to have reached US$951 billion at end-2008, 25 per cent up from US$758 billion in 2007 and three-quarters up on the 2006 total (with dividends ranging between 15 per cent and 20 per cent in 2008). By end-2010 it was observed that total *shari'ah*-compliant assets are closer to US$1 trillion, although, like all financial markets, the *sukuk* market growth declined slightly in the years 2009 and 2010. By the middle of 2011, the market is showing signs of faster growth again.

To put this in perspective, if we stack one-dollar bills vertically, one trillion is equivalent to the distance to the moon! However, this represents less than 1 per cent of global total financial assets denoted as conventional bonds, although the GDP share of Muslim-majority countries is variously estimated to be about 13 per cent of the world GDP. There is room for growth in this market. Demographic statistics suggest that Muslims constitute 22 per cent of the world population.

According to data from Standard & Poor's, new *sukuk* issuance in 2009 increased to US$23.3 billion compared to US$14.9 billion in 2008. However, the listed ones are only a small fraction of total *sukuk* issuances – at the end of 2009, the total public listed on some of the main exchanges was roughly around US$54 billion only: Malaysia (US$17.6 billion); Nasdaq Dubai (US$16.3 billion); London (US$9.9 billion); Luxembourg (US$7.3 billion) and Bahrain (US$2.8 billion). This highlights the non-traded institutional ownership of most *sukuk* instruments at this initial stage of market development.

The geographic spread of *sukuk* issuance showed a marked resurgence in Asia in general and Malaysia in particular, with 54 per cent of the total volume. Saudi Arabia also saw an increase: US$3.1 billion in 2009 compared to US$1.7 billion in 2008.

Interestingly, market turbulences associated with the global financial crisis led to a recovery in USD issuance, which reached US$7 billion in 2009 from only US$1.5 billion in 2008. Also, the *sukuk* structures that dominated the market in 2009 were *ijara* and *murabaha*.

9.2   POTENTIAL OF THE *SUKUK* MARKET

9.2.1   The Global Financial Crisis has Led to a Shift in References

The worldwide Islamic banking sector has grown at more than 10 per cent annually over the past 10 years, from about US$ 150 billion in the mid-1990s to about US$1 trillion by end-2009. The sector was not completely immune to the financial crisis as it was earlier expected, especially given the low prevalence of complex structured products and regulatory and prudential rules discouraging exposure to sub-investment grade investments, to name a few.

However, post-crisis there has been a shift in investor preference – a move towards less risky investment positions as the investors tend to become more risk averse. There is evidence of demand for the adoption of more ethical principles in investment and the conduct of the banking and financial system, stronger corporate governance and more transparency and disclosure in terms of risk-sharing.

9.2.2   Demographic and Growing Population

The Muslim population is growing fast as economic development is taking place at a much faster speed than in the recent past. The current share of this population is variously estimated to be 22–24 per cent in the world. There is growing demand and awareness of Islamic finance, and globally every major financial centre is turning its attention to Islamic finance, the greatest demand being driven in those countries with strong Muslim populations.

A report from the Pew Forum on Religion and Public Life last year estimated that 1.57 billion Muslims populate the world (about 22 per cent of the world's population), with 60 per cent residing in Asia. So in Asia and the oil-rich GCC (Gulf Cooperation Council) regions this market will grow faster than in other regions. This report took three years to compile, with census data from 232 countries and territories, and showed that 60 per cent of Muslims are based in Asia and 20 per cent live in the Middle East and North Africa.

The key features of the Muslim population are that they are young and fast growing. The other common feature is that they live in countries with low banking and financial penetration rates. For example, only one out of every 10 households in Egypt has a bank account. This highlights not only the challenge but also the potential for Islamic finance in tapping into those regional markets, providing solutions for the non-banked and un-financed populations.

9.2.3 Mainstreaming Islamic Finance: Example *Shari'ah*-compliant Mutual Funds

One of the key challenges is how to mainstream Islamic finance and provide more retail products that appeal to the masses. This can be enabled by the introduction of more *shari'ah*-compliant mutual funds, *shari'ah*-compliant money market instruments/hedge funds and such.

9.3 POTENTIAL FOR THE *SUKUK* MARKET

9.3.1 Public Finance

Governments and central banks in the region should introduce *sukuk* as part and parcel of the public finance/debt management framework. Governments should develop the debt markets for their financing needs. They need to use *shari'ah*-compliant instruments, particularly in the GCC, where there is a high level of dependence on oil and gas for revenues.

The use of *sukuk* will provide regional governments with an alternative source of funding to smooth out volatile revenues from energy price fluctuations and diminish macroeconomic and financial vulnerability. The recent crisis saw the introduction of counter-cyclical fiscal policies in the Gulf region, making public debt management a priority.

9.3.2 Infrastructure and Development Projects

The MENASA (Middle East, North Africa and South Asia) region is characterized by a young and fast-growing population and for them the government needs to provide essential infrastructure, for example education, health, transport, power and water.

According to MEED Projects, in the Gulf region alone, about US$2.8 trillion worth of infrastructure projects are in the pipeline for the coming 15 years.

Given the planned expansion plans of the GCC governments, and the commitment to implementing strong infrastructure, such as the GCC Rail

Network, GCC Power grid and so on, infrastructure funding through *shari'ah*-compliant finance is clearly a highly attractive source for such investments.

Given the ease with which capital market products transcend geographical borders, *shari'ah*-compliant financing projects which originate in one country can source investors globally. The potential is strong and the funding is likely to be mostly from local investors in the region.

9.4   BASIS FOR THE ISLAMIC SECURITIES MARKET

Sukuk markets are already established; what needs to be put in place is a multi-currency, multi-country and multi-user market that is open to investors worldwide. This is also a strong case for the development of local currency money and debt markets including s*ukuk*. This will also enable central banks to control liquidity in the markets through open market operations, enabling active monetary policy management.

In recent years, there has been a growing interest in issuing local currency *sukuk*, specifically in Malaysia, Kingdom of Saudi Arabia and Indonesia, which all have sizeable economies, local currency liquidity and locally driven issuance markets. In 2009, these three markets outperformed other markets in terms of local currency *sukuk* issuances.

9.4.1   Issues

Lack of standardization: high set-up and transactions costs
These factors result in higher set-up and transaction costs and lengthier time faced by financial institutions offering *shari'ah*-compliant products, leading to less efficient markets and a preference for conventional products.

Liquidity
Lack of liquidity leads not only to limited trading opportunities, but also to less efficient pricing of *sukuk*. To improve liquidity, the most important requirement is market-makers; the central banks in the region need to be actively involved in the markets; institutional investors need to be permitted to move in and out of the markets freely.

Regulatory convergence
Currently, there is no uniformity across or within countries in the regulation of *shari'ah*-compliant banking and financial activities. Regulators

need to cooperate to ensure convergence of regulation in the absence of a single global regulatory regime. The lack of regulatory uniformity and convergence results in fragmented markets, lack of a level playing field, the possibility of regulatory arbitrage and, more generally, less innovation and fewer barriers to cross-border transactions. Generally, when products transcend the boundaries of the country of origination the regulations and legal requirements of the recipient jurisdiction must be adhered to. In the context of Islamic finance, the added component of *shari'ah* adds a further consideration, that of seeking to ensure that the *shari'ah*-compliant product remains *shari'ah*-compliant in the recipient jurisdictions.

Defaults: framework for insolvency and creditor rights
The recent instance of defaults and near-defaults with respect to *sukuk* raises the question of how to deal with investor and creditor rights in this context, as there has been an absence of legal certainty. By contrast there is a long history and experience in dealing with defaults (both sovereign and corporate) in the conventional bond markets, given that they have been in existence for some 200 years.

Government and central banks must take initiative
Governments and central banks need to take the initiative in developing the potential of the Islamic securities market by developing the legal and regulatory framework as well as by developing issuance programmes.

The Dubai International Financial Centre (DIFC) is actively addressing a number of the issues facing Islamic finance.

Level regulatory playing field for Islamic finance
The Dubai Financial Services Authority (DFSA) has developed a unique *shari'ah* systems model, which provides an appropriate regulatory structure to ensure compliance not only with international regulatory standards, but also *shari'ah*. The DFSA regime provides:

- clarity and certainty across wholly Islamic financial institutions and Islamic windows;
- integrated regulatory structure conducive to the cross-sectoral nature of Islamic finance;
- a level playing field in Islamic finance – all institutions subject to the same standard of regulation.

The DFSA is working with regional and international regulatory bodies and entering into cooperation and information-sharing arrangements with other regulators and counterparties.

Compliance with international standards
Compliance is needed with international standards such as risk and capital
adequacy requirements set out by Basel, as well as Islamic finance industry guidelines and applications specified by the Accounting and Auditing
Organisation for Islamic Financial Institutions (AAOIFI) and the Islamic
Financial Services Board (IFSB) for accounting treatment of Islamic
transactions.

**Mutual recognition agreements (DFSA–Malaysian SEC): 'Islamic
passport'**
The DFSA has signed a unique Mutual Recognition Agreement with
Malaysia's SEC model, the first of its kind, which helps to facilitate the
cross-border flow of Islamic funds. Not only does this open and increase
the investment space between the Gulf and Malaysia, but it also increases
the accessibility of issues and enables mutual recognition of products and
services.

Islamic finance passport proposal
Time is also right for the creation of an 'Islamic passport', similar to the
EU experience. The Markets in Financial Instruments Directive (MIFID)
concept of a 'European financial passport' should be developed for the
Islamic financial industry as well:

- GCC moving towards greater economic and financial integration
- Starting point could be a GCC Islamic Finance Passport:
- IFIs would have 'passporting' potential
- Regulated Funds passport
- *Takaful* and Re-*Takaful* passport

Legislation: trusts (*waqf*s); REITs
The DIFC has introduced a legal and regulatory regime that aims to
support the development of Islamic REITs (Real Estate Investment Trusts)
and other funds such as Collective Investment Funds and Investment
Trusts that are *shari'ah*-compliant. The Trust Law also helps in the
creation of *waqf*s.

NASDAQ-Dubai: listing of hilal IFC *sukuk*
One of the biggest milestones last year was the listing on 4 November 2009
by the International Finance Corporation, an affiliate of the World Bank,
of an Islamic bond (or *sukuk*) on NASDAQ-Dubai, the international
exchange located within DIFC.

The Hilal *sukuk* offered by the IFC set a milestone for Islamic finance and for financial markets in the GCC, as this was the first time that a non-Islamic financial institution was issuing a *shari'ah*-compliant security for term funding (a fact all the more important considering that the IFC has a strong reputation on international markets and impeccable credentials).

By issuing a *sukuk*, the IFC and the World Bank have recognized *shari'ah*-compliant finance and securities as bona fide, valid, and acceptable financial instruments.

Hawkamah: taskforce corporate governance IFI
The DIFC is also one of the founding institutions of the Hawkamah Institute for Corporate Governance, which provides assistance to Islamic finance institutions on enhancing their corporate governance arrangements and structures. In one of their latest initiatives, Hawkamah, with the support of a number of Islamic Financial Institutions, has set up a Task Force on Corporate Governance of Islamic financial institutions (IFIs).

Hawkamah developed a survey questionnaire to take stock of the existing CG frameworks of Islamic Banks and Financial Institutions throughout the MENA region and distributed it to over 90 banks and FIs in the region. The Accounting and Auditing Organisation for Islamic Financial Institutions (AAOFI) is a member of this taskforce, and the IFSB is also involved in the initiative.

Educational initiatives: Islamic workbooks; scholar training
Given the strong growth of the industry, trained Islamic scholars are in short supply, leading to an oligopolistic industry structure of *shari'ah* boards. It is imperative to develop more human capital in the Islamic finance space. The DIFC's Centre of Excellence has taken an active role in the introduction of Islamic finance courses and programmes and an Islamic Finance qualification. The DIFC has introduced Islamic finance workbooks available on its website.

The bottom line is that while Islamic finance has been recognized, it has not entered mainstream finance and there is a lack of innovation in terms of products and structures. What is needed in the medium term is the mainstreaming and standardizing of Islamic finance for a population that is based in countries and jurisdictions that are under-banked and under-financed.

10. *Sukuk* industry development in the Bahrain capital market

Sat Paul Parashar

10.1 INTRODUCTION

This chapter provides an overview of *sukuk* industry development in Bahrain. The industry in Bahrain is quite small compared to global markets. It is quite small even compared with the Bahrain banking industry and capital markets. Indeed, the Bahrain debt market itself is quite small, given its recent development and also given its size, though potential is there in the long run as a financial centre. Interestingly, *sukuk* constitutes the lion's share of the Bahrain debt market. The number one issue facing Bahrain's *sukuk* industry, and for that matter the Bahrain debt market, is absence of market liquidity. The Central Bank of Bahrain (CBB), the Liquidity Management Center (LMC), and the International Islamic Finance Market (IIFM) are actively focused on this and other issues.

As noted in an earlier chapter, in recent years Bahrain has rapidly become a global leader in Islamic finance, playing host to the largest concentration of Islamic financial institutions in the Middle East. Bahrain also plays host to a number of organizations central to the development of Islamic finance. These are the Accounting and Auditing Organization for Islamic Financial Institutions (AAOIFI); the Liquidity Management Centre (LMC); the International Islamic Financial Market (IIFM), and the Islamic International Rating Agency (IIRA). The Islamic banking assets have rapidly increased to constitute about 11 per cent of the total banking assets in 2010 compared to 1.8 per cent in 2000. While the issue size of listed bonds and *sukuk* constituted about 1.4 per cent of the total banking assets in 2010, listed *sukuk* constituted about 91 per cent of the listed debt securities.

The remaining part of this chapter is organized in five sections. Section 10.2 discusses the development of the Bahrain *sukuk* industry vis-à-vis the global *sukuk* industry. Section 10.3 highlights the pioneering and active role of the Bahrain government in the development of the *sukuk* industry in Bahrain. Section 10.4 analyses Bahrain's secondary market for *sukuk.* Section 10.5 highlights major issues of interest for further development of the *sukuk* industry and the efforts underway in Bahrain. Section 10.6 concludes this chapter.

10.2   BAHRAIN VIS-À-VIS THE GLOBAL *SUKUK* INDUSTRY

In order to appreciate the development of the *sukuk* industry in Bahrain, let us first take a look at developments in the global *sukuk* industry. Table 10.1 shows global *sukuk* issues over the last five years. The table highlights the fact that the global *sukuk* issues were clearly affected by the global financial crisis of 2008. While 2006 and 2007 witnessed significant year-on-year growth in global *sukuk* issues, 2008 experienced a serious dent. This was equally true of domestic and international *sukuk* issues. It is, however, interesting to note that the domestic issues tended to suffer less than international issues. While in 2008 international issues, year-on-year, were down by 85 per cent, the domestic issues were down by 54 per cent. The 2009 numbers signify recovery in the global market, with international *sukuk* issues clearly leading the domestic issues. It is also worth noting that the domestic issues over 2005–2009 have been less volatile (or more stable) than international issues.

Let us now take a look at the Bahrain *sukuk* industry vis-à-vis the global *sukuk* industry. Table 10.2 shows global and Bahrain issues over the last five years, 2005–2009. It highlights that the *sukuk* issues as a percentage of global issues have continuously grown from 1.4 to 5.3 over the 2006–2009 period. In 2005, Bahrain's share of global *sukuk* issues was much higher, at 9.2 per cent. Examining the 2001–2009 period, Bahrain issues present a share of 3.9 per cent of global issues. Clearly, despite Bahrain gaining a

Table 10.1   Global sukuk *issues, 2005–2009*

Year	Domestic (US$ billion)	International (US$ billion)	Total (US$ billion)
2005	8.7	3.3	12.0
2006	17.9	10.6	28.5
2007	35.0	13.8	48.8
2008	16.2	2.14	18.34
2009	17.9	8.7	26.6

Source: Reports of International Islamic Financial Market (IIFM).

Table 10.2   Global and Bahrain sukuk *issues, 2005–2009*

Year	Bahrain (US$ million)	Global (US$ million)	Bahrain/ Global (%)
2005	1113	12077	9.2
2006	418	28502	1.4
2007	1137	48808	2.3
2008	891	18392	4.8
2009	1405	26584	5.3
2001–2009	5947	150360	3.9

Source: Reports of International Islamic Financial Market (IIFM).

leadership position in terms of presence of Islamic financial institutions and international standards bodies, its *sukuk* industry remains relatively small. Domestic issues, however, have been less volatile (or more stable) than global *sukuk* issues.

10.3   BAHRAIN GOVERNMENT ROLE IN PIONEERING *SUKUK* ISSUES

The Government of Bahrain has been a pioneering and active issuer of *sukuk*. It has been issuing *sukuk* since 2001. Table 10.3 provides a brief view of the Government of Bahrain *sukuk* issues over the last ten years to 2009.

Table 10.3 highlights the fact that the two main types of *sukuk* regularly issued by the Government of Bahrain are Islamic leasing securities (*ijara* or leasing-type) and *al salam* (a deferred delivery). The new issues of Islamic leasing securities have grown from (Bahrain Dinar) BD37.6 million in 2001 to BD507 million in 2009, which is more than 13 times. The new issues of *al salam* have, however, tapered off in 2009 to the levels of 2001. In terms of balances outstanding, over 2002–2009, Islamic leasing securities have always far exceeded *salam*. This is no surprise. After all, Islamic leasing securities are issued to meet long and short-term funding needs, while *salam* securities are issued to meet very short-term needs.

10.4   BAHRAIN SECONDARY MARKET FOR *SUKUK*

The Bahrain Stock Exchange (BSE) provides the processes for listing and trading of *sukuk* instruments in Bahrain. Table 10.4 presents statistics on

Table 10.3   Government of Bahrain sukuk *issues, 2001–2009*

BD/Million	Islamic leasing securities			*Al salam* Islamic securities		
Year	Matured	New issue	Balance	Matured	New issue	Balance
2001	0.0	37.6	37.6	37.6	65.8	28.2
2002	0.0	75.2	112.8	112.8	112.8	28.2
2003	0.0	180.5	293.3	112.8	112.8	28.2
2004	0.0	134.0	427.3	112.8	112.8	28.2
2005	141.7	156.4	442.0	135.2	152.0	45.1
2006	90.0	120.0	472.0	180.0	180.0	45.1
2007	120.0	155.0	508.6	54.0	54.0	18.0
2008	191.6	191.6	507.0	72.0	72.0	18.0
2009	154.0	507.0	860.0	72.0	72.0	18.0

Source: Central Bank of Bahrain.

debt securities listed on BSE in 2010. It shows that *sukuk* constituted 70 per cent of the number of issues listed and 91 per cent of the total issue size of debt securities listed. Clearly, *sukuk* dominates the listed debt market in Bahrain.

It is also interesting to note that the US dollar is the dominant currency of *sukuk* and conventional bonds listed on BSE because US$-denominated *sukuk* constituted 67 per cent in number and 73 per cent in issue size, while US$-denominated bonds constituted 50 per cent in number and 81 per cent in issue size.

10.4.1   Types of *Sukuk* Listed on BSE

Table 10.5 shows the types of *sukuk* listed as of 2010. *Ijara sukuk* clearly dominate the issues. They constituted 67 per cent in numbers and 71 per cent in issued value. The other listed instruments are, namely, *musharaka* (share-like), and *manafa* constituted only a small fraction.

Table 10.6 presents data relating to issuers of *sukuk* listed on BSE, in 2010. It reveals an interesting observation. While, in terms of number of issues, the government of Bahrain and the corporates have equal numbers, in terms of issued value the total of corporate issues clearly dominate. In terms of numbers of issues listed, the government of Bahrain and the corporates issued 45 per cent each, but in terms of issued value the government of Bahrain and the corporates held 34 per cent and 62 per cent, respectively.

We analysed time-to-listing of *sukuk* issues of the government of Bahrain and the corporates listed as of 2010. The time-to-listing is defined

Table 10.4 Debt securities listed on Bahrain Stock Exchange, 2010

Issuer	Size (Mn)	Coupon rate/return	Date of issue	Date of maturity	Date of listing
Alba	US$200	1.3635% p.a.	18/06/2003	15/03/2013	26/06/2003
BMA	BD 40	5.125% p.a.	20/07/2004	20/07/2014	10/8/2004
CRESC	US$100	US$ 6 month LIBOR + 1.25% p.a.	12/5/2005	12/5/2010	21/06/2005
BCF-5	BHD 10	0.85% above the 6 months BIBOR	15/06/2005	15/06/2010	6/7/2005
Esterad	US$25	1.25% p.a. over LIBOR for 6 months	20/07/2005	20/07/2010	24/08/2005
Government *sukuk*	US$230	5.6% p.a.	21/01/2005	21/11/2011	24/01/2006
Dar	US$100	7.347% (6- m US$ LIBOR plus 2% Margin)	27/10/2005	26/10/2010	28/06/2006
BCF-6	BD 10	0.95% above the 6 months BIBOR (min of 3% p.a.)	19/06/2006	19/06/2011	20/07/2006
Golden Belt	US$650	Six Months US$ LIBOR plus 0.85% P.A	15/05/2007	15/05/2012	27/06/2007
Dar	US$1000	LIBOR + Margin 2.25% p.a. Payable quarterly	16/07/2007	16/07/2012	14/02/2008
Govt. Leasing *sukuk*	BD 95	(30) basis point over LIBOR payable every six months	3/10/2007	3/10/2012	21/2/2008
Govt. Leasing *sukuk*	BD 165	3.75% p.a.	24/09/2009	24/09/2012	15/10/2009
IFC *sukuk*	US$100	3.037% payable every six months	3/11/2009	3/11/2014	4/11/2009

Source: Bahrain Stock Exchange.

Table 10.5   Types of sukuk *listed on BSE, 2010*

Type	Number	Issued value (%)
Ijara	6	71
Musharaka	1	3
Manafa	1	23
Other	1	3
Total	9	100

Table 10.6   Issuers of listed sukuk *on BSE*

Issuer	Number	Issued value (%)
Sovereign	4	34
Corporate	4	62
IFC/World Bank	1	4
Total	9	100

Table 10.7   Time to listing of sukuk *issues during 2004–2009*

Issuer	Average days to listing over 2004–2009
Government	55
Corporate	135

as the days elapsed between the date of issue and the date of listing. While the time-to-listing for issues listed on BSE varied from one day to 246 days during 2004–2009, the average days to listing for government *sukuk* issues during this period was 55 days (Table 10.7). The time-to-listing for corporate *sukuk* issues was 135 days. Such a time-to-listing would signify that the concern for trading and liquidity of these issues must be low. The absence of trading activity data on the BSE website reaffirms these concerns and implications.

10.4.2   Pricing of *Sukuk* Listed on BSE by Type

The *sukuk*, similar to debt securities, may be priced on a fixed rate or floating rate basis in some cases. Table 10.8 presents pricing data relating to different types of *sukuk* securities listed on BSE during 2005–2009.

It highlights the fact that the fixed rate and floating rate basis of pricing of *sukuk* in Bahrain has been equally common. However, when looked at

Table 10.8   Pricing of sukuk *listed on BSE by type over 2005–2009*

Type	Fixed rate		Floating rate		Total	
	No.	% Value	No.	% Value	No.	% Value
Ijara	4	36	2	64	6	100
Musharaka	0	0	1	100	1	100
Manafa	0	0	1	100	1	100
IFC/World Bank	1	100	0	0	1	100
Total	5		4		9	

Table 10.9   Pricing of sukuk *listed on BSE by issuer over 2005–2009*

Issuer	Fixed rate		Floating rate		Total	
	No	% Value	No	% Value	No	% Value
Government	3	76	1	24	4	100
Corporate	0	0	4	100	4	100
Total	3		5		8	

by type, in terms of number, the fixed rate has been more common for *ijara sukuk*, while the floating rate has been more common for *musharaka* and *manafa sukuk* securities. It is equally interesting to note that, in terms of value of issues, the floating rate has been more common than the fixed rate.

Table 10.9 presents pricing data relating to *sukuk* issued by the government of Bahrain and the corporate as listed on the BSE during 2005–2009. It highlights that the government of Bahrain has predominantly adopted a fixed rate basis of pricing of *sukuk*, both in terms of number and issue value. The corporates have, however, adopted a floating rate basis of pricing of *sukuk* issues, without exception. This is more due to the different types of securities being issued by them.

The Bahrain secondary market for *sukuk* is essentially illiquid. The BSE web pages do not display any *sukuk* trading data. It is believed that some trades do happen on a bilateral basis for which no data is readily available.

10.5   DEVELOPMENT OF THE INDUSTRY

In our view, the development of the *sukuk* industry in Bahrain may require attention to following issues:

- How can liquidity be created in the Bahrain secondary market for *sukuk*?
- What would be a good pricing benchmark for *sukuk* trading?
- Can asset-based *sukuk* be *shari'ah* compliant?
- What needs to be done to develop Bahrain into a *sukuk* international hub?

In this connection, it is worth mentioning that efforts are already being made in those directions by the Central Bank of Bahrain, the Liquidity Management Centre (LMC) and the International Islamic Financial Market. It is also worth noting that Bahrain has been one of the first countries to have created a repo facility specifically for Islamic banks: it is also the first to issue *salam* contracts. Worldwide, Bahrain is considered the second hub after Malaysia.

The Liquidity Management Centre (LMC) has been established for the purpose of facilitating the investment of the surplus funds of Islamic banks and financial institutions into quality short and medium-term financial instruments structured in accordance with *shari'ah* principles.

As per its founding mandate, LMC aims to develop an active secondary market for all transferable Islamic investment instruments. LMC's activities in this area revolve around assisting prospective buyers and sellers of *sukuk*. The LMC bid/offer registration and display service, and its indicative *sukuk* bid/offer table have been very helpful in providing *sukuk* pricing data and benchmarks. The last updated bid/offer table on LMC web pages is dated 7 May 2008. The issue of inadequate price data and benchmarks thus persist.

In order to provide liquidity to the market, LMC had initially launched an open-ended Short-Term *Sukuk* programme (STS) in 2004 and this has grown steadily. The Bahrain government's *al-salam* securities also serve liquidity management purposes. LMC is also committed to playing a key role in the creation of an active and geographically expansive Islamic inter-bank market which will assist Islamic financial institutions in managing their short-term liquidity.

In addition, the LMC works to attract assets from governments, financial institutions and corporates in both private and public sectors in many countries. The sourced assets will be securitized into readily transferable securities or structured into other innovative investment instruments. The depth of such a securitization and interbank market will assist in developing Bahrain into an international *sukuk* hub.

IIFM is a non-profit market standard-setting body of the Islamic Financial Services Industry (IFSI). It is supported by several central banks/government agencies and leading financial institutions. The objective of

IIFM is to unify the Islamic Capital and Money Market (ICMM) segment of the IFSI. IIFM's primary focus lies in the standardization of products, documentations and related processes.

The Master Agreement for Treasury Placement (MATP) devised by IIFM in 2008 facilitates cash flow, commodity flow, together with title flow, and thus *shari'ah*-compliant treasury placement. IIFM is currently leading a project to develop an Islamic repo structure that will further facilitate short-term liquidity management.

10.6　CONCLUSION

It may be in order to mention that, despite gaining a leadership position in terms of presence of Islamic financial institutions and the international Islamic finance development institutions and bodies, the Bahrain *sukuk* industry remains relatively small. Bahrain issues over the last ten years, 2001–2009, constituted only about 4 per cent of the total global *sukuk* issues. In relation to the total banking assets as well as market capitalization of listed companies, the listed debt including *sukuk* constitutes a small fraction. However, *sukuk* constituted 70 per cent of the number of issues listed and 91 per cent of the total issue size of debt securities listed on the Bahrain Stock Exchange. Clearly, *sukuk* dominates the listed debt market of Bahrain.

The government of Bahrain has played a pioneering role in the development of the industry in Bahrain. The first *sukuk* issued in Bahrain in 2001 was a sovereign issue. While *ijara* and *salam sukuk* have been regularly issued by the government of Bahrain, *ijara sukuk*, in terms of balances outstanding, is the dominant type. *Ijara sukuk*, as a percentage of total listed securities, also dominates the Bahrain market.

Private issues by corporate *sukuk* equal government *sukuk* in terms of number of issues. However, in terms of issued value, corporate *sukuk* constituted 62 per cent of the total listed market. The real issue facing the market is lack of market liquidity. Hardly any trading has been taking place in recent years. (This is not as severe in Kuala Lumpur, the main *sukuk* hub.) The other major issue facing *sukuk* is the absence of good pricing benchmarks.

The Central Bank of Bahrain, the Liquidity Management Centre and International Islamic Finance Market have undertaken initiatives to enhance market liquidity and develop pricing benchmarks, but this is still work-in-progress. At the end of the day, ideology apart, investors seek maximization of risk-adjusted returns. The investor will be happy to go for a *sukuk* or a conventional bond, as long it helps to maximize their risk-adjusted returns. That would be the final test for *sukuk* markets to develop, match and surpass conventional bond markets.

REFERENCES

www.aaoifi.com
www.bahrainstock.com
www.cbb.gov.bh
www.iifm.net
www.lmcbahrain.com

11. Bond pricing practices in the *sukuk* market in Malaysia

Meor Amri Ayob

11.1 INTRODUCTION

Conventional bonds are issued as pure debt instruments to fund investments by individuals, corporations – meaning legal personae – agencies of governments and governments in what are highly developed conventional bond markets with four centuries of experience in funding borrowers' demand for cash. The total value of the international bond market is estimated to be about US$67 trillion, while that of national bond market capitalizations is about US$87 trillion, and the bonds are traded in a large number of markets. The investor (the funder) receives a *fixed* interest payment during the economic life of a bond, and the initial fund is paid back at the end of the maturity period as being equal to the par value of the bond at the time of the issue. Variations to fixed coupon payment bonds are found in variable interest-rate bonds benchmarked to some basic market rates such as minimum lending or the London Interbank Offer Rate (LIBOR).

The conventional debt market is essentially one that follows this structure with some minor modifications such as the pure discount bonds or bills or convertible bonds. The conventional bond market is very old, and recorded history shows that bonds have been issued by kings for thousands of years. The five factors in such a bond issue are: (i) a fixed face value; (ii) a payment of a sum of money at regular intervals to investors as *coupons*, be it a fixed sum or variable if tied to a benchmark; (iii) a traded market value of the bond if the bond is a public issue; (iv) a current yield based on the coupon and the market price; and (v) the term to maturity of the bond. In the case of conventional bonds, there are established theoretical valuation models that are founded on time-value mathematics, which make the market-revealed prices to be compared with theoretical values.[1] This is not yet the case in *sukuk* securities since the fundamentals of the conventional cash flows cannot be equated to *sukuk* cash flows.

Sukuk securities could somewhat mistakenly be compared to conventional bonds because they have only four of the characteristics in common with the conventional bonds. The one key characteristic that they do *not* share is the pre-agreed fixed or variable *rewards* similar to coupons, which are based on the interest rate. *Sukuk* security cannot be designed with reference to a fixed or variable pre-agreed reward based on interest except in two common cases. Those too are not interest rates: the reward has to be based on other principles such as lease rental payments, or profit shares or claim to a portion of the incomes the issuer puts in a Special Purpose Company (SPC). The SPC has physical assets which form the asset-backing of a *sukuk* issue, on which, unlike in conventional bonds, the *sukuk* holder has ownership rights from day one of the issue. This makes this new Islamic debt securities very different from the conventional ones.

Therefore, in Islamic finance, the principle that interest is not used to price financial securities is pervasive and important. So, the prohibition of interest does not allow the issue of *sukuk* as pure debt security. Islamic legal principles embodied in *shari'ah* (Islamic jurisprudence or common law) allow the issue of financial assets that derives its return from an underlying real asset (or usufructs) of the SPC, and the SPC is owned by the *sukuk* holders. This is thus an asset-backed issue unlike the conventional bond issue, where asset backing is implicit only under certain conditions and it is not formal.[2] Only when a borrower fails to service the loan can the holder of a conventional bond take legal action to possess the assets of the company, although in non-listed private debt markets debt-holders could easily overcome the need to obtain court approval. In Islamic finance, no security can be issued if there are no assets to which the *sukuk* holders can have ownership claims! That is a no-go zone.

This provides the opportunity to issue financial assets that are similar to bonds known as *sukuk*, meaning *funding certificates of entitlement* to the returns on the underlying real assets (asset-backed) in the SPC. This new form of debt contracting (for that is what it effectively is) is now gaining popularity as an alternative source of funding sought by governments (as sovereign issues) and more importantly as private sector funding sought mostly by private corporations. In Malaysia, the private *sukuk* issues emerged as the largest source of private sector financing shortly after the 1997 Asian financial crisis: the savings rate in this economy is very high, so it is easy to tap funds using this mode. Corporate *sukuk* form a substantial portion of this source of funding in this market, which accounts for 65 per cent of the world *sukuk* market in some 12 locations.[3] The demand for this risk-sharing funding using equity-type, as will be explained later, *sukuk* is now more apparent after the failure of the debt-security markets that contributed to the 2007 global financial crisis. The use of *sukuk* is often lauded as a cure for profligate government borrowing, in the face of the sovereign debt debacle facing the world economy in 2011.

Developed countries such as Germany, France and Japan, amongst many other non-Islamic countries, have recognized the potential contribution of *sukuk* arrangements. The structuring of *sukuk* offers more security to the investors since part of the assets of the issuer are separated as being owned by the s*ukuk* investors. Thus, it serves as a signal to differentiate the quality of the *sukuk* issuer as being somewhat superior to the non-*sukuk* issuers who are not able to set aside assets to assure investors that the issue will be serviced adequately because the assets are transferred to the *sukuk* holders. In the case of conventional bonds, the bond issue has the risk of not being repaid in full when the issuing company defaults, whereas a sound *sukuk* arrangement would have to ensure that the assets backing the issue are sufficient for servicing the investors from the start to the end. Islamic banking needs to move towards restoring credibility and stability to the international financial market, and this feature makes it a sound form for debt arrangement for profitable ventures.

The design of *sukuk* is similar to the securitization of assets in the conventional markets, where a pool of assets is built and securities are issued against the pool. In this case the *sukuk* certificates are issued against either a single asset or a pool of assets. The *sukuk* certificate holder (the investor in the conventional sense) will benefit from the cash flows generated by the underlying assets that are transferred until repayment to the lenders via a special contracting arrangement. The tradability and the negotiability of the issued certificates depend on the nature of the underlying assets. For example, if the *sukuk* is issued against a pool of cash or debt-like instruments, it cannot be traded in the secondary market as it could involve *riba* (usury) when trading debt securities. In the Islamic legal principles in *shari'ah*, debts can only be traded at face value with no extra payment of any kind or in any guise. However, if the underlying assets are physical assets and financial rights are enshrined to the *sukuk* holders, then *shari'ah* allows the *sukuk* certificates to be traded in secondary markets.

The fundamental difference of the *sukuk* from the conventional bond is that the bond represents a pure debt of the issuer whereas the *sukuk* represents the ownership stake in the defined underlying assets or project held in escrow by the SPC. The implication is that, unlike the fixed coupon payment (which is not conditional on the performance of the underlying asset or project) promised to conventional bond holders, the periodic payment to the *sukuk* holder is not fixed, but accrues only if there are cash flows generated by the underlying asset or project. And at maturity or end of the project, the assets are sold back to the original seller at a predetermined price (so it is also known ahead of time) and the *sukuk* holders can sell back their certificates to the issuer at the face value of the certificate. However, this is a general process. In practice, there are variations depending on the type of financing contract used to create the underlying asset.

This chapter is organized as follows. In section 11.2, we provide a brief description of the market for *sukuk* in Malaysia where the pricing issue is of paramount importance to creating a sound market for the investing public. Section 11.3 is devoted to a discussion of the pricing concepts: this is followed by a discussion of the types of securities in section 11.4. Actual applied procedures are detailed in section 11.5. An industry example is then described in section 11.6 before the chapter concludes.

11.2 GROWTH OF THE *SUKUK* MARKET IN MALAYSIA

The initiative to introduce the *shari'ah*-compatible bond-like financial asset was first initiated in 1978 by the Jordanian Islamic Bank, followed by a number of issues in Pakistan in the 1980s, when Pakistan introduced Islamic finance. However, the first successful introduction of Islamic bonds was by the Malaysian government in 1983 with the issuance of Government Investment Certificates (a central bank note) and later renamed as Government Investment Issues. It was not until the late 1990s that an asset-backed security in the form of *sukuk* was formally developed and issued in Malaysia and also in Bahrain. Since then, the global demand for *sukuk* has grown rapidly to more than US$200 billion, but this is still less than 1 per cent of the total value of the global conventional listed bond market of about US$67 trillion.

Malaysia dominates this market with about 65 per cent of the global *sukuk* market followed by the Cayman Islands (11 per cent), Saudi Arabia (7 per cent), Bahrain (5 per cent), Indonesia (5 per cent) and the rest shared by other countries.

The Malaysian *sukuk* market has grown by more than 80 per cent in the last five years and has an annual growth of more than 30 per cent (see Figure 11.1). As of 2010, there are 1381 *sukuk* issued in this market, of which the largest corporate *sukuk* issued is by Binariang, which is worth RM20 billion or about US$650 million. In 2011 another issue was for US$1 billion. Fifty-three per cent of the *sukuk* issues are by private sector, 41 per cent by government and quasi-government agencies and the rest by the country's central bank, the Bank Negara, and other financial institutions. Of the 53 per cent corporate issues, 48 per cent resemble conventional bonds, 2 per cent have a corporate guarantee and only 3 per cent are asset-backed securities, so 97 per cent are asset-based.

Total *sukuk* and bond issuance

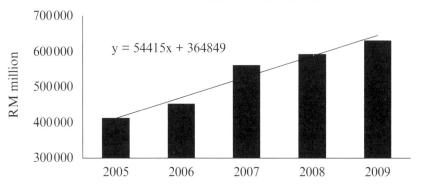

Figure 11.1   Growth of sukuk *and bonds in the Malaysian market*

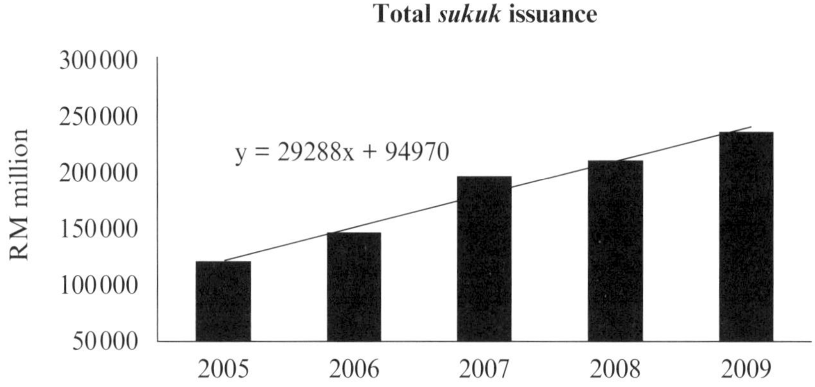

Total *sukuk* issuance

Figure 11.2   Growth of sukuk *market only, Malaysia*

From the plots in Figures 11.1 and 11.2, the phenomenal growth rates reported in the last five years are expected to continue unabated for the foreseeable future due to the nature of the domestic economy which requires substantial infrastructure and capacity building, all requiring large capital outlay. Based on simple regression analysis, the projected growth in *sukuk* will add an additional RM95.0 billion (US$31 billion) into this market per annum.

In terms of contract types, more than 30 per cent are *al bai bithaman ajil* or BBA. More than 20 per cent of the *sukuk* are issued based on a *murabaha* contract, that is a cost-plus sale contract similar to a mortgage contract repayable in instalments. Thirteen per cent are issued based on

Facilities by contract types

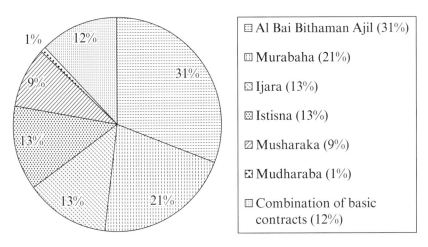

⊞ Al Bai Bithaman Ajil (31%)	
⊞ Murabaha (21%)	
⊠ Ijara (13%)	
⊞ Istisna (13%)	
⊠ Musharaka (9%)	
⊡ Mudharaba (1%)	
⊞ Combination of basic contracts (12%)	

Figure 11.3   Types of sukuk *facilities in the Malaysian market*

istisna (working capital) contracts, another 13 per cent are based on *ijara* (lease) contracts, 9 per cent are based on *musharaka* (share-like) contracts, 1 per cent is based on *mudaraba* and the rest is a combination of these basic contracts (see Figure 11.3).

11.3   VALUATION: THEORY-BASED VS MARKED-TO-MARKET VALUATION?

The valuation of conventional bonds is carried out using the well-entrenched present value theory which is suitable given the finite period, some form of fixed coupons, and a face value recovered at terminal period. Since this four-centuries-old traded debt instrument has assured fixed interest payments over the tenure of the bond – irrespective of what happened to the profits of the borrower – and a fixed sum of capital returned to the bond investor at the end of the maturity period, it is convenient to estimate the present value of the bond, provided the required returns on bond investment are available, for which there are agreed benchmarks available. The present value is then compared to the market value of the bond to indicate any mispricing and therefore opportunity to earn arbitrage profits.

The same is not true for *sukuk* securities as the cash flows to investors depend on the performance of the underlying assets escrowed via the SPC, and though the formula for distribution of the cash flows to bond investors is negotiated and fixed, the real quantum of cash flows received by bond investors is not fixed, and is only declared after the cash flows are earned. Besides the non-fixed nature of cash flows to the bond investors, there is also an issue of the discount rate to estimate the present value of *sukuk*. Similarly, the loss, if not due to negligence of the borrower, is also shared by the *sukuk* investor.

These factors introduce a degree of uncertainty, which probably explains why a *sukuk* bond of equal rating and tenure to a conventional one trades for a higher yield (the yield for the same term and same rating is about 7 basis points to 150 basis points higher in trade markets). To date there is no valuation theory that is applicable to value *sukuk* in their original form (full compliance with the required *shari'ah* principle) and this has led to the valuation of *sukuk* using the valuation concept for conventional bonds. Though the market is aware of the fundamental differences between *sukuk* and conventional bonds, the unique features of the *sukuk* are unaccounted for in the current valuation of *sukuk* (Meor, 2010) to provide a guide for the investors in this market.

11.4 TYPES OF SECURITIES

To date the Accounting and Auditing Organisation of Islamic Financial Institutions (AAOIFI) has recognized a large number of different type of *sukuk*, namely, the *ijara* (lease contract) with ownership right to use, *salam* (advance payment for goods to be delivered later), *istisna* (contractual agreement to manufacture goods to be delivered later), *murabaha* (cost-plus financing of assets), *musharaka* (share-like partnership), *mudaraba* (profit–loss sharing), *muzaraah* (for share cropping), *musaqah* (irrigation loan) and *mugharasa* (agriculture/seed planting).

However, in practice the majority of the *sukuk* issued in Malaysia are *al bai bithaman ajil* or BBA, the *mudaraba*, *musharaka*, *salam*, *istisna* and a combination of these basic contracts. These contracts are briefly discussed to provide a clear understanding of the nature of the financing involved in each contract, also to make clear that the pricing of such instruments using the conventional models is fraught with danger.

The *al bai bithaman ajil* or BBA contract is an innovation of the Malaysian market. This contract is based on sale of an asset to the investors, with a promise to buy back the asset in the future at a predetermined price that includes a pre-agreed profit margin. The issuer issues the *sukuk* to investors to formalize the arrangement. This type of contract is not accepted by the Bahrain regulatory framework and other Middle Eastern countries as they perceive it as non-*shari'ah*-consistent as there is an element of tradability of debt created through this arrangement and it is based on an underlying financial asset rather than a tangible asset.

The *murabaha* or cost-plus contract is usually used to purchase assets on credit. Usually the purchaser (or the entrepreneur who does not have the cash to buy a machine directly) of the asset makes an arrangement with a banker to purchase the asset from an owner and sells the asset back to the purchaser at a price that comprises the cost plus an agreed profit margin. The entrepreneur will then purchase the asset from the banker and arrange a periodical payment schedule to service the loan. To be *shari'ah* consistent, the contract should be an original sale and not just a financing arrangement, which requires the banker to own the asset before selling to the entrepreneur.

The *istisna* contracts are used to facilitate the manufacture of an asset (for example, aeroplane or ship-building) or construction of buildings, roads or a similar infrastructure at the request of the buyer. Both the manufacturer and the buyer agree on the price and the payment schedule and specification of the asset.

The *salam*-based contract is usually used for short-term financing of underlying assets, and is based on spot sale (*salam*) and/or deferred payment sale (*bay' al-muajjil*) or deferred delivery sale (*bay' al-salam*) where the investor undertakes to deliver a specific asset which will be sold to the client at an agreed profit margin. For example, a special vehicle is set up to buy, say, petroleum on a spot price basis and the purchase price is entirely paid up front from the proceeds of the issued *sukuk* certificates. The SPC will then sell the oil at a later date to the beneficiary of the oil on a certain designated delivery date. Since *salam sukuk* results in a purely financial claim that is not linked to the underlying asset, the *shari'ah* only allows such securities to be traded at par value. This affects its trading in the secondary market and investors are forced to hold this security until maturity. This contract resembles the conventional forward contract (which is not permissible by *shari'ah*) except that in case of the *salam* contract, payment it is made in advance and in the case of the latter payment it is usually settled at the delivery date.[4] The *salam* contract was allowed as a special case during the Prophet's time to avoid farmers and traders being forced to take usurious loans. It is considered less onerous than the usurious loan.

The *ijara* contract is a contract of sale of the 'the right to use the asset' for a specified period, which includes lease of tangible assets as property and goods. It also includes the hiring of personal services for a fee. The title of the asset remains with the owner (or the lessor in the case of a lease) and it is a *shari'ah* requirement that the asset is owned by the lessor for the duration of the lease, and no compound payments of any form are allowed to the lessor in the case of default or delay in rental payment.

The *musharaka* contract is a partnership contract involving an equity-type funding arrangement that combines both the elements of investment and management, which implies that two or more persons combine their capital and labour, share profits and losses and have similar rights and liabilities. In fact, *mudaraba* is a special type of *musharaka* contract with reference to partnership of capital and labour with agreed-upon rights and liabilities. Though *musharaka* is commonly recognized as an equity partnership in both Islamic and conventional finance because of its profit-sharing basis and risk-sharing basis in ways similar to owning a common stock, there are various forms of partnerships that can be designed based on different terms and conditions for the partners, so *sukuk* comes in handy in engineering a variety of contracts different from the common stock. For example, the partnership could be classified based on the level of partners' rights and liabilities and/or capital contribution and management.

11.5   PRICING CONCEPTS AS APPLIED

To date there is no special method or process that is used to price *sukuk* in the market place. The so-called market value is determined by either a fair value (of a similar security in the market) or the negotiated price between the buyer and seller that is usually determined through the methods that are applied to conventional bonds: the turnover statistics are shown in Figure 11.4.

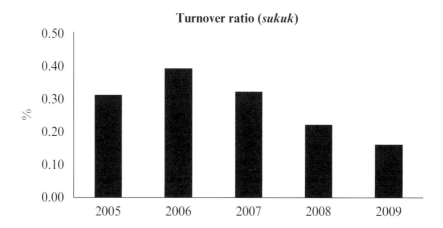

Figure 11.4   Turnover ratio for Malaysian sukuk

The estimation of the *sukuk* prices is made more difficult by the illiquidity of these instruments, as most are bought and kept until maturity. Meor (2010) records that the turnover ratio for *sukuk* averages about 0.67 per cent in the market and has been on the decline since 2005.

In fact, the fair valuation practice in the market is based on the recent arm's length market transactions and relative comparisons with peers and benchmarks. From the accounting perspective, the Financial Reporting Standard 139 is applied, which is approved by regulators and is a device to capture market value for reference purposes only.

There are currently four common market practices used to price bonds in the Malaysian market. These are the Yield to Maturity (YTM) curve pricing, the Individual Quotation Approach, the Model Approach and the Hybrid Approach. The first two approaches are quote-driven and except for YTM all other approaches are used to price individual bonds. Basically, all approaches are based on procedures similar to those in pricing conventional bonds in the market, that is, finding the discounted value of future coupons and the face value. For investors, their decision making is not based on the awareness, as far as is ascertained, to comply with the *shari'ah* principle, but completely on the yield level and the credibility of the issuer. The issuers are more interested in issuing bonds at the lowest cost, and if the bonds issue has to have a face lift to include characteristics that are *shari'ah* linked to attract investors there seems to be a perfect match for both the buyer and seller of the *sukuk*.

The Bond Pricing Agency Malaysia (BPAM) prices bonds based on some benchmark rate and an element of credit spread (see Figure 11.5). The benchmark is not disclosed but takes into account the market price of risk, and the credit spread incorporates the credit, liquidity and structural risk.

The market risk arises in the form of unfavourable price movements (in this case the benchmark rates such as the London Interbank Offer Rate (LIBOR)) which have a potential impact on the bond value over the economic life of the bond. The credit risk is the potential risk that a counterparty will fail in its obligations in accordance to the agreed terms, which includes the risk arising in the settlement and clearing of transactions. This risk is assessed based on some form of structured analysis and scoring.

The liquidity risk relates to the ability to trade the instrument at the fair market price within a reasonable time frame and is measured based on some method (i.e. turnover ratio) using past trade and trade quotes. The structural risk relates to the terms and conditions on the bond and the probability that the parties concerned will be able to comply with stipulated terms. The credit spread will help assess the risk and will be used with the benchmark to value individual bonds.

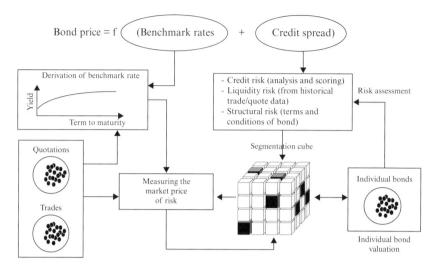

Note: 'Fair value' is the amount for which an asset could be exchanged, or a liability settled, between knowledgeable, willing parties in an arm's length transaction.

Figure 11.5   Pricing bonds and sukuk *by Bond Pricing Agency Malaysia*

There are many models used in pricing bonds based on the mark-to-model approach. All bonds with varying coupons, maturities and various embedded options are priced using sophisticated methods that are based on coupons (or fixed interest payments and not profits), and therefore not suitable for *sukuk*, even though the same formulations, as a convenience, are applied to price *sukuk*. For *sukuk*, the performance of the underlying assets is essential to the valuation and therefore the focus is more on the investor, unlike the conventional bonds where the focus is mainly on the issuer. In Islamic bonds, secondary notes are used to estimate profit payments as no interest payment is allowed. There are extra elements of risk such as compliance risk and regulatory risk that need to be accounted for in the valuation. The market practices of valuing *sukuk* are based on the premise that if the *sukuk*'s cash flows and its corresponding variables are correctly identified, then the current models can be used to value *sukuk*.

In the case of conventional bonds, the credibility of the issuer or the potential of the issuer to honour its obligations (default risk as usually indicated by the ratings agencies) and potential market conditions determine the yield (required returns on the bond investment). Therefore the price of the bond in the market is taken as a fair value. For *sukuk*, the risk-sharing requirement in the investment should lower the risk and therefore the yield on the bonds, but in practice investors in *sukuk* demand higher yields (or rate of return) compared to conventional bonds with a similar risk and maturity.

This could be due to many possible reasons, but the most likely factors are the uncertainty of this relatively new product, illiquidity of *sukuk* and regulatory and governance issues of markets trading these instruments. There is also great concern among conventional investors (who provide a substantial demand for *sukuk*) about the lack of transparency, comprehensive risk-management procedures and standardization of contracts and accounting standards of products in the Islamic finance industry (Askari et al., 2009).

11.6 AN EXAMPLE: KL SENTRAL SDN BHD (KLSSB)

Below is the schematic of the *sukuk* transaction involving **KLSSB** with Kuwait Finance House (KFH) totalling RM720 million under a *musharaka* concept in 2007 (see the following lists) some key considerations in pricing a *sukuk*, as in bonds:

1. Bond has pricing issue on asset pricing (see Figure 11.6)
    a. Forward pricing of assets require a forward rate benchmark of asset class; and
    b. Consideration must be taken for counterparty risk at the end of the contract.
2. Bond has pricing issue on asset's embedded option
    a. Asset volatility and term structure of asset class, for example, equity industry index volatility (see Figure 11.7, next page);
    b. Asset data greatly needed; and
    c. Optionality of the put/call feature.

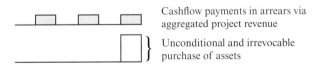

> Cashflow payments in arrears via aggregated project revenue

> Unconditional and irrevocable purchase of assets

Figure 11.6   Cash flow patterns of even and balloon payments

In reality, the market only looks at the market prices of KLSSB as a fixed payment bond to legal maturity disregarding other asset issues.

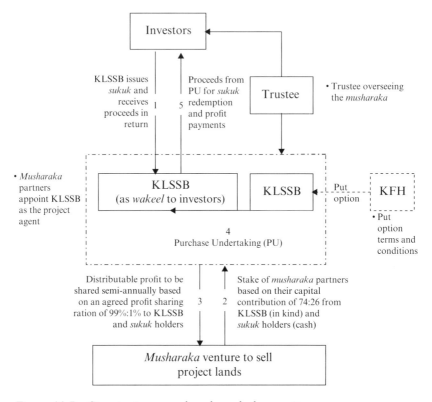

Figure 11.7   Structuring a musharaka sukuk *security*

In fact, there are many more unaccounted Islamic features in current market valuation. Below is a short list of what is missing in the market:

- inclusion of asset volatility;
- term structure of asset;
- floating rate mechanism for the forward rate agreement in the unconditional and irrevocable purchase of asset at maturity;
- prepayment risk modelling;
- counterparty risk modelling.

11.7   CONCLUSION

This chapter discussed the bond pricing issue in the *sukuk* market in Malaysia: similar concerns are relevant in other markets. Malaysia accounts for 65 per cent of global *sukuk* and the domestic *sukuk* market is growing at a steady rate of 30 per cent per annum. Though there is an infrastructure set to ensure the *sukuk* are *shari'ah* consistent, at this stage of the development of the market, this is not 100 per cent possible and hence efforts are made to make the *sukuk* as much *shari'ah* compliant as possible. This also involves important issues like pricing of *sukuk* as a special instrument, when in fact pricing signals are obtained as if these are seen by investors as straight bonds. To date there is no model or method devised to value (or price) *sukuk*, which are Islamic bonds with peculiar characteristics different from conventional bonds, though both are fund-raising instruments in the capital markets involving both the issuers (borrowers) and investors (bond holders).

We documented that *sukuk* are of various types based on the cash flow patterns, maturity and the purpose of the issue, but in general they are a securitized security involving a special vehicle that acquires assets with the *sukuk* proceeds and the cash flows generated by the assets are distributed to the *sukuk* holders based on a pre-agreed formula. The assets are owned by the *sukuk* holders for the maturity of the *sukuk* and are disposed at the end of the bond maturity period based on market value, with no elements of guarantee of capital of any sort. These characteristics require a valuation method (or model) that incorporates these *shari'ah*-based principles, and since none is available yet, currently the market value of *sukuk* is based on the conventional models.

Four methods of pricing *sukuk* are currently in practice, namely, the yield curve, the individual quotation, mark-to-model and hybrid approach. All these models are used for valuing conventional bonds. The market decomposes a *sukuk* cash flow and its risk variables using current available models to value *sukuk*. It has become an acceptable market practice with blessings from the relevant *Shari'ah* Advisory Council and other relevant regulatory authorities. The probable reason for this permissibility is due to public interest and also the current challenges facing the Islamic finance industry, which makes it difficult to have a *pure* Islamic valuation system in place for application purposes.

For example, (i) the lack of consensus among religious experts on the issues of application of the laws based on different interpretations and different schools of thought in Islamic finance, and (ii) the lack of liquid secondary markets for *sukuk* instruments further complicates standardization of the product and processes. Lack of liquidity, a limited set of approved instruments, and no ready provisions for risk management, or in short, the lack of proper infrastructure has allowed experts to improvise by introducing the *shari'ah*-required characteristics on conventional products. Using the current conventional methods to value these *shari'ah*-compliant products in the market is an attempt to provide investors with indicative information, given the questionable application of conventional bond models.

A lot more work is required to make *sukuk* fully compliant with *shari'ah* principles and tradable like conventional bonds. The challenge is to prepare the proper infrastructure to originate Islamic financial instruments that are not just *shari'ah* compliant but *shari'ah* consistent. This might be easier to construct if the instruments are designed in identifiable cash flow patterns, but will be a greater challenge in economies where both Islamic and conventional systems are run concurrently, Malaysia being such a case. These are the challenges the *sukuk* market needs to address in the next decade to develop the status of the global Islamic capital market.

NOTES

1. Any standard modern finance textbook would reveal that the first theoretical model was developed in 1952 by a Harvard professor, Williams. Between then and 2011, more theoretical models have been developed for more and more financial assets. However, by assuming that the Islamic *sukuk* are akin to the conventional bond issues, both practitioners and ratings firms apply the conventional valuation formulae to estimate the theoretical values of *sukuk* certificates. We are of the view that this is misplaced knowledge because cash flows accruing to fund providers vary in nature, and in risk sharing the *sukuk* has to have its own valuation theorems.
2. In a 2009 landmark decision of the standard-setting organization in Bahrain, this principle has been re-stated. Thus, asset backing is re-emphasized as critical to this new type of bond while the previous practice of 'asset-based' interpretation that led to some malpractices has been outlawed since 2011.
3. As at 2011, three more markets have taken steps to introduce *sukuk* certificates once the legal framework has been reformed: Hong Kong, Seoul and Australia.
4. Futures are permissible in Islamic finance under strict conditions. There are tests for its permissibility. First, it could be shown that the use of futures mitigates the pain or sufferings of a community. The value of futures should not be based on a bet resembling gambling, and the contract is only permissible to be drawn if there is at the time of contract real evidence that there is going to be a future value. For example, a futures contract on a wheat farmland is permissible if there is flowering on the plant and there is likelihood of a real harvest. Merely making a bet without evidence of likely future value is akin to a gamble, so such futures have a heavy riskiness (*gharar*), resembling a gamble. A wheat futures contract would certainly reduce the loss to a community of farmers but then the farmers could not wrongly induce a financier to write a contract without evidence that there is a future value. This is the principle of full disclosures for a contract to be binding.

BIBLIOGRAPHY

Askari, Hossein, Zamir Iqbal and Abbas Mirakhor (2009), *New Issues in Islamic Finance and Economics, Issues and Challenges*, Singapore: John Wiley & Sons (Asia).

Archer, Simon and Rifaat Ahmed Abdel Karim (eds) (2007), *Islamic Finance: The Regulatory Challenge*, Singapore: John Wiley & Sons (Asia).

RAM Rating Services Berhad (2009), *Malaysian Sukuk Market Handbook; A Guide to Malaysian Islamic Capital Market*, Kuala Lumpur, Malaysia: RAM.

Meor Ayob, Meor Amri (2010), 'Science of sukuk valuation', paper presented at the Symposium on Sukuk Financial Instruments at Dubai International Financial Center, Dubai.

Iqbal, Zamir and Abbas Mirakhor (2007), *An Introduction to Islamic Finance: Theory and Practice*, Singapore: John Wiley & Sons (Asia).

12. Origination, issuance, marketing and listing of *sukuk* securities

Mohamed Ariff and Shamsher Mohamad[1]

12.1 INTRODUCTION

The first Malaysian *sukuk* as a new Islamic financial debt security was issued as a private sector issue by Shell Company (M) Bhd, and raised RM125 million (US$45 million) in 1990. However, *sukuk* had been introduced earlier in Saudi Arabia and Pakistan back in the 1980s, but the debut of the 1990 issue was after the institutional development of the market for *sukuk* in several locations in the Middle East and Southeast Asia, and which is now in major financial centres such as in London and Zurich. In 2010 we witnessed very large markets that structure *sukuk* under proper regulations, established *Shari'ah* Boards and certification by properly established regulatory authorities, in the case of trade securities, making it possible to trade this new type of debt in secondary markets in a number of locations. The s*ukuk* securities markets have grown rapidly, with both public issues and private sector issues, and have been a very popular fund raising mode in Malaysia since 2000.

Hence, this Islamic funding instrument is providing finance to both private and public sector investments, and is increasingly becoming a popular means of raising capital to be repaid over a defined period. The market has grown very rapidly and has a predicted growth of about 15–20 per cent per annum for some years to come.

Sukuk securities are found in some twelve so-called Islamic bond markets in twelve legal jurisdictions stretching from the Philippines to London. However, there are only five significant locations where most of the issues are found. As at end-2009, these locations account for 5 per cent of the market in Bahrain; 11 per cent in the Cayman Islands; 5 per cent in Indonesia; 7 per cent in Saudi Arabia; and 65 per cent in Malaysia; therefore just 6 per cent are located in some 7 smaller market places such as Abu Dhabi. In the financial press, Islamic financial centres are recognized to be in Malaysia and Bahrain. The total value of all issues across the world is reported by one source to be about US$1200 billion in 2010, including the much larger private issues.

What is a *sukuk* (singular *sakk*)? It may be described succinctly as a financial security representing a claim on physical assets of a borrower with potential income streams as well as a market value. This item stretches from short-term financing modes by central banks to similar account receivables financing that can be used to finance a firm. Some of these take a similar form to almost bond-like issues with regular pre-agreed payments in *ijara*, or lease-type contracts using lease payments as rewards for the fund providers. *Sukuk* could be a more complex capital-raising instrument similar to the more understandable common-stock-like issue of share ownership with claims to physical assets of an entity over a limited period of time.

Hence, *sukuk* are not, as some writers have dubbed them, Islamic bonds! This new Islamic financing product can be engineered to raise money for diverse economic activities by (i) providing some form of claim over part or all of the physical assets of an entity based on (ii) some form of agreed payments, which depend on the income streams of the assets backing the financing. The pay-off will be based *not* on interest but on lease payment, or profit-share-basis or as repayment of the sum lent with a given increase at the time of liquidation of the contract.

In this chapter, we mainly provide an introduction to the primary market-making process for listing the security in an exchange, although a *sukuk* may be designed to be held to maturity without being listed or traded in an exchange. The latter form of *sukuk* funding is mainly done by a financial institution acting as a middleman to arrange one or more private fund providers to provide financing directly to an economic entity on any one of the three bases of servicing the financing arrangement (lease-like payments; a pre-agreed profit-share ratio; a balloon payment that is more than the amount raised originally).

In the next section, the reader will find a description of the primary market-making steps, which, in conventional banking terms, is investment banking. Section 12.3 identifies the regulatory process and the parties to the contract in the design of a new issue by an investment banking process. In section 12.4, the reader will find the activity chart that shows the details of the securitization process before the listing is done in the case of publicly-listed *sukuk* securities. Section 12.5 provides an actual example of *sukuk* issues while the chapter ends with concluding remarks in section 12.6.

12.2   PRIMARY MARKET-MAKING PROCESS

What is the investment banking process used to securitize a *sukuk* issue? Investment banking involves a set of regulated financial activities that an investment bank (a merchant bank) undertakes on behalf of a customer to conduct (i) due diligence valuation of the assets of a company, which is the estimation of the likely market value of the company's assets via accounting, legal and financial assessment of the company as a going concern in order to (ii) place a price per security of the company to be sold to the public for the purpose of listing and trading a security of a hitherto privately-owned company. Such a process leads to initial public offers, IPO, of a portion of the authorized shares of a company to the public. Similarly, an issue of debt financing also undergoes the same process of due diligence, and determination of the funding issue in the case of *sukuk* security.

Presently, in the case of the investment banking process for a *sukuk* security, the first thing to note is that (i) *sukuk* is a form of fund-raising arrangement that could be used to raise money from the public over a finite period for example, or over a few months as in the case of Malaysia's Islamic Investment Certificates issued by the central bank. (ii) It can also be used to raise money over longer periods of time (but not into infinity as in the case of common stock) with an arrangement to service the *sukuk*-holders with periodic payments over several years.

This second type of funding arrangement may also be based on another principle called *mudaraba* or *murabaha sukuk*, which provides slightly different forms of payments unlike the regular lease-like payments of *ijara*, which is a popular kind of *sukuk*. (iii) Other forms of *sukuk* arrangements can also be engineered, apart from these two types. The income for servicing the investors is required to come from a Special Purpose Company (SPC), which receives part or all incomes from the overall profits of the economic entity issuing the *sukuk* security. (iv) In the case of a *musharaka sukuk*, the periodic payment is akin to dividends paid to common stockholders, but the amount of dividends must come from a pool of money from the profits of a company, paid into the SPC.

In this case the financiers also become active managers of the economic entity raising the money, whereas under the other forms of *sukuk*, the financier does not take active ownership-based management actions. The SPC is the vehicle on which the *sukuk*-holders will legally have claims for both servicing the financing arrangement as well as for repayment of the sum raised in a *sukuk* issue. The bulk of the financing is more of the second type described and is characterized by regular payments coming from earnings escrowed to the SPC by the company. The original sum raised is repaid at the maturity of the security. Much of this chapter will be focused on the second type of security more than the other two basic types. For simplicity's sake, let us assume that these four are the basic forms of financing arrangements under *sukuk*, although in practice *sukuk* lends itself admirably well to many more complex financing arrangements than the four simple ones we are going to describe in this chapter.

12.2.1   Global *Sukuk* Market

As stated earlier, *sukuk* is a very recent innovation in Islamic finance, and judging by the size of the market in its 20-year history, it is likely that it will not only grow rapidly, but also take many different forms in its attempt to engineer its arrangement to suit the characteristics of particular financing needs of various forms of borrowers.

12.3   REGULATORY FRAMEWORK, MALAYSIA

The number of issues increased fourfold from 2005 to 2007, Bloomberg reports. After a year of decline during the global financial crisis period in 2008 – issues declined by more than half – there is sign of increased interest in new issues in 2009 (see Figure 12.1). Press reports suggest that the number of issues has crept back to the pre-crisis level. The size of the market by country as at 2010 is given in Figure 12.2. Malaysia has emerged as the number one Islamic *sukuk* market by capturing two-thirds of the market share: see reports from IFIS. The Islamic debt market is but a decade old, and its spread across more countries and by size is likely to take place in the next decades.

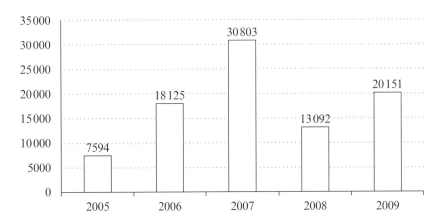

Figure 12.1   Global sukuk *issues over 2005–2009*

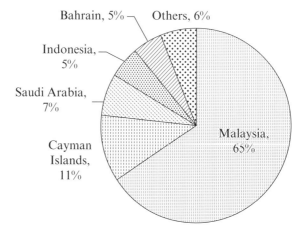

Figure 12.2   The global share of the sukuk *markets by country*

Who are the parties issuing and buying the issues? The key parties to the contractual arrangement in *sukuk* securitization are described here. The Securities Commission, SC, is the regulatory body that approves a *sukuk* issue in Malaysia. In each of the major *sukuk* markets, there are defined authorities that are in charge of approving *sukuk* issues: the Bahrain Monetary Authority is the regulator in Bahrain. The underwriter of the issue is normally a merchant bank, also called the *arranger* in *sukuk* literature, who prepares the Information Memorandum and the Trust Deed required to be lodged with the SC for approval of the issue. This practice is borrowed from similar norms established during the 70 years of the growth era of investment banking. In a sense, this body is at the apex of the regulatory process. The Information Memorandum is the result of the arranger making an assessment required in law as the due diligence process.

This requirement spans across compliance with accounting requirements, land codes for the land held by the issuer, *shari'ah* codes governing *sukuk*, securities laws, lease laws, taxation and stamp duty laws, and others. This is the core of the due diligence process that leads to the establishment of credibility of the issuer resulting in an estimate of the value for the assets of the firm wishing to issue the security.

The trust body has to be established, and this may require the arranger having a good enough reputation to have access to quality trust institutions, usually large banks, to serve as the trustees as reliable and financially sound bodies to provide confidence to the investors.

The regulatory framework has been well developed to first secure investor protection in the products designed and issued by the market players:

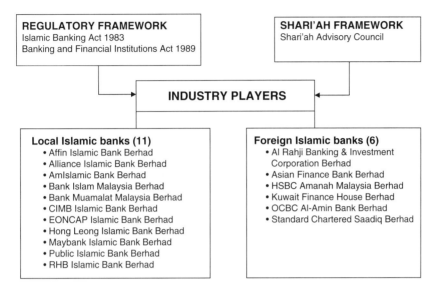

Figure 12.3   Regulatory framework and the market players

see Figure 12.3. The two sides of the regulation refer to the enabling legis-
lations and the requirement that the products designed pass the approval
of the *shari'ah* scholars: in practice, the *shari'ah* board ensures that the
contracts, once issued, are in fact operationally managed as specified at
the time of approval. Thus, there is continued supervision of the *shari'ah*
board located in the bank issuing the securities. Islamic banking activities are controlled both by the banking laws originally covering only the
conventional banking and by the specific laws that only apply to Islamic
banks.

A special requirement is the appointment of a *shari'ah* adviser to advise
on the structure and documentation of the *sukuk* issue as to compliance
with the known *shari'ah* provisions applicable to the *sukuk* issue. This is
a difficult area, and the party involved has to be objective in providing
advice on the legality and bona fide nature of the security as an Islamic
instrument requiring compliance of the issuer regarding the following:

i.   permitted economic activities;
ii.   avoidance of usury;
iii. avoidance of interest dealing;
iv.   avoidance of ambiguity to remove information asymmetry;
v.   risk-sharing;
vi.   avoidance of uncertainty approaching gambling-like chance-taking.

Comprehensive Regulatory Framework	Tax Incentives

Islamic Banking Act 1983
  • Government Funding Act 1983
  • Takaful Act 1984
  • Banking and Financial Institutions Act 1989
  • Labuan Offshore Laws 1990
	The Government is encouraging issuers to issue *sukuk*. Through tax deductibility of expenses incurred in raising *sukuk* adopting *ijara, istisna, mudaraba, musharaka* principles until YA 2015.
	Cost incurred and income received by the Special Purpose Company set up for the purpose of *sukuk issuance* is exempted.

Tax Neutrality
  • To facilitate more *sukuk* issuance, the government has amended tax legislation to provide tax neutrality.
  • Profits in Islamic transactions to be treated similar to interest in conventional financing.
  • Islamic financial instruments are essentially constituted by sale, purchase, lease and investment instead of lending and borrowing.
Tax legislations must recognize these types of sale and treat them similarly to conventional instruments.
	• For Investors, MIFC provides tax exemption and withholding tax exemption on profit received by non-residents investing Islamic securities approved by Securities Commn.
	• Stamp Duty exemptions – 20% exemption on instruments used in Islamic financing.
	• Stamp Duty exemptions for all instruments relating to the issue of, offer for subscription of, or invitation to subscribe to Islamic securities approved by SC.

Figure 12.4   Incentives for Islamic sukuk *securities investors*

Besides these fundamental principles that apply to Islamic financial transactions, there is also the vexing problem of lack of consensus on experts on some aspects of *sukuk* securitization. Should or should not a *sukuk* be tradable? If traded, is it legal to trade away from par value? These and a few other issues are still unsettled despite the fact, or perhaps because of the fact, that this industry has a very short history, having had no time to time-test principles and practices.

In addition to the above, further parties involved are: the issuing entity, which in most cases is the government or agencies of the government or private companies. The issuer has certain expectations for the issue, the payments to the payee, and so on. These are to be solved objectively, for example by discussion, as well as through market-making processes needed to pre-discover prices before the issue is approved and sold to the investing public. Finally, investors form the most important group in this form of contract.

These investors are motivated to first of all have a higher yield than they could get in conventional bond markets in so far as the terms of *sukuk* are expected to provide a premium over conventional bond markets. This is a tricky area since benchmarking what is relevant yardstick can be tricky especially in public issues more so than in private issues not involving an exchange listing.

As is evident from the information in Figure 12.4, there are certain tax law changes that ensure that Islamic banking is given the same level playing field as conventional banking. One significant legislation is the stamp duty exemption which means that in the case of certain products, Islamic banking products get to apply stamp duty on a par with conventional products. In fact, this is the main stumbling block for entry of Islamic banking in most Western-law-based tax regimes.

12.4 *SUKUK* SECURITIZATION PROCESS

Figure 12.5 is a schematic diagram of the securitization process for issuing an Islamic *sukuk* security in Malaysia. What this depicts is a complex case where the time to complete an issue may be as long as a year or more, as in this case. The average time to issue and listing is estimated as reported in another chapter to be about 140 days. One important thing to note is the role of *shari'ah* intervention in the issue process. That ensures the ethical bases of product designs.

It is easy to identify the milestones of an issue process as depicted in Figure 12.5. The appointment of a merchant banker by a client is the first step that starts the process. Our studies of this process show that it takes about 14 weeks from this step to the completion of the issuance when an issue gets listed and traded in Malaysia: this is considered too long compared with the time taken in conventional bond issues. Shortening the time

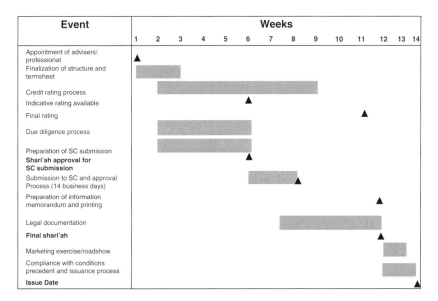

Figure 12.5   Securitization process applied to Islamic financial products, Malaysia

needed has been identified as an urgent priority, so the AAOFI has come up with a prototype agreement to speed up the process. The second step is the setting of terms of the underwriting arrangement with the client.

Once this formality is over, the client knows the fee involved, and the terms of the contract for the issuance: the fee is about 2–4 per cent of the issue value. The third activity is a bundle of activities relating to the rating of the issuer, which is essentially the establishment of the credit standing of the issuer regarding the issuing company's ability to service the funding via the SPC. The fourth activity is the most important one, relating to due diligence that will lead to the Information Memorandum and application to the SC.

The fifth activity relates to the set of activities needed for *shari'ah* approval as part of submission to the SC. As remarked earlier, this is an area which is still evolving in definition, standards and also guidelines for decisions, so much so that this part of the process may have greater risk than other parts of the process. The next two steps are the final ones. With the due diligence done, and *shari'ah* work completed along with the rating decision resulting in a grade being assigned to the issuer, the arranger is in a position to first consult the client as to the application that will be made to the SC for the issue. Here some degree of consultation and education takes place between the two parties in order to bring the arranger and the issuer to agree on the specifics of the application as determined by the two parties. Some compromises are made, and a decision is made on all outstanding problems relating to the issue. The final stage is the SC approval leading to the listing of the issue (if it is a public issue).

The arranger undertakes the important step of launching a marketing programme to ensure that the issue is well publicized, attracts the attention of likely investors, and the book-making process is carefully done to price the issue correctly. Upon appointment of advisors and professional parties, the next step includes the finalization of the structure and term-sheet. The arranger(s), with advice from the *Shari'ah* Adviser, will be responsible for advising on the suitable *sukuk* structure based on the approved *shari'ah* principles to best suit the underlying nature of the financing and commercial requirement of the transaction. Another factor to be considered in structuring a *sukuk* would be the nature of the issuer's business activities. The nature of the business will dictate the kind of assets that will be suitable for the SPC to hold. A financial institution issuing a *sukuk* will have securities and not real assets to back the SPC, just as a property firm may have rentable properties that could be income-producing to service the loan so the property is likely to be attached to the SPC. Also, the latter type of firm would find an *ijara*-type security more suitable than a *musharaka sukuk*.

Islamic banking and finance comprise many types of activities: banking, asset management, *sukuk* market, and so on. Similarly, in the Islamic debt

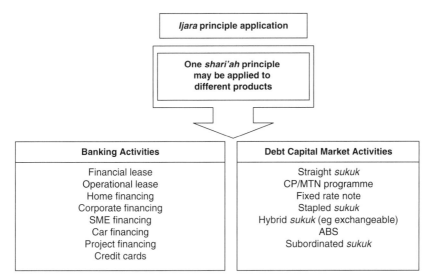

Figure 12.6   Shari'ah *principles are flexible in application*

capital market there are straight, hybrid and stapled *sukuk*, for example. A singular *shari'ah* principle such as the one applied to *ijara* can be used to facilitate various activities and is not just for leasing activities, this is as illustrated in Figure 12.6. As is evident, there are several types of *ijara* contracts that come under the broader principle of *ijara* contracting.

Figure 12.6 is an illustration of how a single principle of leasing as in *ijara* can be used to design different securities under *shari'ah*-consistent design. For example, the *ijara* principle establishes that a set of assets in the SPC can be used to service the loan with regular (despite the incomes of the SPC being not exactly equal to the) pay-off to investors as well as pay the terminal payment of the loan from the SPC assets. This can be used to design capital market securities for trading, much as a bank may use the same principle to provide housing loans at one end of the product design to small and medium enterprise financing. This versatility is often not explained in the popular press, which tends to give an impression that the Islamic securities are rather staid instruments; but they are not at all.

12.5   A CASE: GUTHRIE RAISING US$150 MILLION

In this section, we highlight one issue as a case for illustration purposes. It is the Guthrie Corporation issue of an *ijara sukuk* for US$150 million: see Figure 12.7.

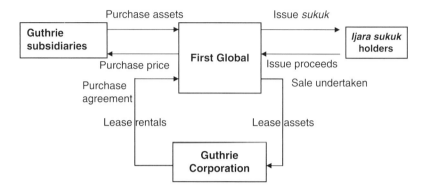

Figure 12.7   The case of Guthrie Corporation sukuk *issue for US$150 million*

First Stage: First Global *Sukuk* Inc. (First Global) purchased plantation lands (assets) from Guthrie's subsidiaries and issued *sukuk* to evidence the *sukuk* holders' undivided beneficial ownership in the assets. First Global paid the purchase price to Guthrie's subsidiaries with proceeds from the *sukuk* holders, the investors who would obtain the proceeds less the fee. First Global leased the assets to Guthrie and in return received lease rentals. Guthrie issued an undertaking to purchase the assets under certain events at a predetermined exercise price. First Global issued an undertaking to sell the assets. This process conforms with the Islamic securitization requiring ownership of assets of a borrower before the loan can be made.

This is how the Special Purpose Company was formed to facilitate the passing of assets of subsidiaries of Guthrie to the SPC. Once this was done, this contract went one step further to engage the borrower to agree to purchase the assets at a pre-agreed price that would equal the loan proceeds for repayment purpose, at the maturity time of the debt. This is the First Stage of the issuance at the time of origination.

The *Second Stage* involves the servicing of the loan agreement. In this stage, there are periodic payments (pay-off as termed in this book) to be made to the security holders. First Global paid the purchase price to Guthrie's subsidiaries with proceeds from the *sukuk* holders. First Global leased the assets to Guthrie and in return received lease rentals. Guthrie issued an undertaking to purchase the assets under certain events at a predetermined exercise price. First Global issued an undertaking to sell the assets.

In *Stage Three*, matters relating to liquidation of the debt are dealt with. On maturity, Guthrie purchased the asset from First Global.

Guthrie made a payment on the residual amount to First Global. First Global distributed the proceeds to *sukuk* holders. That is, the agreement by Guthrie to purchase the assets at a predetermined price was now activated, so that the sum of money was then paid off to the investors to redeem the loan. What has this achieved? This is a neat arrangement to pay back (under *ijara*) a sum exactly equal to the funding at the start of the loan agreement. Other arrangements could also be designed: for example, instead of periodic payments at regular intervals (a matter bond investors are used to in conventional lending, so this design is attractive) the agreement could be to pay the loan and a sum based on a certain profit share of the rental proceeds at the terminal period. In the latter case, the contract will not be a standard *ijara*, but then it is equally possible to vary the pay-offs to suit the income patterns of the firm that seeks the loan.

12.6   CONCLUSION

This chapter provides an introduction to the actual securitization process in structuring Islamic financial products. The investment banking process has been adapted to this purpose with additional features relating to adherence to principles that are unique to the structuring of Islamic products. We have noted how in practice (i) firms provide ownership to part of the assets of a firm securing the loan while also (ii) ensuring pay-offs to suit the particular income streams of the debtor; and (iii) how the maturity payment is paid off to the fund providers through a pre-agreed sale agreement.

The *sukuk* markets have now come of age with very large funds being raised in Malaysia and elsewhere. The expertise needed for securitization comes mainly from the investment banking laws and practices already in place in most financial centres. Adding the laws necessary to enable Islamic financial entities to operate on a level playing field with the conventional entities is a first step in starting to make a *sukuk* market feasible in any location. As already noted in another part of the book, the market is growing at 20 per cent per annum, and it is projected to grow even faster when more developing countries learn to organize *sukuk* markets to tap local and regional capital to develop infrastructure and to assist small and medium enterprises to create jobs to expand their economies. The Islamic Development Bank, as shown in another chapter, is providing specific help with funds for this purpose, which is an admirable role in the development of poorer countries.

NOTE

1. This chapter is based on information provided by Mr Shamsun A. Hussein, an indus-
    try professional, who presented the paper at the Dubai International Financial Centre
    Symposium. The paper was drafted, then edited and finalized with his permission to use
    the information presented at the time the paper was presented. He declined to have his
    name included for reason(s) not revealed to us; we wrote the first draft of this chapter and
    showed it to him before getting his permission to include it in this book.

13. The role of IDB in Islamic capital market development

Salman Syed Ali Khan

13.1 INTRODUCTION

The unstated but significant hallmark of Islamic capital market development is to keep finance relevant to economic activities to maintain justice and fair play for all members of the society. By avoiding financial transactions based on a pre-agreed interest rate, unnecessary risk-taking by following the principle of *gharar* and by adherence to certain fair trade and exchange rules, Islamic finance provides a means for orderly financial contracting. The development and smooth functioning of Islamic capital and money markets depend on the sustained efforts of all the stakeholders in an economy as in conventional finance. Thus, private business firms and financial institutions, governments and multilateral financial organizations as well as individual savers, the investors, all have important roles to play in their respective contexts.

The Islamic Development Bank (IDB), which is a multilateral development finance institution, is actively contributing towards the orderly development of Islamic capital markets at national and international levels. To understand the role of the IDB in the development of Islamic capital markets, it would be useful first to know the IDB and its mission while understanding the issues and challenges in Islamic capital market development. Development banking uses *sukuk*-type instruments in its multilateral financial activities, so a discussion of IDB in a book on *sukuk* is relevant just as it is appropriate to cover other forms of market-making for *sukuk* securities in this book.

Therefore, in section 13.2 we provide a brief introduction to the IDB: its purpose and mission. Section 13.3 highlights issues and challenges to orderly development of Islamic capital markets. Then section 13.4 describes the role played by the IDB in the development of such markets locally and internationally through its initiatives to create new products, establish support institutions, conduct research, and provide policy advice.

13.2 INTRODUCTION TO THE ISLAMIC DEVELOPMENT BANK

The Islamic Development Bank is a development finance institution created for the purpose of fostering economic development and social progress of its 56 member countries and Muslim communities in non-member countries in conformity with the *shari'ah*. The IDB has been in operation since 1975 and currently has 56 countries as its member countries, ranging from the Middle East, Africa, Asia, the Asia Pacific region, and also from South America. More than 1.5 billion[1] people live in this group of countries, accounting for one quarter of the world's population.

However, the real gross domestic product (GDP) of this group constitutes only 6 per cent of world output, although in purchasing power parity terms, it is about double this ratio.[2] Most of these countries fall in the categories of developing or least developed countries. On the positive side there exists much diversity across these countries in terms of education, population, products, income, and financial sector development.

Against this backdrop the mission of the IDB is noble but colossal, as it is 'committed to alleviating poverty; promoting human development, science and technology, Islamic banking and finance; and enhancing cooperation amongst member countries, in collaboration with its development partners.'

To accomplish its mission and provide development financing, the IDB makes use of a variety of means. Most commonly it uses project finance, loans and technical assistance aimed at development of basic infrastructure, education, healthcare and other social sector institutions as well as agriculture and industrial sectors. It uses trade finance to enhance intra-trade among OIC (Organisation of Islamic Countries) nations. It also supports the private sector through separate affiliate entities like the Islamic Corporation for Development of Private Sector (ICD), Islamic Trade Finance Corporation (ITFC), and Islamic Corporation for the Insurance of Investment and Export Credit (ICIEC). The IDB also provides equity investment and lines of financing for the development of Islamic financial sector institutions. Support for research and development of Islamic economics, finance and banking as academic disciplines and as practicable alternatives is provided through the Islamic Research and Training Institute (IRTI). The Institute also takes care of the capacity building of member countries towards macroeconomic development through various training programmes.

To do all this, the IDB has limited financial resources relative to its needs but it possesses a vast strength in the form of firm commitment of its staff to the noble cause and obtains determined support from its member countries. Continuing progress of the institution over the last 35 years testifies to this statement. The authorized capital of the IDB stood at 30 billion Islamic Dinars (equivalent to US$45 billion) in 2009, up from 2 billion Islamic Dinars at its inception in 1975. The subscribed capital and paid-in capital in 2009 stood at 15.86 billion and 3.6 billion Islamic Dinars (US$22.5 billion and US$5.4 billion) respectively.[3] In addition the independent affiliated entities of the IDB Group such as the ICD, ITFC and ICIEC have their own capital.

The total development related exposure of the bank at present is approximately US$5.3 billion, which is diversified across 56 member countries with project financing constituting about 67 per cent and trade financing about 32 per cent of development assistance. The most commonly used modes of financing employed by the IDB in its operations are: leasing, instalment sale, *istisna* (pre-manufacturing of equipment and civil works financing or pre-shipment export financing), equity participation, lines of financing to Islamic financial institutions, and loans. By using Islamic financing modes in its operations the bank not only helps in socio-economic development but also contributes to the development of Islamic finance in general.

In fact, existence of a vibrant and developing Islamic finance sector will contribute in many ways to improve and scale up the size of the IDB's development financing operations. It will help in further resource mobilization, increasing the access to finance, and will contribute to broad-based inclusive economic growth of its member countries. In this context development of Islamic capital markets at national and international levels and introduction of new capital market products and instruments are quite important for resource mobilization by IDB as well as by its member countries to promote long-term economic and social sector development.

13.3   ISSUES IN CAPITAL MARKET DEVELOPMENT

Capital markets provide the opportunity to fund long-term projects through a variety of long and medium-term funding instruments. Tradability of these instruments provides an exit opportunity, thus attracting short-term investors as well to enter what is in essence a long-term investment market. Ideally these markets exist to directly link the fund-surplus units with fund-deficit units, thus it channels savings into economically productive investments. However, the reality is that these markets do not exist in a developed form in many of the IDB member countries. Moreover, where they exist, whether in developing or the developed countries, they can be misused if not properly guided. The inception and development of capital markets require time, effort, and an environment of trust and security conducive to promoting investment and spurring economic activity. Not only is the legal framework and rule of law important in this context but often some credible entity has to take a lead by moving in first and launching some products. This will boost the confidence of others and help in the building of trust and hence a market in those products.

The role of the government and that of the big firms becomes crucial here, as their active support can ease the creation of such markets. Similarly, proper functioning of these markets requires development of a society-wide willingness to take economic risks, and adherence to ethics so essential to well-functioning Islamic financial contracting, which induces internal controls and formation of appropriate regulations that provide external control. These elements ensure that the capital markets will serve the cause of economic development and may not be used only for speculative purposes.

At present, there are four main challenging issues in the development of Islamic capital markets at the national level of member countries as well as at the international level. These are: (1) creation of a wide range of Islamic financial products; (2) creation of an appropriate legal and regulatory framework along with the political will to implement it; (3) creation of supportive infrastructure institutions; (4) general enhancement of social and political stability. Additionally, introduction of fixed income products and the creation of a market in them will require: (a) development of trust; (b) initiative by the governments; and (c) initiatives by international and national level financial institutions. We will briefly discuss these issues before highlighting the role of the IDB in the development of Islamic capital markets.

A wide range of products are needed to complete the market. 'Completing the market' is a technical term reflecting the situation when it is possible for offered securities to span across various risk-and-return profiles and to achieve various maturity levels (see Figure 13.1).

This can be done by combining independent and distinct characteristic financial products. Therefore, increasing the diversity of financial products is important. However, increasing the number and quantity of similar products is also useful to achieve more liquidity and accessibility for investors.

The Islamic financial asset classes, which are easily available at present to the investors, range from private equity with long maturity and high returns, to demand deposits which have the shortest maturity and no returns, as in the case of current (checking) accounts. The class of assets such as shares, real estate and investment deposits lie in between these

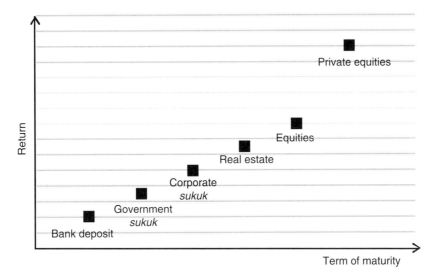

Figure 13.1   Completing the market, a schema

two categories. Fixed income Islamic securities such as *ijara* (lease-type) *sukuk* and other more complex types of *sukuk* are few and far between. Introduction of such products would contribute both towards greater spanning and more liquidity.

Another challenge for a well-functioning Islamic capital market is to create an appropriate *legal and regulatory framework along with a strong political and societal willingness to implement it.* The existing regulatory frameworks governing the capital markets in most of the IDB member countries are such that when they allow trade in shares they also allow interest-based securities, provide better protection to interest-based transactions, allow short sales, options and futures contracts, and also tolerate trading rules that are repugnant to *shari'ah.* This is a challenge faced in the present phase of development under the dual systems found within which Islamic finance is operated. Though most of the existing rules and regulations for the conventional capital market products will be equally applicable to Islamic capital market products, some changes and fine tuning will be required for Islamic products. Moreover, financial markets have become interdependent and internationally linked, therefore the regulatory changes suited to Islamic capital markets need to be recognized across regulatory jurisdictions and even in the conventional financial markets.

Rules without the power to implement them are pointless. While it is true that development of appropriate laws and regulations promote the financial sector and capital market growth, the laws that lack enforcement and resolve of the political authorities to enforce lose their effect. This was as true in ancient Rome as it is true today.[4] Development of Islamic capital markets therefore requires a strong resolve by the governments and regulatory authorities of the countries to make the change, given the fact that the conventional regulatory framework and the conventional financial system are strongly entrenched. Hence continuous advocacy, policy advice to governments along with creating awareness among finance professionals and the public at large are quite important to create good understanding and the necessary will for the change.

Appropriate supportive infrastructure institutions are a must to facilitate Islamic capital markets to further reduce structuring and transaction costs. Every system creates its own institutions and develops its own culture of doing business. The culture it creates helps perpetuate the system itself. Compare kingdoms with democracies; compare capitalism with socialism; this fact underlies their differences and is responsible for their continuation over time until some significant change occurs through evolution or revolution.

In the present-day capital markets it is much easier to finance purchase of stocks through interest-based borrowing than through profit-sharing arrangements. It has become easier to sell securities that one does not own than to own and then resell, which is required under Islamic finance. It has become cheaper and simpler to lend and then securitize the loan portfolio than to invest and securitize the real assets. In such situation, creation of a supportive infrastructure is a must in order to develop a vibrant and growing Islamic capital market. This infrastructure will be in various forms such as: creation of an appropriate legal framework along with the establishment of institutions such as *shari'ah* courts; development of appropriate regulatory and supervisory principles, rules and processes along with the establishment of powerful regulatory and supervisory bodies to implement them; standardization of accounting conventions for Islamic transactions; creation of information processing institutions similar to credit bureaux but that produce business competency and trust ratings; trading platforms that ensure completion of trade in full-form before securities are re-traded.

Conflict resolution mechanisms are needed along with arbitration institutions and banking tribunals to resolve business disputes quickly if they arise. Most importantly, creation of a large number of education as well as training institutions are needed to develop human resources at all levels and to bring out trained manpower in Islamic economics, finance, *shari'ah* and other related subjects and practices.

Political stability, removal of abject poverty and security are preconditions for development of trade as well as for the development of capital markets. Many IDB member countries suffer from internal or external conflicts, poor governance, as well as natural disasters that are leading to political instability, poverty, social disharmony or all of them together. This situation is itself a hindrance in the development of Islamic finance in general and in the development of Islamic capital markets in particular.

13.4   ROLE OF THE IDB IN DEVELOPMENT OF ISLAMIC CAPITAL MARKETS

The IDB has taken several initiatives within the scope of its mission and operations to develop Islamic finance in general and to develop Islamic capital markets in particular. On the products side several initiatives were taken to introduce new *sukuk*. These *sukuk* were launched both for resource mobilization for the IDB's development assistance programmes as well as for its treasury management purposes which will go a long way towards building the market by encouraging flotation of *sukuk* by many other players.

On the institutional development side, the IDB has taken initiatives and helped in the creation and workings of various important infrastructure institutions to enhance growth of Islamic finance. On the research frontier, it constantly generates new thinking and creates a network of researchers, scholars and practitioners to continuously contribute towards the development of Islamic finance and capital markets. Through the IRTI it organizes research conferences, orientation and training courses, as well as publishing research papers, books, monographs and reports. Through cooperation between the IRTI and other departments of the IDB it is contributing in industry events to create awareness and coordinate the efforts of various entities. On the policy side, the IDB is playing an active role in providing guidance to the private sector as well as to its member country governments.

13.4.1   Products

Traditionally the IDB's development finance activities were funded from its shareholders' equity. However, anticipating the increasing requirements of the IDB's development assistance needs to its member countries and in order to scale up its operations, it entered into capital markets in 2003 when the first IDB *sukuk* was launched. Since then it has issued several *sukuk* to mobilize resources. The debut *sukuk* of IDB issued in 2003 was an *ijara*-based *sukuk* where the underlying assets were a portfolio of IDB investments, the majority of which comprise *ijara* and *istisna* agreements with a small portion being based on *murabaha* receivables. This was the first *sukuk* of its kind, at the time reflecting a portfolio mixture of different types of assets against which the *sukuk* were issued. The term to maturity of this debut *sukuk* was five years, with semi-annual payments with a fixed rate of return of 3.625 per cent per annum. This *sukuk* was planned to be issued only to raise about US$300 million. However, due to its high demand it was oversubscribed and hence the actual issue size was raised to US$400 million.

Given the AAA credit rating of the IDB and its wide sovereign share-holder base, the *sukuk* issuance by the IDB can not only facilitate fund mobilization for the bank itself but it also has the potential to raise funds from international markets for its member countries at lower capital costs than would be possible for individual members themselves. This credit enhancement possibility has not been utilized so far.

Another innovation to the *sukuk* products by the IDB was the creation of Medium Term Note (MTN) *sukuk* issue. *Sukuk* generally require long documentation, execution of a large number of contracts, implementation of procedures, and marketing for each issue. All this is costly and raises cost of issuance per *sukuk* issue. Instead of this, if a standing set of documentation and contracts can be finalized at the outset, and medium-term *sukuk* are issued in small tranches as and when they are needed, it will be more cost effective and also provide flexibility in size, issuance and rate. This is the crux of the MTN programme. In 2005 IDB established a US$1.0 billion MTN programme, which was increased to a US$1.5 billion MTN programme in 2009. The first issue under the MTN programme was made in 2005, and US$500 million were raised from the market. This issue provided semi-annual payments to its holders on a floating rate, 6-month LIBOR plus 12 bps (0.12 per cent). The issue had a five-year maturity which ended in July 2010.

The second issue under the same MTN programme was made for US$850 million in 2009. This issue had a tenor of five years with a fixed rate of 3.172 per cent per annum on a semi-annual payment for the *sukuk* holders. A swap of the fixed rate into floating rate of 6-month LIBOR plus 31.5 bps (basis points) was made immediately after allocation, which was geared towards risk management. There were several objectives in addition to mobilization of resources that IDB tried to meet with this issuance.

While funds of US$850 million were raised to meet the operational needs of the IDB, a tighter pricing was also achieved within the market conditions and the pricing differential between IDB *sukuk* and other supranational papers was also narrowed. Another objective was to obtain a wider geographical distribution of *sukuk* over a diversified investor base.

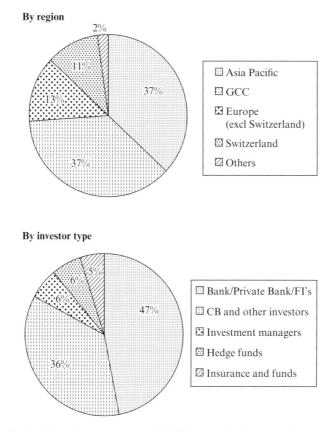

Figure 13.2   Distribution of second MTN tranche by region/investor type

This was also achieved as the *sukuk* was picked up 57 per cent in Asia Pacific; 37 per cent in GCC; 13 per cent in Europe (excluding Switzerland); 11 per cent in Switzerland; and 2 per cent in other regions.

By investor type 47 per cent of the issue was bought by banks and other private financial institutions, 36 per cent by central banks and other investors, while 6, 6 and 5 per cent respectively was picked up by investment managers, hedge funds, and insurance funds. Figure 13.2 shows the distribution of this second NTM tranche (2009), whereas Figure 13.3 gives geographical distribution of the IDB's debut *sukuk* (2003).

In addition to the US dollar-denominated *sukuk*, the IDB has also issued *sukuk* in the local currency. In this regard two tranches of Malaysian Ringgit *sukuk* were issued (RM300 million or US$99 million) in 2008 and (RM100 million) in 2009 amounting to a total of RM400 million under a

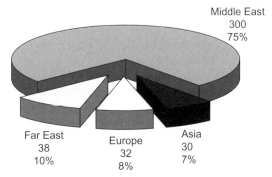

IDB's debut *sukuk*
(Total Allocation - US$400 Million)

Middle East
300
75%

Far East
38
10%

Europe
32
8%

Asia
30
7%

Figure 13.3   Distribution of IDB 2003 sukuk *and first MTN 2005 tranche*

RM1000 million *sukuk* programme in Malaysia. In 2010, this local currency MTN programme was also listed on Bursa Malaysia under exempt regime (that is, it is listed but not exchange traded).

The listing represents further support from the IDB Group for the Islamic finance market. It is also an example of close collaboration that IDB maintains with many regulators and local banks for the development of Islamic capital markets. In the present case the listing involved close collaboration between Bank Negara Malaysia, Securities Commission Malaysia and Bursa Malaysia. Another local currency issue made by the IDB was in Singapore dollars; it was a SDG200 million private placement transaction in Singapore under the US$1.5 billion MTN programme.

These efforts of launching innovative *sukuk* on a regular basis, denominated in international as well as local currencies, with an effort to diversify across investor types and geographical regions are expected to contribute to the development of the Islamic capital market not only through the products introduced by the IDB, but by encouraging other players to take an active role and bring about more products that will further develop the market.

13.4.2 Infrastructure Institutions

Another important role played by the IDB in the development of Islamic finance in general and for capital markets in particular is that it facilitated and promoted the creation of various infrastructure institutions at international level. It provides continuing support to these institutions for their work through participating on their boards, providing technical assistance, and at times also funding their activities. Prominent among such institutions that were created under the lead role of the IDB are the Accounting and Auditing Organization for Islamic Financial Institutions (AAOIFI), International Islamic Financial Market (IIFM), Liquidity Management Centre (LMC), Islamic Financial Services Board (IFSB), International Islamic Rating Agency (IIRA), and Arbitration Centre.

Each of these infrastructure institutions is supporting the Islamic finance industry in important ways. The AAOIFI takes the lead in developing accounting, auditing and governance standards for Islamic financial institutions and for their products. It also brings out ethics and *shari'ah* standards for such products and financial contracts. To date the AAOIFI has brought out 23 accounting, five auditing and six governance standards. It has also published two codes of ethics and 30 *shari'ah* standards that serve the Islamic finance industry in general.

However, quite a few of these standards are directly relevant to capital market products and transactions, particularly those that relate to *ijara* and other types of *sukuk*, *istisna* and tradable securities. The AAOIFI also helps in developing professionals for the Islamic financial services industry through professional certification programmes in its standards. Another institution, the IIFM, was created to develop Islamic capital markets at international level and increase coordination between financial markets of the member countries. This institution has also contributed in increasing the awareness of Islamic capital market issues, and recently endeavored to create standardized master agreements for tradable financial and hedging products.

The Liquidity Management Centre, LMC, was created to help solve the short-term access liquidity problem faced by many Islamic banks. The LMC brought out various tradable as well as non-tradable instruments for liquidity management. However, to date it has achieved only limited success. Another institution, the Islamic Financial Services Board, brings together banking sector regulators (central banks) as well as the capital market regulators of various countries to harmonize regulations of the Islamic financial sector across countries and to help develop the banks and financial markets in a stable way.

Rating of financial products and of the issuing institutions is quite important in making a market in tradable securities. The International Islamic Rating Agency (IIRA) was created for this purpose to incorporate credit as well as *shari'ah* and ethical issues in its rating criteria. Amicable and swift resolution of any dispute is quite important for the efficient functioning of financial markets. The cross-jurisdictional nature of the parties and the cross-border nature of transactions in capital markets involving different legal systems, *shari'ah* and conventional laws pose a problem.

The International Islamic Centre for Reconciliation and Arbitration (IICRA) was created to avoid costly litigation in various courts and to help in arriving at a negotiated resolution of financial and commercial disputes that may arise between financial and commercial institutions or between them and their clients.

13.4.3   Research and Training

The Islamic Research and Training Institute (IRTI) is an independent entity of the IDB Group responsible for extending the frontiers of knowledge in Islamic economics and finance. It also provides training services to develop capacities of IDB member countries in economic development, alleviation of poverty and establishment of Islamic finance. It also serves as a data and resource centre in these areas. The IDB, through the IRTI, is furthering research and capacity-building in Islamic capital markets, which is one of its areas of focus. Numerous seminars, papers and workshops addressing financial products for Islamic capital markets have been completed, resulting in many innovative yet practical ideas.

For example, the concept of *ijara sukuk* first appeared in one of the papers by an IRTI researcher in the late 1980s and in IRTI conference proceedings during the early 1990s. The Institute had conducted some pioneering research in Islamic financial products and markets in the past. In recent years, IRTI has produced several works on Islamic capital market products, market development and regulation.

It has conducted two major conferences on Islamic capital markets, one in Jakarta and one in London, and a few smaller workshops with IIFM in Bahrain, Karachi and Kuala Lumpur on *sukuk* products. Involvement of outside researchers, practitioners and *shari'ah* scholars creates a strong and growing network of interested individuals and institutions who keep the torch of knowledge and research alight. In addition, the IDB through the IRTI is also contributing to dissemination of knowledge and delivery of training in Islamic finance. A number of these training programmes and awareness seminars have addressed *sukuk*, other tradable Islamic financial products, and capital market development issues.

13.4.4   Policy Advice

Helping member countries in formulating their policies for Islamic financial sector development, including the development of Islamic capital markets and their products is an important aspect of the IDB's work. For example, in the recent past, a 'Ten-Year Master Plan Framework for Development of Islamic Financial Services Industry' was prepared by the

IRTI and IDB in cooperation with many member countries and multilateral development finance institutions. One important aspect of the Ten-Year Framework was to provide stages for the development of Islamic capital markets, taking into account the fact that different member countries are at different levels of financial sophistication and varying states of economic development.

The recent financial crisis in 2007–08 also provided the IDB with an opportunity to present a case for Islamic finance including Islamic capital markets, both to a Muslim and non-Muslim audience in member as well as non-member countries. The stability features inherent in the Islamic system tend to appeal to all audiences as they became receptive to new ideas after the crisis.

Recently, the IDB through IRTI and its other entities has provided policy advice to a few member countries on issuance of *sukuk*. It has made presentations to their parliamentarians, regulators and finance professionals to increase their awareness and answer questions. These policy dialogues and awareness seminars go a long way towards creating the necessary will for development of Islamic capital markets. Without the existence of a strong will among the political leaders and economic managers of the countries, Islamic capital markets will develop only slowly.

The last of the requirements for Islamic capital market development are political stability, improved governance and sustained economic growth. This we hope will come with time, with the efforts of the general public and with the interplay of a large number of factors, including a conscious following of Islam. The overall economic development agenda followed by the IDB for its members including the use of *awqaf* and *zakah* as tools for poverty alleviation should bear fruit.

NOTES

1. As of 2008 data reported in *Key Socio-Economic Statistics on IDB Member Countries*, Statistical Monograph No. 30, IDB (2010).
2. As of 2008 data the total real GDP of IDB member countries amounted to US$2.4 trillion, reported in *Key Socio-Economic Statistics on IDB Member Countries*, Statistical Monograph No. 30, IDB (2010).
3. IDB (2010), *Islamic Development Bank: 36 Years in Service of Development*.
4. Ulrike Malmendier (2009), 'Law and Finance "at the Origin"', *Journal of Economic Literature*, **47**(4), 1076–108.

14. Prospects and challenges of developing *sukuk* Islamic debt markets around the world

Mohamed Ariff, Munawar Iqbal and Shamsher Mohamad

14.1 INTRODUCTION

The *sukuk* securities or Islamic asset-backed debt securities truly started to be offered in organized markets as publicly listed instruments only in 2000, so at the time of writing it is a 12-year-old market. There is a record of its first private issue in 1978 in Saudi Arabia, after an article in *Islamic Economic Studies* some years earlier had suggested this instrument to be a suitable and safe debt instrument with safeguards for investors and being consistent with ethics long since forgotten in issuing debt instruments in past Islamic empires. It has since been widely accepted as an Islamic financial product for debt-raising with one important principle, namely asset ownership of part of the assets of a borrower which gives this instrument asset backing, a unique feature in debt markets. Historical reference to *sukuk* is found in the records of the Abbasid Empire established in circa 900 soon after Islam spread to the Byzantine region in what is known today as Jordan, Iraq, Palestine and Syria.

The *sukuk* instrument has in the contemporary period become an ethics-based Islamic financial instrument already issued either as private issues or as public issues in some 12 locations as at 2010, to provide both short- and long-term funding arrangements. Four more financial centres are actively putting together reforms as at 2011 to start markets for issues of this new instrument. In terms of *sukuk* market size, Malaysia has particularly emerged as the major player with international interest in raising large sums of money in a manner different from that of conventional debt market. Bahrain, though it has about 5 per cent of the same market by value, is none the less the second Islamic finance hub if the presence of other Islamic financial institutions in Bahrain are taken into account. In just a decade, therefore, the total *sukuk* issue of nearly 2000 cases amounts to US$1200 billion, or just under 2 per cent of the international bond market issues: see BIS source cited in Chapter 2.

Broader press reports suggest that this market is growing at an annual rate of 20 per cent, while the conventional bond market is not growing at more than 5 per cent per year. In fact issues of conventional bonds and *sukuk* declined significantly during 2007–2009 during the Global Financial Crisis. From the comments of some of the contributors to this book, it appears that the room for growth in this market is to be found mainly in the 56 Muslim majority countries and in international hubs such as the UK, Switzerland, Hong Kong, Singapore and so forth, where private issues by high net worth investors and governments are driving the growth because of the reputational quality of these centres lending credibility to issue quality.

If the GDP share of such Muslim-majority countries is taken as about 13 per cent of the world GDP in PPP terms, it is possible to suggest that the room for future development of this market is to be found in the less banked and less securitized centres in North Africa, the Middle East, Central, South and South-East Asia. The future prospects will be from harnessing the savings of Muslim populations for funding development in each of the 56 Muslim majority nations. This would also require transaction costs to be lowered, the financial infrastructure to become more efficient, and the returns to investors to be higher than they are at present during this early phase of building the market. These issues have been documented, in particular the current high yield in *sukuk* securities compared to identically rated conventional bond markets.

In this chapter we examine the prospects for this predicted growth in section 14.2. The issues confronting this market are discussed in section 14.3. The chapter ends with comments on important issues confronting the *sukuk* as a special Islamic debt financing instrument as well as a special type of equity instrument to raise entrepreneurial capital.

14.2 PROSPECTS

The most commonly-structured *sukuk* debt instrument is the *bai bithaman ajjal mudaraba* or BBA, which dominates as the most popular issue in Malaysia. This *sukuk* instrument has the normal structural features – finite period, profit-share, SPC, and so on – but it provides pay-offs at regular intervals at a *constant growth* rate starting as a normal annuity payment from the first period. It is asset-based, but not necessarily asset-backed (an important issue that has been just resolved with new rulings) and is also traded in exchange markets. Available statistics suggest that there is a great deal of interest in this instrument, which is being fine-tuned to be consistent with the AAOFI regulations after the 2008 notice of possible violation of some principles, in particular the need for asset-backing rights of the lenders.

The other popular security is the *ijara sukuk*, which derives its pay-off as fixed payments (similar to the conventional bonds) at regular intervals with pay-off of the original sum borrowed at the maturity period (see Chapter 12 for a case) so it is akin to the lease payments in conventional leases. Available statistics suggests that this is the most dominant instrument in Bahrain. Issues in Dubai are mainly Islamic products, whereas in Malaysia there is a vibrant conventional bond market that exists side by side with the *sukuk* debt market: see Ariff, Cheng and Neo (2009).[1] There are four more instruments that are issued, but these form a minor portion of the *sukuk* markets.

The prospect for growth of these two popular and the other four less popular specialized securities is good. For example, private corporation issues, which dominate the BBA and *ijara* issued by both governments and private firms, are mostly tradable issues in exchanges, and are more appealing to investors for one good reason. The *yields are higher* than in the similarly-rated conventional bonds by an amount ranging from 20 basis points to about 200 basis points in some cases. These instruments are also easier to track since the pay-offs are, though legally not fixed, predictable with less uncertainty even at the maturity value since that too is *fixed* (a point of continuing debate) in most cases. In the BBA, the pay-offs grow at constant rates, and in the *ijara*, the pay-offs are received as fixed cash flows. These two instruments are likely to be attractive fund-raising instruments at this early stage of the *sukuk* debt market development. Given the 12-year history, investors need instruments that are very close to those of conventional bonds for them to have confidence.

Use of this market to raise public finance is also increasing, but not as fast as the demand by private firms. That this instrument is ideal for securing domestic debt by giving *ownership of state assets to the public* via the SPC at the time of issue of the instruments is an attractive idea to raise vast sums of money from the public for projects that benefit the public while also providing incomes to the savers. Note that the savers placing their savings in bank savings accounts earn just about two-thirds of returns compared to returns achieving after placing them in *sukuk* instruments. First, *sukuk* instruments avoid currency risk in sovereign debt issued in foreign currencies, so they are less risky. This is especially true in the post-Breton Woods era from 1973, and since 2011, given the worldwide revulsion for sovereign debt raised without reference to the ability of the states to have sufficient incomes to service the loans: the debate on overhang of sovereign debt has been raging across the world since October 2010. Second, the public has a stake in the assets of the government so they would be less reluctant to finance the government, expenditures as such expenditures would benefit the very same people.

Look around the Muslim countries, where there is too much foreign borrowing while infrastructure demands are still high, yet this new instrument is ideal for raising the money needed instead of raising taxes to do the job. But little is known about how in historical periods this instrument was used to raise public finance: some reference is found in Chapter 5, though specific details of how much and for what purposes are not yet researched. So there is a need for a search of the archives in Arabic, French, English, Turkish and Urdu languages to understand this matter.

Another attraction is that the *ijara*-type *sukuk* are ideally suited to raise long-term funds by agencies of governments such as electricity companies, toll-road operators as well as by governments with SPCs holding treasury assets or usufructs that provide incomes to investors where default is less likely. The fact the yield is higher for this instrument than an equivalent conventional note ensures that the investors would favour this over the conventional bonds, whether the buyer is a Muslim or non-Muslim, in any of the 56 IDB member countries. The wealthy lenders are seeking high returns for their savings in private *sukuk* marketing centres in Zurich, London, Frankfurt, and elsewhere.

If infrastructure funding is suitably met by *sukuk*, then these countries need to build the infrastructure for the *sukuk* market to function well so they can speedily tap the funds from the savings of their people for infrastructural development of the type the Islamic Development Bank is promoting across 56 member countries. Instead of borrowing in foreign currencies, and so incurring a high-risk funding fraught with exchange rate risk, from the World Bank or IBRD (some from the infamous Paris Club), sourcing the money in one's own currency would be much less risky.

Complex instruments have their own use in the Islamic debt market. The income patterns of economic agents are variable, so the structuring of products must match the patterns of the income stream. A manufacturer may need working capital to get its product on the shelves. Such a funding need is ideally matched in *istisna sukuk* as working capital: a joint venture deal with no certain income would find a *musharaka sukuk* ideal.

Banking regulation requires some level of statutory reserves in OIC countries. That means there is a market for local instruments to be held by banks to meet the reserve requirements, not forgetting additional reserves needed as liquidity reserves. Therefore, the prospect for central bank issues of bills and notes for reserve and liquidity purposes will be well served by Islamic Investment Notes. This is found in Malaysia but is not yet found in most other places. Thus, complexity is needed, but at this early stage of *sukuk* debt market development, any contract that looks like conventional bonds is more likely to be appealing to investors, which explains the popularity of the BBA and *ijara sukuk* as the most popular ones. As pointed out by Nasser Saidi, there is an urgent need to build infrastructure and market process to tap the savings of the public through these short- and long-term instruments. The prospect for growth in these instruments is very attractive, and will happen in the next decades.

Further specialized contracts are attractive in toll road construction, in agriculture, mining, and so on. *Istisna, salam* and other special contracts offer higher yields than in conventional finance to tap needed funds in those several critical areas of rural development in many OIC (Organisation of Islamic Countries) nations. The *salam* contract, a forward contract based on SPCs owning the future assets, was first issued in Bahrain, and it is finding its way in other markets as well. Several financing situations in agriculture and mining would ideally find these contracts a suitable means of raising money. Special project funding is possible with *istisna* contracts to provide working capital during the building stage turnkey projects as working capital while, after the building is done, an *ijara* contract would raise the money for governments to buy the turnkey projects in building schools, ports, airports and roads. There is a good prospect for these contracts if properly marketed.

14.3 HOT-BUTTON ISSUES FOR DEVELOPMENT OF THE MARKET

Throughout this book, the contributors have identified critical issues for the continued and orderly development of Islamic financial markets and specially *sukuk* markets. In this section, an attempt will be made to highlight the issues and pinpoint strategies for resolving these issues. We identify seven priority areas for attention.

14.3.1 Regulatory Plurality

The conventional debt market spans some 110 countries with public trading of very *standard* bonds developed over some 400 years. In a typical day funds amounting to US$500 billion are easily raised because the markets are well established and have high liquidity: notably there is a great deal of standardization of different products. Despite its already very established nature, the AOSCO (Association of Securities Commissions) as a coordinating body provides a large number of continued improvements and uniformity to the regulatory framework under which exchanges are organized and trade is made in an orderly fashion. The Islamic products markets are not yet coordinated since there are many regulatory bodies, and the products are also not standardized. This increases uncertainty and, more importantly, increases contracting costs.

In Islamic finance, there are some 12 *sukuk* locations with more already getting ready to enter this market in the near future, so this number is likely to increase in the near future as there will be many more OIC countries scrambling to secure funds in the next decades as economic development is already picking up in all these countries. In Islamic finance, there is a multitude of market regulators but no single coordinating body. There is one regulatory body in each of these locations, yet there has been no attempt to have a common regulatory framework until recently in 2008, when regulatory differences prompted some attempts to cobble a degree of cooperation. It is still a work in progress, and an AOSCO type of international body is needed in addition to the rule-making body formed in 2008. This state of affairs is not conducive to investor confidence.

Yet there is no consensus to have a coordinating organization for the purpose of law-making and for supervision and enforcement. This issue needs to be addressed quickly; if not, the domain privilege enjoyed by each market regulator, for example Malaysia, will prompt less cooperation at later stages of development when parties would want the status quo to prevail. A suggestion is to work with the IOSCO to study the feasibility of working with that body to engage in this urgent need for regulatory oversight.

14.3.2   *Shari'ah* Opinions Too Many

A somewhat similar issue to the above has been raised with regard to *shari'ah* supervisory matters. While there are national *Shari'ah* Boards or Councils in each of the market locations, there is less coordination in terms of documentation and standardization of *fatwas* (opinions) already issued as clear guides in understandable forms: we may develop the kind of tax matter rulings that are found in government tax office opinions on questions on taxation issues as are often published as tax opinions in developed countries. Neither is there a central consultative body to smooth differences before differences or non-compliance become a thorny issue at the level of the market. Potentially, any dispute (such as the 2008 *fatwa* on asset-backing) becomes a red flag for investors to raise their guard against investment in these markets.

Critical reports point to the existence of some 300 *shari'ah* experts dominating the market place and earning an unjustified amount of money, which has often been described in less complimentary terms. There is a crying need to train professionals in an accredited manner by reputable institutions to stem the tide of the dominance of the market by religious scholars with little understanding of economics or finance. That in fact makes their advice suspect, and introduces a severe element bordering on orthodoxy in what is a straightforward commercial transaction responding to the changing situations requiring re-interpretations of rules developed for a different era in Islamic empires of the past before the advent of modern instruments such as bonds.

14.3.3   Basic Fundamentals in Designing *sukuk*

Munawar Iqbal is perhaps the first to provide a common theme, a kind of set of minimum conditions, for designing Islamic financial products. He does this by identifying ten precepts that must be obeyed in any design of Islamic products. He even gives further assurance that following the ten precepts would make a product pass the test of being *shari'ah* consistent, not just compliant, almost always. This is the first time that such a broad-based guideline is attempted for *sukuk* markets: see Chapter 4. More discussion and agreement on this sort of framework will enhance the reputation of the product design process, given the personal interest of compensation of *shari'ah* experts who depend on the institutions employing them and paying them. There is an incentive for this group of experts not to address this matter because it is too complex to be reduced to simple rules.

Despite the claims of *shari'ah* experts, these design principles are simple and ought to be simple, as they have been practised for centuries to suit the changing circumstances in the commerce of Islamic countries. The only complexity in decision-making is their relevance to modern-day conditions in financing modern economic activities. This key issue should receive careful scrutiny in each regulatory site because the principle of conscious deliberation to amend principles to suit changing circumstances is a long established legal tool in Islamic jurisprudence. Yet the current crop of *shari'ah* experts seem to be unable or more likely unwilling to go beyond quoting the past principle developed centuries ago, long before the West took over financial transactions in Muslim countries. Because of presumed complexity promoted by self-interest of such experts and also the locked-in positions they enjoy as insiders of financial institutions, the average time taken to design *sukuk* securities is twice as long as in other debt markets.

The cost of transactions is too high with so many side contracts in what is at the centre just a debt contract. No one has yet identified the average cost of originating a *sukuk* security taking into consideration the exorbitant fees of the experts. In major investment banking centres, the cost of origination is about 0.75 to 1 per cent of the issue cost in conventional bond markets. There is no documentation of cost in *sukuk* issuance. Standardization attempts of the type recently made by the AAOFI indicates that regulators and market players are aware of this issue. Speedy research and solutions to this problem will assist in the development of the *sukuk* markets.

14.3.4   Origination, Marketing and Listing

This is a highly developed area with years of innovations in the regulatory framework to protect investors. Procedures for valuing the securitization process to ensure correct valuation and application of modern book-making procedures to discover market price for initial issue have been developed over 90 years in conventional debt markets. The received wisdom of investment banking over some 90 years has to be adapted to the very *different* provisions in the securitization process in *sukuk* markets. Obviously it is being successfully done, as the reader will have learned from Chapter 12. Yet more is needed.

This is where there is need for innovation. For example, how does an originator estimate the risk of the cash flow pay-offs coming not from the total firm but from the SPC? The current practice is to look at the firm, not the SPC alone. Should not the incomes or market value of SPC assets be more difficult to assess than the incomes of a whole firm, given the portfolio effect being absent in the SPC? Neither is there certainty in the income streams of the SPC, which means that the originator needs far more nuanced understanding of how to model the credit risk embedded in the SPC.

This challenge has not been researched well enough to model how the risk of the SPC should be estimated. Ratings companies have adapted more incorrectly by adopting conventional practices that appear to ignore this special character of *sukuk*, which, we believe, is the root cause of higher riskiness of this type of debt instrument. Hence the higher yield in the market may be explained as being consistent with higher riskiness of *sukuk*.

14.3.5   Islamic Securities Quality Rating

Michael Skully has commented that the challenge to rating a *sukuk* is more complex than is the case of straightforward conventional bonds. This is an important statement, and is a cornerstone of the origination process in *sukuk* markets. Leaving this aside, the marketing of such instruments should seek to reach the clientele in a very different way from conventional debt markets. Putting up a roadshow in ways similar to that in conventional bond issue origination is not the way to approach this ethics-based investment promotion. As far as it could be verified, marketing the issues has targeted the same clientele as in the conventional bond markets except for the nicety of holding roadshows in high-net-worth locations in major Muslim cities. Is that meeting the call for ethical investment?

14.3.6   Liquidity of *Sukuk* Instruments

A market expert has estimated in this book that the liquidity of listed *sukuk* instruments is less than 1 per cent of the outstanding value! Another, a regulator, has commented that the market is one where the securities are held to maturity and about 40 per cent of the issues are taken up by financial institutions. These statistical facts appear to suggest that *sukuk* markets need to think about how to spur liquidity. Without liquidity markets are known to die, and *sukuk* markets have not been there long enough to assure that such a fate is unlikely. In futures exchanges one in seven new financial futures products fail for lack of liquidity. Given the fact that even conventional bond issues have low liquidity, it behoves well to investigate how serious are the liquidity shortfalls in Islamic financial instruments as well as if there are sufficient issues for institutions to hold as reserves. This is an area of urgent research priority.

Lack of liquidity is perhaps another reason why the yields in the *sukuk* markets are significantly higher than in the bond markets for an identical term and quality rating. We tend to think that the higher yield is actually coming from the higher-risk profit-share basis of *sukuk* design and not from illiquidity. But this needs to be verified, and there is thus a need to do this as a serious inquiry to retain investor confidence in this market. Apart from these, structural changes need to be introduced – for example market makers need to be appointed to create liquidity. Another alternative would be to have quotes at which market makers would buy an issue; this information should be posted by specially appointed brokers and dealers. Liquidity is a priority area for sustaining markets, and this requires careful analysis.

14.3.7   Public Awareness of Application

It has been some 21 years since the first private *sukuk* was offered in Malaysia (Shell Corporation issue in 1990): public-traded issues have come on stream from 2000. Yet the public awareness of the basics of *sukuk* instruments is poor, literature is not available even at the counters of banks. What the customer gets is a tiny pamphlet extolling the virtues of instruments, and hardly any attempt is made to provide technical details to customers either at the window or at public promotion gatherings. One should compare the expense and publicity given to new issues of shares in stock exchanges. A lot of money is raised via the *sukuk* issues, much more than in share markets. Yet the promotion effort, even in the major Malaysian market, is not as extensive as is seen in conventional fund-raising events. Something is not entirely right.

A public awareness programme is a way to educate the public, especially the masses whose small savings may add up to a lot if they are convinced by the usefulness of the instruments and made aware of the significant higher yields and higher risk of *sukuk* securities. Mass marketing was the way the finances for the World War were secured in the 1940s and that is in recorded history, for example how designers invented the flower bond. Efforts in this direction have to come from associations and individual Islamic financial institutions, especially the larger ones, funding public awareness campaigns. Perhaps it would lead to more demand for *sukuk* debt instruments when the average Ahmad and his family have a stake in the market. That would also increase the acceptance of the new products as more discerning clients would find them useful.

For example a diminishing *musharaka sukuk* is an ideal instrument for elderly people to buy high-yielding annuity type investments and earn a high return over a finite period. Such instruments, if traded in exchange markets, can yield funds for medium-sized firms from the public. Such instruments can be a boon to old retirees who are about to take out large savings from pension funds such as the employee provident funds or superannuation funds.

14.4   CONCLUSION

Early stage growth statistics from the experiences of new financial instruments (for example the derivative instruments in the 1980s) suggest that at the take-off stage, their growth rates are exceptional. So is the case of *sukuk* markets, where the growth rate is reportedly in excess of 20 per cent per year. One of the contributors to this book estimates a time trend that shows a very high demand for many more years, in fact, decades to come for *sukuk* financing to grow. Hence, growth is likely to be a big driver for this market, and that is a good thing, we all agree.

On the supply side, we have increasing revenues which ends up as savings in governments and in private savings in more and more growing

OIC economies. Traditional sources – bonds and fixed deposits – are extremely low in yield, especially since 2007, after the recent great financial crisis. Average yields for a AAA rated bond rarely exceed 5 per cent. So, savers as investors are looking elsewhere to increase their investment returns. By providing asset ownership in the firm, to which the investors lend their money, *sukuk* offers greater safety than is the case in bank deposits and conventional bond markets. But, given the low visibility of what *sukuk* is, it is unlikely these advantages will be known to investors, unless it is promoted as a selling point while also ensuring that investor protections are in place in times of default. For example, Dubai World did not provide investor protection although some of the debt was held as *sukuk* certificates at the time this company's investors were about to experience either a haircut or a re-negotiation of debt, although SPC was in the contract! This innovative product as a reasonably safe lending instrument should be promoted by the industry, as should the institutions developed to enhance investor protection as intended in the design of the products.

Although just six types of securities are actually being offered to-date – these do exist in the 12 centres – there are eight more complex instruments that could be issued as the market instruments to market them slowly to suit special needs of firms needing special types of funds. In other words, more complex instruments to meet diverse needs of firms will emerge soon. One worrying trend is the dominance of two basic types: *ijara* and BBA. The reasons for this, though not yet known from any well-designed research, are perhaps to do with investors at this stage of market development. The investors appear to desire instruments *closer* in character to the conventional bonds, which have been familiar instruments for centuries. In fact these two popular instruments are very bond-like, making them easy to value and for pre-issue yields to be estimated.

Our opinion is that the market will begin to experiment with more complex instruments just as complex derivatives were designed in the 1990s, whereas the initial derivatives in the 1970s were simple ones that came earlier at the early stage of these markets. Derivative markets grew from just three markets around the world to some 60 markets in 2011 selling about 1700 products. All this happened in just over 44 years. Hence, complexity in the *sukuk* market is likely to be the next challenge to come.

In short, not only is the prospect for sustaining the high growth good for Islamic finance; the prospect for more complex instruments to be issued is rather high as we enter the second decade of growth in *sukuk* markets. After all the 48-year-old Islamic banking started with a single product, the two-tier *mudaraba* savings account! This would also be a welcome change since more trained staff are entering the market place with knowledge of designing complex instruments, while the clientele base is also changing dramatically, especially in wholesale private *sukuk* markets, and includes high net worth people as well as ordinary investors.

In terms of prioritizing the issues, we would place the six issues as follows: (1) liquidity and (2) regulatory levelling and (3) shortage of intelligent *shari'ah* experts are likely to be the growing concerns that will occupy a great deal of attention from governments and the market makers, as well as researchers. The investors are watching new developments in respect to these three items. If these issues are not resolved speedily, the progress made to date may reverse because a tower of Babel in the regulatory world and an unwillingness of investors to trade in the instruments in the market are likely to sow discord and slow the build-up of liquidity. That would clearly stunt the growth potential and the future prospects for the industry. There are historical examples of financial market failures when liquidity failures continued to plague new product offers.

With this note of caution, we feel these key issues, and many before them, will be tackled in due course of time to set the *sukuk* Islamic debt market on an orderly growth path in more than the current 12 locations in the world.

NOTE

1. M. Ariff, F.F. Cheng and S.K. Neo (2008), *Bond Markets in Malaysia and Singapore*, Selangor, Malaysia: University Putra Press.

Index